AWARD
HANDBOOK

The Duke of Edinburgh's Award
Gulliver House, Madeira Walk, WINDSOR, Berkshire SL4 1EU
Tel: 01753 810753   Fax: 01753 810666

Third Edition: October 1994 (First Impression)
            January 1995 (Second Impression)
            August 1996 (Third Impression)
            January 1998 (Fourth Impression)

This Third Edition replaces all former editions of the *Award Handbook*.

For additional guidance on the requirements, conditions and programmes, and on the procedure for updating information contained in this book, refer to page 39.

Cover Design by T-Square Studios
Designed and typeset in-house by The Duke of Edinburgh's Award
Photographs by Paul Smith and Tony French, working for the Award under the Halina/Fuji Bursary. Additional photographs reproduced courtesy of:
RSPB, The National Trust, Sporting Pictures (UK) Ltd., The Still Moving Picture Company, Dave Wood
Printed and bound by Sterling Press Limited, Wellingborough, Northamptonshire

ISBN 0 905425 10 3 (paperback) (1st Edition: 0 905425 02 2)

Young people growing up in this modern complicated world have many difficulties to face, and opportunities for personal achievement are often limited. At the same time, parents, teachers, voluntary organisation leaders and employers, who recognize their responsibilities towards young people, also have their problems.

This scheme is intended to help both the young as well as those who are concerned for their welfare. The object is to provide an introduction to worthwhile leisure activities and voluntary service; as a challenge to the individual to discover the satisfaction of achievement and as a guide for those people and organisations who would like to encourage the development of their younger fellow citizens.

I hope that all those who take part in this scheme will find an added purpose and pleasure in their lives. I am quite sure that all those who help to run it will gain that special sense of satisfaction which comes from helping others to discover hidden abilities and to overcome a challenge.

Contents

Foreword

L ast year we brought together two outstandingly successful businesses to form the new Halifax. More than ever we will depend on our young people to help us build this organisation into one which is the first choice in personal financial services. Truly the Biggest and Best.

By supporting The Duke of Edinburgh's Award the Halifax provides the opportunity for young people to develop the self-sufficiency and transferable skills needed in tomorrow's world. Many young people are unaware of their true potential. The Award helps them to identify and build on their existing skills and to develop both as individuals and as team players.

We all know that learning is not necessarily confined to the workplace or the classroom and the Award provides a marvellous learning experience; it isn't just about hard work – it's about fun too!

The Halifax takes great pride in playing a part in the Award's activities and I am personally delighted to be asked to give my support to this edition of the Award Handbook.

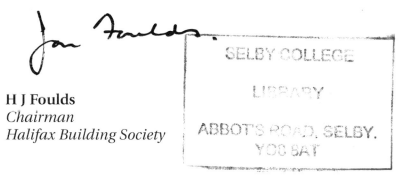

H J Foulds
Chairman
Halifax Building Society

CHAPTER 1
An Overview of the Award Scheme

1.1 OPPORTUNITY AND CHALLENGE

Young people are eager to grasp opportunities for enjoyment, excitement and new experiences. They wish to make their mark in a world where the individual often appears insignificant and are willing to take on substantial challenges if they perceive them to be worthwhile and relevant to the needs of society. They want to prove themselves, to discover new talents and develop their relationship with friends and the wider community.

The Duke of Edinburgh introduced his Award Scheme to encourage and stimulate their enthusiasms and energies by presenting a challenging programme of activities open to young people between the ages of 14 and 25. The Scheme is intended to develop those qualities of maturity and responsibility which will help them throughout their lives, in their homes, in their jobs and in their relationships, whatever their personal abilities or circumstances. The Scheme now operates in over 50 countries; in some it is known by a different title, although the underlying philosophy and basic principles of operation are the same.

To quote HRH The Duke of Edinburgh:
"The philosophy of the Scheme is neither very profound nor very complicated. It is simply this: a civilised society depends upon the freedom, responsibility, intelligence and standard of behaviour of its individual members, and if society is to continue to be civilised, each succeeding generation must learn to value these qualities... Above all, it depends on a willingness among younger generations to find out for themselves the factors which contribute to freedom, responsibility, intelligence and standards of behaviour. These are all rather abstract concepts. The Scheme... has attempted to bring them down to earth; to give individual young people the opportunity to discover these ideas for themselves through a graduated programme of experience."

Challenge is the essence of the concept. The Award Scheme presents to young people a balanced non-competitive programme of voluntary activities which encourages responsibility, self-reliance, personal discovery and perseverance.

The value to the Scheme of Adult Helpers is paramount and fundamental. Adults have a wealth of experiences, abilities and attitudes which can have a profound influence on the development of young people. In Prince Philip's own words: *"If there is one thing which the experience of the Scheme re-affirms and re-emphasises time and again, it is the involvement and dedication of adults that is absolutely critical to its success."*

The Award Scheme

The Scheme itself is not a youth organisation. It is a programme of practical, cultural and adventurous activities designed for use by all agencies having a concern for the development of young people; a programme flexible enough to meet their enthusiasms and aptitudes whatever their background or culture, however plentiful or limited their resources may be.

Participants follow their chosen activities, largely in their own time, with guidance from someone knowledgeable in each subject. Minimum standards of achievement are laid down and when these are met, the participants qualify for an Award. These minimum standards should be exceeded, where appropriate, in order to create a truly personal challenge. A badge and certificate are presented on behalf of The Duke of Edinburgh to mark an attainment which represents the successful completion of a co-operative venture between the young and not-so-young so that, in this way, barriers between generations are eroded.

In gaining Awards, young people learn by experience the importance of commitment, enterprise and effort. They discover a great deal about themselves and come to know the enjoyment of working with and for other people.

The Scheme is voluntary and entry must be a participant's free choice. It is not competitive since individuals are assessed on their own progress, perseverance and achievement and Awards are within the reach of all. The programme is available to all young people whether members of a youth organisation or not. They may take part individually or together with others of their own age group.

This, then, is the essence of the Scheme. Through a commitment to its programmes, young people will be acquiring self-reliance

• Chapter 1: An Overview of the Award Scheme - Opportunity and Challenge

and a sense of responsibility to others, both essential qualities of citizenship. The Award programme is a vehicle for spiritual, personal and social development and the overall benefits of the Award are therefore greater than the sum of its component parts. It is hoped that adults who help young people towards an Award will bear these aspects in mind.

1.2   THE AWARD PHILOSOPHY

It is essential for everyone involved in The Duke of Edinburgh's Award, whether as a participant or Adult Leader, to share a common understanding of the philosophy which underpins all aspects of the Scheme's delivery.

Once a fundamental appreciation of the philosophy has been developed, the more technical conditions and requirements of the Scheme follow naturally. It is important for Leaders and participants to know their way around the *Award Handbook* and use it as a reference, although it is not necessary to know every detail of the requirements. On the other hand, an understanding of the basic principles enshrined in the 'spirit' of the Award must be developed.

The essence of the Award Scheme is that it is 'a challenge to the individual' and not simply another competition in life where success is another person's comparative failure.

Through Adult Helpers sharing their experiences, abilities and attitudes with young people, new relationships evolve which can have a profound influence on the development of young people. They inherit new values and review those they already hold. They come to understand themselves and the contribution they can make to the community. It is therefore the process of participation in the programme, rather than the end achievement of the Award, that leads to personal development and new, well-earned self-confidence.

Above all, the Scheme should be enjoyable for both Leaders and participants. Only in that way will they benefit fully from the experience and continue to develop new-found talents and abilities. 'Personal development' is not a transient concept and it can be diluted if the Award has been approached with grim determination!

The Ten Key Points

Non-competitive
The Scheme is a personal challenge and not a competition against other individuals. The only set standards are those necessary to ensure the safety of participants. The Award programme is based on personal choice and should reflect the abilities and interests of individual participants. No two programmes should be identical.

Available to All
There is one Award which is available to young people who wish to take up its challenge, with no discrimination on grounds of gender, cultural background, religion or political affiliation. An Award is gained through individual improvement and achievement, which means that disadvantaged young people and those with special needs are able to benefit from involvement in its programme.

Voluntary
The Scheme is run by volunteers for volunteers. Every young person makes a free choice to enter the Scheme and must commit leisure time to complete the activities, with the support of a huge network of adult volunteers.

Flexible
The Award programmes can be geared to local facilities and should be designed for individuals taking part. Providing the basic age requirements are met, young people may take as long as they wish to complete an Award and may enter for whichever level of Award best suits them.

Balanced
Whatever the level, there are four Sections which must be completed: Service, Expeditions, Skills and Physical Recreation. There is the additional requirement of the Residential Project at Gold. The challenge is to extend and develop existing abilities and to try something new. Each Section will make greater or lesser demands on participants according to their experience, interests and abilities.

• Chapter 1: An
Overview of
the Award
Scheme
- The Award
Philosophy

6

Progressive
Through its three levels, the Award programme demands more time and an increased degree of commitment and improvement. Young people should also take an increasing role in organising their Award. At Bronze, participants will need strong support from Adult Helpers, at Silver they should be given more independence and at Gold they should be largely responsible for organising their own Award programme with the guidance of adults.

Achievement-Focused
The *Record Book* notes positive achievement and improvement only and it profiles achievement across a broad range of activities. If a participant does not complete the conditions at one time, the opportunity exists to try again.

Marathon not a Sprint
The Scheme demands persistence and commitment and cannot be completed in a short burst of enthusiasm. The time limits for each level of Award are minimum rather than maximum requirements and therefore individuals can work at their own pace, according to the time available, until their 25th birthday.

Process not a Prize
The Scheme is a process of personal and social development and the programme and activities are a means to this end. It should introduce participants to a range of new opportunities, allow them to learn from their experiences and enable them to discover hidden capabilities and talents. The value and significance of the Award to participants is directly proportional to the quality of experience and degree of personal commitment.

Enjoyable
Above all, it is important that both young people and their Adult Helpers find participation in the Scheme enjoyable, exciting and satisfying. The intention is that participants should pursue Award activities in their future lives and not be discouraged from ever trying them again!

1.3 GENERAL CONDITIONS

1.   Three Levels of Award
There are three separate Awards – Bronze, Silver and Gold.

2.   Four Sections
For each Award, participants have to fulfil the requirements of each of four Sections:

Those Sections and their aims are:

SERVICE
To encourage service to others.

EXPEDITIONS
To encourage a spirit of adventure and discovery.

SKILLS
To encourage the discovery and development of personal interests and social and practical skills.

PHYSICAL RECREATION
To encourage participation in physical recreation and improvement of performance.

There is an additional requirement at Gold level only for a:

RESIDENTIAL PROJECT
To broaden experience through involvement with others in a residential setting.

Activities in the four Sections are intended to complement each other and so provide a balanced programme reflecting different aspects of young people's development. There are minimum periods of time for which the chosen activities have to be sustained and the detailed conditions for each Section of the Award are given in the following chapters. Young people should be encouraged to set themselves personal challenges beyond the minimum requirements according to their abilities and talents.

3.   Age Range
The age range for the programme is from the 14th to the 25th birthdays.

4. Minimum Ages

The minimum starting ages for Awards are:

BRONZE -	14 years
SILVER -	15 years
GOLD -	16 years

At **Bronze** level, some discretion is given to Operating Authorities to permit a few who would be just too young to enter but who are part of a larger group over this age, to make a start with their friends. (This concession is primarily intended for those in schools or youth groups who plan their activities on a group basis for the year ahead).

At **Silver,** some discretion is given to Operating Authorities to permit those who have completed the Bronze Award to make a start on the Silver Award just before their 15th Birthday without imposing an artificial delay.

At **Gold,** no activities may be counted for the Gold Award before the 16th birthday.

5. Maximum Ages

The latest date for entry into the Scheme is the 23rd birthday and the upper age limit for all Awards is the 25th birthday, by which time all activities to count for an Award must be completed.

Extensions: Extensions to the upper age limit can only be considered where illness, accident or unavoidable circumstances make it impossible to complete an Award by the 25th birthday, in which case requests are to be referred by Operating Authorities via Territorial and Regional Offices to the National Award Office for consideration. The participant will be required to write stating the circumstances for requiring an extension and, if the application is successful, extra time will be allowed which must not be further exceeded. Extensions will not be granted if the participants fail to meet the requirement because they have been wrongly advised by an Adult Helper. At Gold level, participants are expected to be largely responsible for their own programme.

• Chapter 1: An Overview of the Award Scheme - General Conditions

6. Qualification

The *earliest* ages for qualification for each Award are:

BRONZE	All Entrants	14½
SILVER	Bronze Award Holders	15½
	Direct Entrants	16
GOLD	Silver Award Holders	17
	Direct Entrants	17½

7. Entry

The purchase of an *Entrance Pack,* containing a *Record Book,* from a recognised Operating Authority marks entry and the starting point in the Scheme. Activities undertaken before obtaining this book will not count towards an Award, unless undertaken during the previous three months in accordance with the conditions of the appropriate Section with a view to entry into the Scheme and provided the age requirements are satisfied. Details of activities undertaken are recorded in the *Record Book;* it forms a record of progress through the Scheme, verified by the adults who have carried out the assessment in each Section.

8. Leisure Time

The Scheme is essentially an introduction to leisure time activities. The programme should be voluntarily undertaken during those parts of the day, week, month or year, when the choice of activity is at the option of the participant and purely voluntary, and the effort made within personal, rather than directed, time. Although a participant's interests within school, formal training or work will often stimulate and sustain a commitment to one or other of the Award's many programmes or activities, training within normal curriculum or working times for examination or career advancement purposes cannot be counted for an Award. A participant must show adequate evidence of voluntary effort and a substantial contribution of leisure time.

9. Exemptions

If they meet the basic age requirements, young people may enter for whichever level of Award is best suited to them. They may enter direct for the Bronze, Silver or Gold Award but there are obvious benefits for those participants who progress through successive levels of Award. Those who have completed all Sections of a

Bronze or Silver Award and go on to attempt the next higher Award will be exempted from some aspects of training in the Expeditions and Skills Sections.

Participants should, however, be encouraged to complete all Sections of a particular Award before embarking on a higher Award.

It is possible to work for a Section of the next higher Award before completing all other Sections of a lower Award, as long as the participant has reached the minimum starting age for the higher Award. In these circumstances, the exemptions cannot be claimed until the lower Award is achieved.

1.4 HISTORICAL DEVELOPMENT

The History of the Award Scheme

"In the summer of 1938, I found myself walking five miles, as fast as I could, along country roads in Morayshire. I had never done anything like it before and I fervently prayed I would never have to do anything like it again. It so happens that my prayer was answered because I was completing - successfully as it turned out - a section of the Moray Badge, a direct ancestor of what has become known as The Duke of Edinburgh's Award".

This, in His Royal Highness The Duke of Edinburgh's own words, describes the origins of the Scheme. From the Moray Badge (1934) grew the County Badge Scheme (1941), a system of awards devised by Kurt Hahn, the great German educationalist and Prince Philip's Headmaster at Gordonstoun.

Prince Philip developed Kurt Hahn's ideas and philosophy and launched The Duke of Edinburgh's Award for Boys in 1956 under the Leadership of Sir John (now Lord) Hunt.

The Duke of Edinburgh's Award is now in its fourth decade with more young people taking part than ever before, while retaining the same fundamental aims and philosophy.

The First Decade - experiment and growth

By September 1957 over 7,000 boys had entered the Scheme and a flood of enquiries led to the establishment of The Duke of Edinburgh's Award for Girls in 1958. This broadened the educational base of the Scheme and provided a focus on the personal and social development of all young people. It was launched under the direction of Phyllis Gordon-Spencer who was instrumental in its implementation and became its first Secretary. She later became Senior Deputy Director of the Award Scheme.

The operation of the Scheme was delegated to responsible bodies who were trusted to uphold the standards and conditions of the Award. As Prince Philip said, *"I would rather scrap the Scheme altogether if I felt I could not trust the operators."*

In 1960, the Scheme was established as a Charitable Trust with His Royal Highness The Duke of Edinburgh as Patron. There was greater emphasis on training and leadership, particularly in adventurous activities, to ensure the safety and competence of participants.

By 1961 the Scheme was seen as an extension of secondary education with 16 per cent of schools participating.

During the next few years, the Scheme was heavily promoted in schools, voluntary youth organisations and industry. By 1966, the expansion of the Scheme led to its regionalisation in the United Kingdom. Parallel schemes were also developed internationally.

The Second Decade - development and expansion

By the late 1960s, it was clear that, in its attempt to cater for all young people, the programme had become over-complicated. The trends in education towards mixed schools, clubs and joint activities made the continuation of two separate schemes, for young men and for young women, inappropriate.

In February 1969, at a press conference in Buckingham Palace, Prince Philip launched an integrated single Award for both young men and young women aged 14 to 21 (later extended to 25). The Service, Expeditions and Interests Sections were available at all levels to everyone whilst at Bronze and Silver young women took

Design for Living and young men Physical Activity. At Gold all were given the choice of either Section and in addition were required to complete a Residential Project.

Alfred Blake, then Director, used his special understanding and experience of Local Government to steer the Award through the Local Government reorganisation of 1974.

The Third Decade - into the 80's

Robert Heron headed up yet another major revision shortly after he took over as Director. In order to reflect changes in society and demand for total equality of opportunity, Award conditions were amalgamated into a single programme for both sexes. A simple four Section format was devised:

- Service
- Expeditions
- Skills
- Physical Recreation

– and the Residential Project at Gold was retained.

The new structure offered:

- A simpler programme, easier to operate and the same for all participants.
- A wider range of choices to cater for many different tastes.
- A balance between physical and non-physical activities designed to appeal to Leaders and result in increased participation by young people.

The Sections have remained in this format since 1980 and the formula has proved to be increasingly successful with young people and Adult Helpers.

The first International Award Forum was held in 1982 in Edinburgh and was attended by delegates from 19 different participating countries. The International Award Office became the International Secretariat with the aim of promoting the Award world-wide.

• Chapter 1: An Overview of the Award Scheme - Historical Development

The Fourth Decade - available to all

Under the leadership of the Director, Michael Hobbs, the Award Scheme has made great efforts to raise its profile to appeal to a wider audience and to extend the range and quality of opportunities for participation.

The number of participants has grown steadily and more young people, from a wider diversity of backgrounds, are entering the Scheme than at any time in its history.

His Royal Highness The Prince Edward has established a Special Projects Group committed to raising money and interest in the Scheme. The funds have been targeted at innovative projects in deprived urban and remote rural areas, new initiatives involving ethnic minority groups, young people with special needs and young offenders, and collaborative developments involving sports and arts associations.

Under the banner of a 'Charter for Business', substantial efforts have been made to raise funds and increase the involvement of industry and commerce in the operation of the Scheme. Exciting new initiatives are developing at national and local level as a result of the new and thriving partnerships.

Promotional and operational literature and materials have been redesigned to reflect the changing face of the Award. New training materials have been devised to focus on the quality of delivery of the Scheme but there have been no significant changes to its basic structure or conditions.

The challenge for the decade is to continue to develop the Scheme amidst the changing social, political and educational environment.

CHAPTER 2
Structure of the Award Scheme

2.1 THE NATIONAL FRAMEWORK

His Royal Highness The Duke of Edinburgh is Chairman of the Board of Trustees which governs The Duke of Edinburgh's Award programme.

The Scheme nationally is an association of bodies and individuals, not an organisation with a hierarchical structure. This association acts as the custodian of the Scheme; it determines the criteria and maintains the integrity and quality of the Award. A consultative and advisory framework comprising the National Advisory Committee, Territorial and Regional Committees, the Sectional Advisory Panels and the biennial General Council offer advice to the Trustees through the Award's Directorate.

The Scheme in the United Kingdom is administered on behalf of the Trustees by the Award Headquarters in Windsor which deals with matters of overall policy and central administration.

The main functions of Headquarters are to:
- Administer and monitor the delivery of the Scheme nationally.
- Co-ordinate the development of policy, serve as secretariat of Advisory Committees and Panels, and organise General Council.
- Produce operational, promotional and training literature and materials.
- Issue Operating Authority licences to suitable applicants.
- Initiate national projects to broaden the reach of the Award.
- Ensure Award conditions and programmes are appropriate and relevant in a rapidly changing society.
- Arrange Gold Award Presentations.
- Organise training courses and conferences on a national level and co-ordinate the Assessor Accreditation Scheme.

There is also a Fundraising Department, based in London, charged with raising sufficient funds to allow the Headquarters and Territorial and Regional Offices to carry out their functions.

• Chapter 2:
Structure of
the Award
Scheme
- The National
Framework

In addition, there are Territorial Offices in Scotland, Wales and Northern Ireland and seven Regional Offices covering the North East, North West, Midlands, East, South East, South West and London. These Offices have delegated responsibility from Headquarters in most matters and their main functions are to:

- Provide information, advice and assistance to Operating Authorities, Operating Units and Assist Organisations in the Region and oversee Wild Country Panels.
- Actively promote the Scheme to all potential users and initiate new developments.
- Liaise and establish working relationships with Local Government Officers, Industrial Executives and Award Officers together with other Award users, and act as a focus of information for enquiries on Award conditions.
- Organise courses and conferences on a Regional basis to share good practice, promote new developments and standardise quality of delivery.
- Act as a channel of communication between Award Headquarters and users of the Award Scheme.

Operation

Responsibility for the operation of the Scheme is delegated under licence to Operating Authorities who are authorised to grant Awards on behalf of His Royal Highness.

2.2 OPERATING AUTHORITIES & THEIR RESPONSIBILITIES

Any authority, organisation or other body concerned with the education, welfare or training of young people may apply to Award Headquarters to become licensed as an Operating Authority.

• Chapter 2:
Structure of
the Award
Scheme
- The National
Framework
- Operating
Authorities
and their
Responsi-
bilities

In order to obtain this licence, which is subject to review every three years, Operating Authorities have to satisfy the National Award Office that they understand the full implications of the Scheme. They have to be in a position to safeguard its aims and standards, to establish the necessary administrative framework to enable it to function and to ensure its continuity.

Any young person wishing to participate must do so through one of these Authorities, though they do not necessarily have to belong to a particular group or organisation.

Operating Authorities vary in size from national organisations, large companies and Local Government Authorities, to single-Unit establishments such as independent schools and industrial concerns. These smaller Units operate under the umbrella licence of an existing larger Operating Authority wherever this is practicable, in order to maximise the number of opportunities for both young people and Adult Helpers, and to ensure independence of assessment for participants.

User Units

Operating Authorities may sponsor the Scheme in any number of User Units under their control. The various types of Operating Authority and User Units are shown in the following table:

Operating Authorities	User Units
Local Government Authorities	Schools, Youth Clubs, Further Education Establishments, Probation Centres, Leisure Centres, Open Award Centres and other Groups
National Voluntary Youth Organisations	Clubs, Groups, Units etc.
Independent Schools	Schools
Industrial and Commercial Concerns	Companies, Industrial Units, Offices and Local Branches
The Home Office	Young Offenders' Institutions

The programme's flexibility enables it to be operated in a host of different settings because it offers the means of linking a great number of organisations and individuals concerned with young people. Most Units are based on sites which are existing meeting points for young people such as a school or youth centre, an office or probation day centre. Over the last few years, however, there has been a significant increase in the number of Open Award Centres which provide a facility for unattached and independent participants to take part in the Scheme beyond these confines.

An Award Centre, if it is to act as the focal point for the operation of the Award within a particular locality, should be located in a central position which is easily accessible by public transport. Ideally it should be on 'neutral' territory so that young people from the whole area who attend school or college, are employed or unemployed, all feel comfortably able to attend the venue.

There is really no standard format for an Open Award Centre. They come in all shapes and sizes, depending on the number in the group's catchment area and the resources of the local community. In a rural area, a thriving centre may consist of a group of twelve young people meeting in the kitchen of the Award Leader's home whereas in a large urban area the Centre may operate in a sophisticated social setting and involve over a hundred young people in a wide variety of activities. The unifying principle is that they operate an 'open door' policy to all young people to participate fully in the Scheme and the organisation and administration of the Centre. They therefore promote ideal opportunities for effective personal and social development.

As will be seen, the Scheme may be operated in a variety of situations and, because of this, it offers the means of linking together a great number of organisations and individuals concerned with young people.

Responsibilities

Operating Authorities must carry out the following responsibilities:

- Designate a specific person or persons as Award Officer to be responsible for all matters relating to the Scheme within the organisation.
- Authorise the use of the Award programme in as many Units (schools, colleges, clubs, independent groups, factories, offices) under the control of the organisation as required and ensure these User Units maintain the quality, standard and credibility of the Award.
- Advise and update User Units on the operation of the Scheme.
- Approve Instructors, Supervisors and Assessors, before the young person starts an activity, and ensure that they are

• Chapter 2:
Structure of
the Award
Scheme
- Operating
Authorities
and their
Responsi-
bilities

properly qualified or experienced for their roles. The approval of an individual as a suitably qualified Instructor or Assessor rests entirely with the Operating Authority.

- Arrange adequate public liability insurance to cover the legal liability of themselves, participants and Adult Helpers to pay damages to third parties as a result of an Award activity.
- Supply *Entrance Packs* and other literature to User Units.
- Check *Record Books* and grant Awards. (Gold Awards must be confirmed by the appropriate Award Office.)
- Issue badges and certificates and arrange Award presentations.
- Ensure Leaders and all those involved in the Scheme attend training courses on a regular basis. Training for new Helpers is essential.
- Maintain accurate records and statistics on Award participation. Details on the numbers of male and female participants, User Units, adult volunteers and training courses are required every year by Headquarters for publication in the *Annual Report.*

In the case of large Operating Authorities, some of the above responsibilities may be delegated, but overall supervision of all aspects of the Scheme remains with the Operating Authority.

Some Operating Authorities may also be able to:
- Support young people who wish to enter the Scheme but who do not belong to any particular organisation.
- Hold stocks of equipment for use in training and on expeditions.

Further information relating to the functions of Operating Authorities and advice concerning operational and administrative matters and insurance details are contained in the *Operating Authorities' Guide.*

Training

A common understanding of the purpose, structure, content and practice of the Scheme is essential to its effective delivery. Training and briefing of Helpers is an essential responsibility of Operating Authorities and its importance cannot be over-emphasised. Operating Authorities must ensure that training exists at local level for individuals new to the Scheme and must provide refresher courses for experienced Leaders on new developments within the

• Chapter 2: Structure of the Award Scheme - Operating Authorities and their Responsibilities

Scheme and specific skills training for Instructors and Assessors. Large Operating Authorities are expected to mount their own courses or collaborate with neighbouring Authorities in offering a range of training opportunities. The *Over to You* training pack contains a wealth of resource materials to assist Trainers in devising courses.

A training course should be attended by potential users as soon as possible after becoming involved as it can prevent hours of abortive work by adults and ensure that the young people they support derive maximum benefit from participation in the Scheme. This training can be carried out as a series of evening sessions or, as is often the case, at a residential weekend. Training for new Leaders should incorporate the following points:

- The philosophy of the Award.
- Overall structure and general conditions.
- The conditions of the three Awards.
- Operational procedures and methods.

Award videos, promotional and training material help to make these courses more interesting and all resources can be obtained from The Award Scheme Ltd.

Other training events within the Scheme are run at national, regional and local level and Operating Authorities are encouraged to take full advantage of these opportunities. All Expedition Assessors in Wild Country Areas are expected to join the Assessor Accreditation Scheme which is operated on a national basis to standardise and improve the quality of the assessment of Expeditions. Details of courses are published in *Award Journal* and are also distributed from Territorial and Regional Offices.

Award Committees and Associations

Larger Operating Authorities may find it useful to establish a group of users to co-ordinate the delivery of the Scheme at local level and to provide a forum for consultation and discussion.

• Chapter 2: Structure of the Award Scheme - Operating Authorities and their Responsibilities

This group can take the form of a Committee electing officers who fulfil certain roles including Chair, Secretary, Treasurer, Press & Publicity Officer, or may be an informal Award Association or Forum of Unit Leaders meeting two or three times a year.

In addition to an officer of the principal Operating Authority, the membership of an Award Committee should comprise representatives of other local Operating Authorities, a wide range of User Units, Assisting Organisations, Award participants, associated bodies and influential members of the local community.

It should be stressed that Award Committees/Associations are normally consultative and act as agents of the principal Operating Authority. In areas of little Award activity they may, however, with the approval of the Operating Authority, assume the role of a User Unit.

The Committees/Associations are valuable in fulfilling the following functions:
- Promoting the Scheme locally, by recruiting adults, establishing Open Award Centres and use of the media.
- Pooling resources of Leadership, equipment and facilities.
- Helping participants who have started the Scheme under one Operating Authority to link up with another agency to complete an Award.
- Helping independent participants not attached to particular User Units.
- Arranging Award Presentations in consultation with the Operating Authority.
- Maintaining contact with Gold Award Holders.
- Monitoring standards to ensure a degree of uniformity.
- Sharing good practice to improve standards.

2.3 SUPPORTING ORGANISATIONS

Initiating Authorities

Some organisations share a concern for the personal development of young people but their activities are related to one specific Section of the Award. They initiate young people into the Scheme but cannot sustain or support their involvement throughout the Scheme. Outward Bound, for example, share common historical roots and aims, but only deal with the Expeditions and Residential Sections. These organisations have been empowered to enter young people into the Scheme by issuing them with *Entrance Packs* and are able to sign specific Sections of the *Record Book*. However, young people must register with an Operating Authority, usually the Local Authority nearest their home base, in order to undertake their Awards. Initiating Authorities cannot authorise or approve Awards or issue certificates.

Assisting Organisations

There are over 1000 National and International Organisations who have pledged their support to the Scheme and are able to offer assistance in many different specialist fields, such as producing new programmes, giving guidance on technical and safety matters and offering training courses to Award participants.

Further reference to appropriate bodies is made in the detailed conditions for each Section of the Award.

2.4 THE INTERNATIONAL AWARD

Outside the UK, the Award programme is administered by autonomous National Award Authorities which are serviced by the International Secretariat. All NAAs who accept the International Declaration and whose Award programme conforms to the following internationally agreed principles are co-equal members of The Duke of Edinburgh's Award International Association.

The International Declaration is:
'The Award concept is one of individual challenge. It presents to young people a balanced, non-competitive programme of voluntary activities which encourages personal discovery and growth, self-reliance, perseverance, responsibility to themselves and service to their community.'

The fundamental principles of the Award programme are:
- The voluntary nature of participation by young people, without discrimination of any kind.
- The age range of participants, i.e. 14 to 25 years.
- The basic structure of the Award programme, i.e. its four mandatory Sections and its three levels of Award.
- The minimum time requirement laid down for the completion of each Award, i.e. for direct entrants, 6, 12 and 18 months.

Within this framework, National Award Authorities adapt the Award programme to suit the needs of their young people and the resources available.

• Chapter 2:
Structure of
the Award
Scheme
- Supporting
Organisations
- The
International
Award

There are National Award Authorities in the following countries:

- **The Duke of Edinburgh's Award:** *Australia, Bahamas, Barbados, Bermuda, Canada, Cayman Islands, Dominica, Falkland Islands, Fiji, Gibraltar, Grenada, Hong Kong, India, Jamaica, Montserrat, New Zealand, Pakistan, St Lucia, St Helena & Dependencies, St Vincent, Solomon Islands, United Kingdom*

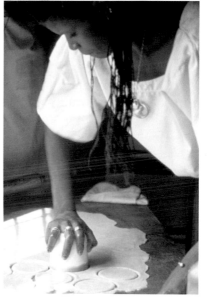

- **The President's Award:** *The Gambia, Republic of Ireland, Kenya, Malta, Trinidad and Tobago, Malawi, Zambia, Zimbabwe*
- **The National Youth Award:** *Mauritius, Sierra Leone, Sri Lanka*
- **Le Mérite International de la Jeunesse:** *Benin, Central African Republic, Chad, Comores, Côte d'Ivoire, Gabon, Guinea*
- **The Benelux Award:** *Belgium, Netherlands*
- **Mérite Jeunesse Bénélux:** *Luxembourg*
- **The Premier's Award:** *Malaysia*
- **The National Youth Achievement Award:** *Singapore*
- **The Namibia Youth Award:** *Namibia*
- **The Gold Shield Award:** *South Africa*
- **Adikarsa Nugraha Cestita:** *Indonesia*
- **The Congressional Award:** *USA*
- **The Crown Prince Award:** *Jordan*
- **The Head of State Award Scheme:** *Ghana*
- **The Israel Youth Award:** *Israel*
- **The Nigerian National Youth Award:** *Nigeria*
- **Premio Infante D.Henrique:** *Portugal*
- **The Prince Makhosini Award:** *Swaziland*
- **The Prince Mohato Award:** *Lesotho*
- **Priz Sénégalais Pour la Promotion de la Jeunesse:** *Senegal*
- **The Source of the Nile Award:** *Uganda*
- **Ordre National du Mérite de la Jeunesse:** *Cameroon*

The Award is also operated by independent Units in a further 20 countries worldwide. For further information contact the International Secretariat.

• Chapter 2: Structure of the Award Scheme - The International Award

CHAPTER 3
Operating the Award Scheme

As with all activities for young people, success in the Scheme depends on good preparation and organisation. The programme must be simply explained and sensibly interpreted both to the young people themselves and to the adults who will help them through the Award programme.

Although at first sight responsibility for running the Scheme may present a somewhat daunting prospect, closer study will reveal the flexibility of the programme and the way in which it can be used to complement current activities and adapted to suit local conditions.

The purpose of this chapter is to offer guidance to users of the Scheme, especially those preparing to adopt it for the first time.

3.1 BENEFITS OF OPERATING THE AWARD SCHEME

Benefits to Organisations

The Duke of Edinburgh's Award is a youth programme which enjoys high public recognition and acclaim. Operating Authorities may use the status and profile of the Scheme to enhance their appeal to young people and extend the range of opportunities within their existing programme.

- The Scheme provides an off-the-shelf accessible programme of activities geared to the development of the individual. It has been finely tuned over the years into an efficient and effective tool. Prince Philip described the Award as 'a DIY kit in the art of civilised living'.
- Three levels of Award provide tangible evidence of success and effort on the part of young people. This has obvious advantages at a time when organisations are required to be more accountable. This progressive approach also acts as a strong motivation for young people.
- The Scheme is a magnet to adults as well as young people. An efficiently run Scheme attracts a large number of volunteers who derive great satisfaction from sharing their enthusiasm, experience and skills. The Scheme bridges the age gap.
- Operating the Scheme encourages the establishment of community networks and links. The Scheme has thrived over

• Chapter 3:
Operating the
Award Scheme
- Benefits of
Operating
the Award
Scheme

the years as a result of the great contribution of many voluntary and statutory agencies. These agencies are usually willing to assist any operator of the Award Scheme.

- The programme is a currency which is accepted nationally and internationally.
- The Award Scheme is concerned with 'empowering young people to take greater responsibility for their own lives, to discover new talents, to advocate on behalf of others and to take positive action in the community,' and therefore has a major contribution to make to the curriculum of the Youth Service.
- As an extra-curricular activity in schools, the Award can act as a value-added component for the personal and social development of pupils enhancing the accepted range of cross-curricular elements.
- The sense of self-confidence, the problem-solving skills and the ability to work as part of a team are valued by employers, not only when recruiting staff, but also when training their existing workforce.

Benefits to Young People

The Scheme gives opportunities for young people to:

- Enjoy a wide variety of physical, creative and aesthetic experiences which encourage their personal growth and development.
- Experience new lifestyles and cultures outside their own immediate neighbourhood, possibly abroad.
- Experience a variety of learning and teaching styles with people from different walks of life.
- Take decisions of increasing complexity and accept responsibility for the consequences.
- Discover new talents and abilities.
- Test values and beliefs.
- Give a continuing personal commitment of service to others.
- Establish and sustain deep and satisfying inter-personal relationships.
- Negotiate their own personal programme of participation, seeking out and researching relevant information, and gradually take responsibility for their own learning.
- Understand their own strengths and weaknesses, assess their personal level of competence, increase their own personal effectiveness and take responsibility for their own lives.

• Chapter 3:
Operating the
Award Scheme
- Benefits of
Operating
the Award
Scheme

- Develop qualities such as enterprise, initiative and leadership which are highly regarded by employers.
- Experience a sense of fun and enjoyment.

3.2   THE ROLE OF THE UNIT LEADER

Adults may have a number of reasons for establishing an Award group. Introducing the Scheme may be seen as a means of deriving a personal sense of satisfaction and enjoyment, fulfilling a requirement of a job description or giving back to others some of the benefits of previous Award experience. Others may wish to introduce the value-added benefits of the Scheme to a group. Whatever the reason, the success of the Scheme in any Unit may depend on the way in which it is first introduced which, in turn, is influenced by the groups of young people to be targeted. Introducing the Scheme demands a different approach in each situation according to whether it is a school or youth group, young people with special needs, those from a particular ethnic group, young adults in the workforce or young offenders. A strategy which will succeed in one situation cannot necessarily be applied to another.

It is essential to remember that, whatever the energies or talents of a particular individual, it is a near impossible task for any one person to run the Scheme and oversee every Section. Although it is necessary for the Unit Leader to act as co-ordinator, operating the programme successfully demands a team approach, whatever the size of Unit, if young people are to be offered a comprehensive range of activities and benefit from a rich diversity of leadership styles.

Responsibilities of the Unit Leader

In every Unit there should be one adult with the responsibility for co-ordinating the work of participants and their Adult Helpers. The Leader need not be involved with the detailed running of any particular part of the Scheme, but should build up a balanced team of helpers to cover different aspects of the Scheme. This will ensure continuity, a pool of expertise and a sharing of responsibilities.

The role of the Leader is partly promotional and partly operational. The responsibilities are to:
- Maintain a knowledge of the Scheme.
- Launch and promote the Scheme.

• Chapter 3:
  Operating the
  Award Scheme
  - Benefits of
    Operating
    the Award
    Scheme
  - The Role of
    the Unit
    Leader

- Liaise with the Award Officer of the appropriate Operating Authority.
- Obtain promotional and operational literature.
- Recruit, brief and arrange the training of Adult Helpers in accordance with the Operating Authority procedures.
- Order and issue *Entrance Packs* from the Operating Authority.
- Plan and co-ordinate a comprehensive range of activities.
- Discuss with participants their choice of activities.
- Obtain parental support and consent where appropriate.
- Comply with the administrative and operational procedures of the Operating Authority and the Award Scheme.
- Understand the insurance arrangements provided by the Operating Authority and the Award Scheme.
- Dovetail Award activities into other Unit programmes.
- Review financial arrangements.
- Record participants' progress through the Award Scheme.
- Help young people to continue the Scheme on relocation.
- Submit *Record Books* to the Operating Authority for authorisation.
- Arrange the presentation of badges and certificates in consultation with the Operating Authority.
- Publicise the Scheme locally.

3.3 SETTING UP THE AWARD SCHEME IN A UNIT

Although is is important to tailor a launch of the Scheme to local circumstances the following ten-point action plan describes the main tasks involved.

1. **Make contact with the local Operating Authority and the Award Officer who may provide:**
   - Knowledge of the Operating Authority's procedures and channels of communication.
   - Knowledge of the local area and opportunities available for young people.
   - Knowledge of local resources including equipment, particularly for Expeditions.
   - Supplies of Award literature.
   - A system for keeping records and administrative support.
   - Contact with other Award users.
   - Access to training courses.

• Chapter 3:
  Operating the
  Award Scheme
  - The Role of
    the Unit
    Leader
  - Setting Up
    the Award
    Scheme in
    a Unit

2. **Recruit and train Adult Helpers who have:**
   - A genuine interest in young people.
   - The ability to communicate.
   - A particular expertise they wish to share.
   - An understanding of the philosophy and conditions of the Award.
   - An appreciation of their responsibilities to young people and the Operating Authority.

3. **Identify a venue which may be:**
   - At a school or youth centre.
   - In an industrial or commercial company.
   - At the local church or other place of worship.
   - In an independent 'Open' Centre.
   - In any meeting room accessible to young people.
   - In the Leader's home.

4. **Develop contacts with local institutions and organisations which may:**
   - Offer activities within the Award programme.
   - Be a source of potential participants.
   - Offer a source of Adult Helpers.
   - Provide equipment/materials.
   - Sponsor events.

5. **Promote the Scheme to young people by:**
   - Using promotional material.
   - Giving talks, video/slide presentations to large groups.
   - Involving Award Holders.
   - Planning an open evening at which young people can 'taste' activities.

6. **Enrol young people who should:**
   - Understand the challenge of the Award.
   - Decide which Award to work towards.
   - Complete an enrolment form.
   - Pay an entrance fee.
   - Receive an *Entrance Pack* containing the *Record Book*.
   - Decide on a personal programme of activities.

• Chapter 3:
Operating the
Award Scheme
- Setting Up
the Award
Scheme in
a Unit

7. **Plan and organise activities by:**
    - Involving young people responsibly.
    - Satisfying individual needs and aspirations.
    - Identifying adults with appropriate skills.
    - Delegating tasks and working as a team.
    - Utilising the resources of the community.

8. **Maintain accurate records by:**
    - Keeping enrolment forms and record sheets.
    - Checking initial details are completed in the *Record Books*.
    - Explaining the purpose of the *Record Book* to adults and young people.
    - Obtaining the Operating Authority's approval of Instructors and Assessors.
    - Adhering to the financial and administrative procedures of the Operating Authority.
    - Monitoring and recording progress regularly.
    - Forwarding *Record Books* to the Operating Authority for approval of Awards.

9. **Establish support networks including:**
    - Parents of participants.
    - Potential fundraisers and local business contacts.
    - Influential members of the local community.
    - Other Award Units.
    - Local Award Committees.

10. **Publicise the Award group by:**
    - Involving participants in planning events and displays.
    - Using the local press/radio.
    - Publicising the achievements of the young people using all available resources and opportunities.
    - Inviting local Councillors and the business community to open evenings.
    - Arranging prestigious Award presentation evenings.

    THEN TAKE A NIGHT OFF!

• Chapter 3:
Operating the
Award Scheme
- Setting Up
the Award
Scheme in
a Unit

3.4 KEY ROLES IN THE OPERATION OF THE AWARD SCHEME

There is a range of key roles in the operation of the Scheme. The following descriptions may be helpful in clarifying what these are:

Territorial/Regional Officers

The Territorial/Regional Officer, as a direct employee of the charity, The Duke of Edinburgh's Award, promotes the development of the Scheme, supports Operating Authorities in carrying out their responsibilities under the licence and monitors the quality of delivery.

Award Officers

The Award Officer is the person designated by the Operating Authority to be responsible for all aspects of the Scheme within the organisation.

Development/Field Officers or Co-ordinators

Operating Authorities often appoint employees or voluntary representatives who are responsible for promoting, co-ordinating and supporting the operation of the Scheme through User Units in a specific geographical area.

Award Unit Leaders

The Award Leader takes responsibility for a group of young people and facilitates their involvement in every Section and at each level of the Award.

Adult Helpers

The Adult Helper assists the Adult Leader in the administration, organisation and operation of a particular aspect of the Scheme.

Instructors

The Instructor, approved by the Operating Authority, helps young people to acquire knowledge of and improve their skills in a particular activity in order to comply with the requirements specified in the *Award Handbook*.

Supervisors

In the Service Section, the Supervisor is responsible for supporting young people by arranging the necessary briefing,

• Chapter 3:
Operating the
Award Scheme
- Key Roles
in the
Operation of
the Award
Scheme

organising counselling sessions and advising on the compilation of the diary, account and, at Gold, the study topic.

In the Expeditions Section the Supervisor is responsible to the Operating Authority for the safety and well-being of the young people during their practice and qualifying ventures.

Assessors

The Assessor, who is appropriately qualified, experienced or accredited, confirms whether young people have fulfilled the conditions and requirements of a particular Section of the Award as specified in the *Award Handbook*.

3.5 ADULT VOLUNTEERS, INSTRUCTORS, SUPERVISORS AND ASSESSORS

Adult participation

The successful operation of the Scheme in any community depends largely on the involvement of a number of adults prepared to devote their talents, enthusiasm and time to help young people discover the enjoyment of Award participation.

Although many are busy people, they are very ready to share their special skills and interests with young people, especially if it is made clear that this is the limit of their involvement and that times can be arranged to suit their own convenience. Adults are often attracted to the idea of contributing to the development of young people and influencing their future lives. The Scheme can act as a rich source of development for adults as well as young people.

The larger the number of volunteers prepared to help, the wider the choice of activities which can be offered to young people. The aim should be to seek a little help from as many people as possible rather than a great deal of help from just a few.

Experience in recruiting adult help has reinforced the value of a personal approach, as opposed to a general call for volunteers, and of specific requests for assistance in a particular capacity or area of interest. Having secured the co-operation of adults it is important to sustain their interest and enthusiasm and to ensure that they fully understand their role.

• Chapter 3:
Operating the
Award Scheme
- Key Roles
in the
Operation of
the Award
Scheme
- Adult
Volunteers,
Instructors,
Supervisors
and
Assessors

Instruction, Supervision and Assessment

The approval of an individual as an Adult Helper or as a suitably qualified Instructor, Supervisor and Assessor rests entirely with the Operating Authority whose procedures must be followed. This approval must be sought before a young person embarks on a particular activity. Suitability in some fields may be indicated by recognised qualifications and in others by the knowledge and experience of the individual. It should not be assumed, however, that, because they are experts in their subjects, they necessarily understand the principles of assessment for the Award.

Briefing and training is essential and the appropriate *Notes for Adult Helpers* leaflets should always be provided. Wild Country Assessors for Expeditions and Explorations should be accredited through the Award's Accreditation Scheme.

Assisting organisations, such as St. John Ambulance, the Police Service or British Trust for Conservation Volunteers, will offer help in various ways including instruction and assessment. The need to establish an extensive network of local organisations who are willing to help cannot be over-emphasised and some useful contacts are included in the following chapters.

Instructors and Supervisors should be suitably experienced people, holding appropriate qualifications where specified in the detailed programmes, and approved:

- For the **BRONZE AWARD**, with the approval of Operating Authorities, by Unit Award Leaders.
- For the **SILVER AWARD,** by representatives of Operating Authorities at local/area level.
- For the **GOLD AWARD,** by representatives of Operating Authorities at Regional (or equivalent) or Headquarters level.

On completion of each individual programme it is necessary for a participant's achievement to be assessed. The Assessor's signature in the *Record Book* certifies that the Award requirements for that Section have been satisfactorily completed.

The basis of assessment is laid down in the detailed conditions for each Section in the following chapters.

• Chapter 3:
Operating the
Award Scheme
- Adult
Volunteers,
Instructors,
Supervisors
and
Assessors

Assessors should be suitably qualified people approved:

- For the Bronze Award, by representatives of Operating Authorities at local/area level.
- For the Silver Award, by representatives of Operating Authorities at Regional (or equivalent) or Headquarters.
- For the Gold Award, by the Headquarters of the Operating Authority.

3.6 RECORD BOOKS

Entrance Packs containing a *Record Book* are issued by the Operating Authority on entry into the Scheme and become the personal property of the participants. One *Record Book* is used for both the Bronze and Silver Awards whilst a separate *Gold Entrance Pack* is used for the Gold Award by both progressive and direct entrants. Purchase of the *Record Book* denotes a young person's entrance into the Scheme and provides:

- Personal Accident Cover for participants in connection with approved Award activities.
- All certificates and badges.
- The services of the Award Offices and Expedition Panels throughout participation in the Scheme.
- Arrangements for Gold Award presentation.

The *Record Book* records details of the activities which have been undertaken. It forms a record of progress and achievement through the Scheme, verified by adults who have carried out the assessment in each Section. Only success and achievement should be recorded. If an Assessor feels that the requirement has not been met, the participant should be encouraged to make further effort, and no entry made in the *Record Book*.

When making entries, Instructors and Assessors should make full and appropriate comments and complete all requested details so that the Operating Authority can check that conditions and requirements have been met.

Leaders must ensure that the following particulars are absolutely correct:
- Name and address of participant, in capital letters.
- Date of birth.

• Chapter 3:
  Operating the
  Award Scheme
  - Adult
  Volunteers,
  Instructors,
  Supervisors
  and
  Assessors
  - Record
  Books

- Date of issue (which is also date of entry).
- Name of Operating Authority.
- Dates when activities were started and completed.

The *Record Book* and *Entrance Pack* contain detailed information on the Award which should be read by participants before they commence any activities toward their Award. The Entrance Pack also includes an interesting selection of promotional items and special offers.

Continuing the Scheme

When young people are leaving school or moving to a new area, it is important to encourage them to continue with the Scheme and to take steps to enable them to do so. The person best able to help in this regard is likely to be the designated Award Officer of the Operating Authority, who will be in touch with all User Units in the area.

Change of Operating Authority

If a participant moves from one area or organisation to another, it is important that the current Operating Authority ensures that the *Record Book* is up to date and forwards the completed detachable page from the *Record Book* to the appropriate new Award office. All entries in a *Record Book* authenticated by the old Operating Authority should be honoured by the new.

Loss of Record Book

In cases of genuine loss, *Record Books* may be replaced and previous entries vouched for by the Operating Authority. Lost badges may be replaced on application to the Award Office; recipients must provide proof that the Award was granted and a small charge will be made.

3.7 AUTHORISATION OF AWARDS AND AWARD PRESENTATIONS

A participant qualifies for an Award when all the requirements in the *Record Book* have been completed to the satisfaction of the Operating Authority.

The *Record Book* should be sent to the appropriate official in the Operating Authority, not to the Award Office, so that the pages headed *'Certificates and Awards'* may be signed.

• Chapter 3:
Operating the
Award Scheme
- Record
Books
- Authorisation
of Awards
and Award
Presentations

At Gold level, the *Gold Award Notification Form*, accurately completed and signed by the responsible person, must also be sent to the Operating Authority who in turn will forward it to the appropriate Territorial, Regional or National Award Office.

Authorisation of Awards is to be undertaken:

- For the **BRONZE AWARD**, by Operating Authorities or their representatives at local level.
- For the **SILVER AWARD**, by Operating Authorities or their representatives at Regional or Headquarters level.
- For the **GOLD AWARD**, at the highest level in each Operating Authority. (Confirmation by the Territorial or Regional Office, or in the case of National Operating Authorities, the National Award Office, is required before final confirmation with the participant.)

Gold Award Holder's Badge

Gold Award Holder's Brooch

Gold Award Holder's Stick Pin

Certificates and Badges

After the Award has been authorised the appropriate certificate and badge may be awarded. The young person is awarded a pin badge for Bronze and Silver. For the Gold Award, participants may choose a miniature stickpin, badge or brooch.

For Bronze level, the Award has produced Sectional Certificates. These may be issued, at the discretion of the Unit leader, with the approval of the Operating Authority, to those young people who need added motivation to participate further. The Certificates provide tangible encouragement as they progress through each Section of the Bronze Award. For young people who are unable for any reason to complete all Sections of the Award, these Certificates provide recognition of their achievement. For the full Bronze Award, however, the *Record Book* must be authorised by the designated Officer in the Operating Authority.

Award Presentations

Gold, Silver and Bronze Badges and Silver and Bronze Certificates should be presented locally by Operating Authorities as soon as is practicable after participants have completed their Awards. Instead of holding separate presentations in various user

• Chapter 3:
Operating the
Award Scheme
- Authorisation
of Awards
and Award
Presentations

organisations and groups, many Local Government Authorities or Award Committees arrange annual presentations of Awards by a notable personality to give status to the achievements of all participants and to provide an opportunity for local publicity.

A young person must not be invited to a Presentation Ceremony until the Award has been authorised at the highest level and, for the Gold Award, confirmed by the appropriate Award office. To obtain this confirmation a completed Gold Award Notification form must be forwarded.

Those who qualify for the Gold Award are invited to a reception held at one of the Royal Palaces. These Presentations represent the culmination of achievement within the Award. Reports of Gold Award Presentations in the local press will raise the profile of the Scheme locally and increase participation in its programme.

When the date of the Gold Presentation is known, and this may be several months after the submission of the form, an invitation package will be sent to the Gold Award holder.

3.8 PUBLICITY AND PROMOTION

The importance of good publicity by press, radio and television concerning the purpose and achievements of Award participants will be obvious to all Operating Authorities. As with all aspects of youth work, no matter how good the concept, the Award Scheme will become redundant if no-one knows about it.

The Duke of Edinburgh's Award Headquarters is able to promote the idea of the Award so that the general public as well as teachers, industrialists, youth workers, young people and their parents are aware of its existence and value.

The Scheme relies on its operators to publicise it locally to those who will actually take up the challenge. The promotion falls into three overlapping categories:

- Promoting a positive image of young people by recognising their achievements and their contribution to the local community.

• Chapter 3:
Operating the
Award Scheme
- Authorisation
of Awards
and Award
Presentations
- Publicity and
Promotion

- Publicising the Scheme to attract new recruits and Adult Helpers.
- Publicising the activities and successes of local Award groups to engage the active support of potential sponsors and of those holding positions of responsibility.

3.9 FINANCIAL ARRANGEMENTS

Cost to the Individual

Entrance Fee: There is an entry fee payable on first joining the Scheme which covers the cost of the *Entrance Pack* and *Record Book*. There is one pack for the Bronze and Silver levels and a separate pack for the Gold.

The Scheme is intended to be a challenge in all respects and it is reasonable to expect that young people should make a financial contribution. This contribution also implies a commitment to future involvement and the entrance fee is a comparatively small sum in relation to the services provided. However, if it acts as a barrier or discouragement to some young people, Operating Authorities are encouraged either to offer a means of paying by instalments or to help young people seek sponsorship locally.

Award Activities: It is usually Award activities rather than the entrance fee which make the greatest financial demands on young people. There is sufficient flexibility in the programme, however, for individuals to choose activities which match their resources. Award participation frequently opens doors to subsidised activities and there are local and national trusts which offer grant aid to individuals. Access to pools of equipment maintained by Operating Authorities or Award Committees can significantly reduce the cost of participation, particularly in the Expeditions Section.

Costs to the Organisation

• Chapter 3:
Operating the
Award Scheme
- Authorisation
of Awards
and Award
Presentations
- Financial
Arrangements

Operating the Scheme can be extremely cost-effective. Finance will be required to purchase operational and promotional literature and it may also be necessary to subsidise the cost of transport to the expedition area or other areas, for basic administration and possibly to reimburse Instructors and Assessors for out-of-pocket travelling expenses.

Policies and practice over the remuneration of Adult Helpers, Instructors and Assessors vary widely, but it should always be remembered that The Duke of Edinburgh's Award thrives on volunteers. Payment to Adult Helpers may undermine this voluntary ethos but Operating Authorities must obviously create their own policy, depending on resources.

Financial Assistance

Private trusts, Local Authorities, or other statutory departments may give assistance through grant aid or loan of equipment. Many Award Leaders find that the national profile and credibility of the Scheme make it possible to recruit the financial support of local industry and commerce, particularly for innovative projects.

Imaginative fundraising events can act as a focal point of the Award Unit programme, galvanising the collective energies of participants and Adult Helpers. The Scheme ultimately thrives on the belief that 'anything's possible'.

3.10 LITERATURE

A wide range of operational and promotional material in the form of books, posters, leaflets in a variety of languages, videos, tape-slide sets, films and souvenir items is available from The Award Scheme Ltd. Details may be found in the Catalogue and Order Form published annually and available from The Award Scheme Ltd or Operating Authorities.

All involved with the Scheme in any capacity should be supplied with, or have access to, the relevant items of Award literature.

The main items for operating and promoting the Award Scheme are detailed below:

Operational Literature

Award Handbook - the principal item of operational literature and essential for all those operating or participating in the Scheme. New editions are published every four years and regular updates are contained in both the *Award News* section of *Award Journal* and in an annual *Award Handbook Update Pack*.

• Chapter 3:
Operating the
Award Scheme
- Financial
  Arrangements
- Literature

Expedition Guide - detailed guidance and advice on all aspects of Expedition training and qualifying ventures at all levels and for all modes of Expedition travel.

Exploration Resource Pack - a loose-leaf pack giving ideas, information and advice for both Exploration and Expedition purposes.

Land Navigation - Route-Finding with Map and Compass - detailed guidance on finding your way and using a map and compass in various terrains.

Workshop - Design and Make Expedition Equipment - a book which shows how to design and make quality expedition clothing and equipment.

Skills Programmes Folder - a loose-leaf folder containing detailed programmes for activities in the Skills Section. Annual *Skills Updates Packs* are available from The Award Scheme Ltd.

Notes for Adult Helpers - a set of five leaflets outlining the conditions for each of the Sections of the Award. They are essential reading for all Instructors, Supervisers and Assessors. Available free of charge.

Over to You - a comprehensive pack of training resource material to assist Trainers in planning and running Leader training courses at all levels.

Operating Authorities Guide - a loose-leaf reference book detailing the responsibilities for all Operating Authorities.

Promotional Material

Award Journal - the Award's magazine is published in January, April and September each year and is free to Operating Authorities. It contains features and editorials on topics of special interest and a calendar of training events and conferences. *Award News*, a supplement within the *Journal*, contains items of operational importance and changes to Award conditions or requirements and information on new publications.

Why Not You? and *Outline* - leaflets outlining The Duke of Edinburgh's Award and the framework of the Award programme.

Help Wanted - a leaflet identifying the need for Adult Helpers and outlining the framework of the Award programme.

The Duke of Edinburgh's Award goes into Business - a leaflet highlighting the benefits of the Award to both employers and employees.

Award Scheme Logo

The Duke of Edinburgh's Award name and logo are registered trade and service marks and should only be used by those authorised to do so. All licensed Operating Authorities are authorised to use the logo and they in turn can authorise Award Units, Local Award Committees and Expedition Teams acting under their auspices. Any other individual group or organisation wishing to use the logo **must** obtain permission in advance from The Duke of Edinburgh's Award Headquarters.

- The logo must only be used in full and must never be redrawn or adjusted manually or by computer.
- The design can be printed in black or two colours (blue and red only as detailed below).
- If printing in two colours, the blue is Pantone 281 and the red is Pantone 199. If printing in the four colour process, the blue is a mix of 110% Cyan, 72% Magenta and 38% Black. The red is 100% Magenta and 65% Yellow.
- The design can be printed in white out of a solid dark blue.
- It can also be printed with the words reversed out (white) from a blue solid with the cypher and flashes in red.

Detailed guidance on how best to apply the design, along with artwork for reproduction, is available from Award Headquarters.

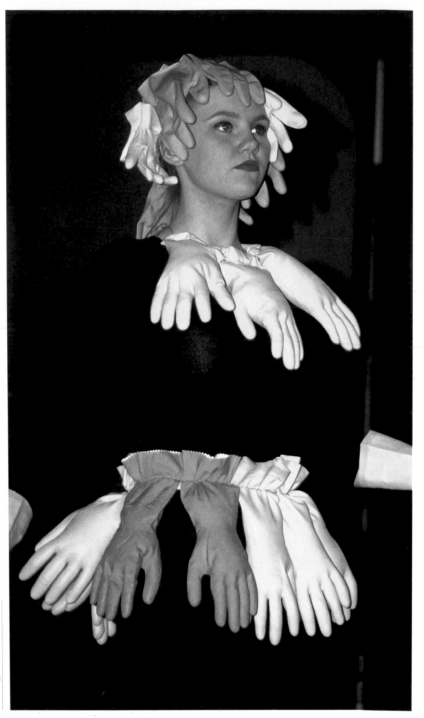

CHAPTER 4
The Award Scheme and Young People

The earlier chapters of this *Award Handbook* have attempted to explore the various aspects of The Duke of Edinburgh's Award, its philosophy, its framework and structure, and its conditions and requirements. Essential as this information and understanding is to an Adult Leader, the Award remains but an imaginatively conceived idea until it is brought to life by its application with young people. The concept of the Scheme has no intrinsic value; its benefits and outcomes are manifested only when young people participate in its programme in partnership with supportive adults.

Leaders should understand the difference between the concept of 'process' and 'task' when working with young people. In its broadest sense, 'process' refers to how things are done rather than what is done. The Scheme is not only a vehicle for developing skills and undertaking a series of challenging tasks, however developmental that may be. The real benefit is derived from a programme when concentration is also given to the process or how the Scheme is operated with young people. The progression towards the self-responsibility, the involvement of young people in planning the programme and organising the Unit, the use of participative methods of delivery all help to maximise the effectiveness of the Award programme.

Working with young people is an adventure; it is not an exact science with magic formulae, easy solutions and simple hypotheses. It is common practice to 'label' and categorise young people with the expectation that they will exhibit pre-determined patterns of behaviour, but this is a mistake. They are refreshingly unpredictable. Award activities add to this unpredictability, particularly if they are challenging and unfamiliar or involve establishing new relationships.

If working with young people is to be an adventure, everyone involved must embrace the challenge. Introducing innovative methods of delivery and new approaches involves a considerable degree of risk, and failure is one of the indicators of performance in the 'risk business'. Adults should celebrate the unique talents and abilities of young people by moulding the Scheme to each individual and avoiding the temptation to fit participants into a preconceived programme with established methods of delivery. As each Award programme is designed to focus on the needs and abilities of individual participants, no two programmes should be identical.

Group rules and peer pressure are powerful influences on young people. Groups frequently trap their individual members in particular roles from which it is difficult to escape. In an attempt to satisfy their need for security, young people sometimes want to stick to familiar activities. They have found something they enjoy but it may be a comfortable routine rather than a developmental experience. Adult Helpers must develop a careful strategy to encourage and support them to try something new. Participation in the Award programme should encourage daring, effort and persistence, attributes which are of value in many aspects of life.

A whole range of human emotions can emerge from working with young people, from concern and frustration to fulfilment and sheer joy. Adult Helpers are almost equal beneficiaries from the Scheme with the participants themselves. In fact, its voluntary ethos determines that, if adults cease to enjoy their involvement, then they will inevitably leave.

It is important, however, for adults to consider and admit the satisfaction they derive from their work. They may enjoy responding to the needs of others, they may find fulfilment in sharing their expertise, they may even gain a sense of importance by helping young people and playing a part in their lives. Danger arises when adults try to be too helpful and take responsibility away from the participants by being 'in complete control' and organising everything on their behalf. They should adopt an unerring principle of never undertaking anything which young people can effectively do for themselves.

4.1 CHOICE AND SUITABILITY OF ACTIVITIES

It is important to remember that, as far as practicable, participants should themselves select the activities they wish to pursue, having regard to the local facilities available. The Award aims to extend experience and one criterion for success is therefore improvement on an individual's starting point. For this reason, work undertaken prior to entering the Scheme cannot count towards an Award.

An essential element in Award participation is the progression through the levels. Young people learn self-reliance and it is the Award's philosophy to empower them to take responsibility for their own programmes and, having gained confidence and experience, apply it to other aspects of their lives. At the higher levels of the Award, an increasing proportion of Award activities should be conducted outside the immediate environment of the Unit.

The Award Scheme sets minimum requirements but, in order for it to stretch abilities, it is important that these are exceeded where necessary to provide a real challenge. One participant's mountain is another participant's hill. On the other hand, the activity should not be so daunting as to present unrealistic expectations and hence reduce rather than build the confidence of young people. The role of the Leader, therefore, is to ensure that the degree of challenge is appropriate to the young person's ability and maturity.

Part of the Award's philosophy is that it is a marathon rather than a sprint and again the times laid down in the *Award Handbook* are minimum requirements. Young people should therefore give careful thought to planning their programmes in order allow themselves time to savour the experience of participation and do justice both to themselves and to each Section. This is not a fast lane Award.

Guidelines on Operating the Sections

The Scheme is designed to allow flexibility but there are, of necessity, some basic principles which must be followed to preserve its framework and integrity.

- **Young people are expected to undertake a balanced programme of activities and follow different forms of activity in each Section.**

• Chapter 4: The Award Scheme and Young People - Choice and Suitability of Activities

For example, although canoe-related options appear in all Sections (i.e. Canoe Lifeguard, Canoe Expedition, Canoe Building, Canoeing, Canoe Residential Courses) it would be inappropriate for an individual to undertake all of these options.

Whilst it is possible to follow the same activity within a particular Section for the three levels, the Award is intended to extend horizons and allow participants to discover new talents. Young people should therefore always be encouraged to try something new when they embark on the next level of Award.

- **If a programme appears in the *Award Handbook* in one Section, it should not be transferred to another for convenience.**

For example, although a participant may help out at a library, Librarianship is listed under the Skills Section and is not transferable to the Service Section.

- **Sectional activities sometimes fall within certain groups. This is for well-considered reasons, very often of safety to the participant or those they seek to help. An activity demanding a course of training or qualification cannot, therefore, be transferred to another group.**

For example, Sports Coaching can only be undertaken as a Service option under the wider Group Three Community Sports Leaders' Award. It is not acceptable for a participant to coach others in Gymnastics by following a Group One Community Service Programme.

Youth work with a Uniformed Organisation is a Group Three form of Service requiring a training qualification at Silver and Gold. At Bronze only it is acceptable to by-pass this qualification by helping within a uniformed organisation under a Community Service programme. At this level, youth work should include supervised assistance with specific activities such as Music, Craft or Badgework.

- **The content and duration of individual programmes should be followed as they appear in the *Award Handbook*, with any variations for those with special needs being made in accordance with the conditions.**

For example, a group of young people with learning difficulties should choose a Community Service option involving more Practical Service, rather than following a simplified Group Three First Aid course with little opportunity for offering practical service.

Young people should concentrate on their chosen Physical Recreation activity and participate for the required minimum rather than 'mix and match' different programmes to achieve the points total.

4.2 DOVETAILING THE SCHEME

It should be remembered that the Scheme is not an organisation, but a programme available to all young people. Its flexibility allows it to be dovetailed into programmes of Units with a wide diversity of aims to act as a 'value-added factor'.

A group can be set up specially for Award Scheme purposes. Equally, established Units such as Scout Groups, Ranger Guide Units and youth clubs, may use the Scheme as an extension of their existing programme of activities. There may be close similarity between some of the activities undertaken by young people for their Awards and those they are required to undertake for special qualifications or badges within their own particular youth organisation. In these circumstances, the activities followed may also count for the Award, provided that the relevant conditions are fulfilled and the young person has joined the Scheme by purchasing a *Record Book*. On the other hand, it is not possible to gain an Award simply by participating in the programme of a youth organisation; additional effort and commitment must be given. As already mentioned, retrospective qualifications are also not permitted because it is the progression from a starting point, however advanced that may be, that constitutes 'success' in the context of the Award.

The Duke of Edinburgh's Award is concerned with relative rather than absolute standards, and is therefore incompatible with progressive competency-based National Vocational Qualifications

(NVQs). A talented young musician, for example, may complete Grade VIII of The Royal School of Music for the Bronze Award whilst another young person just taking up the piano may complete Grade II for the Gold.

Although it is not possible to align the overall Award programme to an NVQ, an increasing number of organisations offering activities in particular Sections of the Award link their standards to NVQ levels. Some participants, therefore, may be able to gain an NVQ through completing that Section.

The Award has developed National Record of Achievement (NRA) forms for Bronze, Silver and Gold levels, to be included in the NRA document introduced by the Government. The document acts as a record of young people's achievements in both National Curriculum and extra-curricular activities. Every young person is given this 'portfolio of experience' on leaving school and, if it is used effectively, it can contribute to the Accreditation of Prior Learning (APL) for NVQs.

The form, which should be completed by participants in consultation with their Award Leaders, provides a summary not only of the activities they have undertaken but of the less tangible but as important skills and qualities they have gained.

4.3 PARENTAL CONSENT AND SUPPORT

• Chapter 4: The
  Award
  Scheme and
  Young People
  - Dovetailing
    the Scheme
  - Parental
    Consent and
    Support

It is desirable to obtain parents' consent for participants under the age of 18, not only to satisfy any requirement of the Operating Authority but also to engage their interest. Parents can often help as Instructors and Assessors (or persuade others to do so), and provide equipment, transport and other facilities. Their support and encouragement may inspire participants to persevere when the initial novelty has worn off.

4.4 GOLD AWARD HOLDERS

Award holders, in particular those who have attained Gold, can give valuable assistance in helping others to gain Awards. Award holders wishing to continue their involvement in the Scheme are encouraged to do so by acting as Award Leaders, Supervisors, Instructors or Assessors or assisting with publicity or fundraising. A list of categories of help which Gold Award holders can provide is summarised in the leaflet *What Next?*

Further details are available from Territorial and Regional Offices or National Award Headquarters.

4.5 YOUNG PEOPLE WITH SPECIAL NEEDS

Everyone taking part in the Scheme is guided by its philosophy and must adhere to the same framework of levels, Sections, minimum time scales and age requirements. This means that there is no separate Award for participants with special needs. Since success is based on partici-pation and development from each individual's own starting point, all participants can benefit from taking part.

There is sufficient flexibility within the conditions and choice of activities available in each Section of the Award to enable young people with special needs to have an opportunity to participate and achieve.

Before they embark on the Award, it is important that potential participants, and their Leaders, have a reasonable understanding of what is required and the level of involvement expected. Responsibility for the safety of Award participants rests with the Operating Authority, and Leaders need to ensure that those entering the Award have an awareness of the activities they will be undertaking and that taking part will not cause irreparable damage to their health.

All young people who choose to participate in the Scheme should be capable of meeting the challenge and should be able to:

• Chapter 4: The Award Scheme and Young People
 Gold Award Holders
- Young People with Special Needs

- Make a commitment and have a basic ability to communicate.
- Have sufficient knowledge, skills, self-reliance and self-orientation, particularly when meeting the requirements of the Expeditions Section.
- Choose their own activities.
- Have the will to take part in the Scheme and not just a willingness to be led through it.

The Leader's counselling skills are of paramount importance in ensuring that individuals are challenged within their capabilities. Where participants have limited mobility or learning difficulties, the training (particularly for expeditions) will probably take longer and may require more practice, research, imagination and ingenuity on the part of both Leaders and participants to complete the chosen venture.

The other Section which may present more challenges for some is the Physical Recreation Section, but there is a wide choice of activities available and the index of activities is not exhaustive. Some participants may wish to choose a sport publicised through organisations promoting sports for those with disabilities.

The conditions laid down in the *Award Handbook* should be adhered to but it is possible to negotiate variations where a participant has a permanent physical or sensory disability. These are more likely to be necessary for the Expeditions Section than for any other. Variations are not permitted on the grounds of learning difficulties alone as the flexibility of the Scheme normally makes them unnecessary.

At all levels any proposed variations must be discussed with, and approved by, the Operating Authority.

At Gold the Territorial/Regional Office or Award Headquarters must be involved in the consultative process to ensure that participants receive effective guidance based on examples of good practice.

The Award programmes are sufficiently flexible to offer something to all young people. For those people whose range of capabilities or age mean that they fall outside the design of the Award, there are a number of other recognised regional and national Awards which may be more appropriate, e.g. The Gateway, Peak, Linx, Castle, Bridge/Mayor's and Caledonian Awards. Moreover, full use should be made of The Duke of Edinburgh's Award Sectional Certificates  which are available on completion of each Section at Bronze and provide recognition of success.

There are times when the Award requires its participants to work as a group. Here it is important to give guidance on forming the group so that each member will be actively involved and challenged at a level relating to their personal capabilities.

The intention of these few paragraphs is to reassure both Leaders and potential entrants that disability is not a barrier to participation. This *Handbook* is the common source of guidance for everyone wishing to operate or participate in the Award.

Note: Guidelines for requesting Variations, information on sports for the disabled, details of other Awards such as The Gateway Award and further guidance on operating the Award for people with special needs can be obtained from the Award's Regional and Territorial Officers.

Service

SECTION

Joe Cornish/National Trust

The Duke of Edinburgh's Award Handbook

Service

S E C T I O N

CONTENTS

Aim of the Service Section

To encourage Service to others.

The Principles

This Section is based on the belief that members of a community have a responsibility to each other and that voluntary help is needed.

Young people should receive briefing and training in appropriate skills, and have some knowledge of the needs of those whom they are assisting. For some young people, it may be the first time that they have been expected and trusted to offer help to others. The value of the Service to young people comes from the experience of training for and giving practical service, and gaining an appreciation of the needs of the community.

Benefits to Young People

Although the specific benefits depend on the choice of activity, the Service Section should offer participants the opportunity to:

- **give personal commitment** by dedicating leisure time to the service of others,
- **appreciate the needs of others and contribute to their well-being** by working with and for people with whom they would not normally come into contact,
- **trust and be trusted** perhaps for the first time,
- **understand personal strengths and weaknesses** by reviewing their performance in training and counselling sessions,
- **increase self-esteem** by receiving positive feedback from peers and adults, and learning to appreciate the value of their personal contribution,
- **overcome prejudice and fears** through building new relationships, questioning attitudes and values, and developing an empathy with others,

- **generate positive community action** by taking a pro-active role in identifying worthwhile Service opportunities which benefit the local community or the environment,
- **care for the environment** through practical involvement in projects,
- **accept responsibility** through a personal commitment to an organisation or member of the community.

Requirements

Participants are required to train for and give service to others. Consideration should first be given to the proposed form of **practical service** to be followed and then to the training required so that the Service can be undertaken with competence and insight.

This training may take the form of **either** briefing and counselling sessions leading directly to practical service of a non-specialised nature, or of a specialised training course as preparation for practical service in that field.

Forms of Service

The Service Section offers young people a wide choice according to their abilities, personal preferences and the opportunities available. The choice of Service activity should reflect a young person's individual interests, talents and capabilities but also challenge personal attitudes and build on previous experiences. The various forms of Service are set out in three categories to facilitate choice.

An activity listed in Groups Two and Three **cannot** be followed as a Service programme in Group One. The required training for Group Two courses **must** be completed and the appropriate qualification **must** be attained for Group Three.

Forms of Service

GROUP ONE
Service with a substantial element of practical involvement

- Children
- Elderly People
- People with Special Needs
- Other People in Need
- Environment
- Fundraising

GROUP TWO
Service requiring specialised training

- **Animal Welfare**
  - Care for Animals
- **Emergency Services**
  - Ambulance Service, Civil Aid, Fire Service, Police Service
- **Leadership in the Community**
  - Award Scheme Leadership, Service through Religious Education, Youth Work
- **Rescue**
  - Cave Rescue, Coastguard Service, Lifeboat Service, Mountain Rescue
- **Safety**
  - Cyclist Training Instruction, Home Accident Prevention, Road Safety

GROUP THREE
Service requiring a specific qualification

- **Care in the Community**
  - Child Care, First Aid, Home Nursing
- **Leadership in the Community**
  - Dance Leadership in the Community, Expedition and Mountain Leadership, Sports Leadership, Youth Work - Uniformed Organisations
- **Life Saving**
  - RLSS Life Saving, Surf Life Saving
- **Rescue**
  - Canoe Lifeguard, Rescue Coxswain

SERVICE
INTRODUCTION

• Forms of Service

Conditions – Summary

GROUP ONE
(Service with a substantial element of practical involvement)

- Briefing

- Practical Service

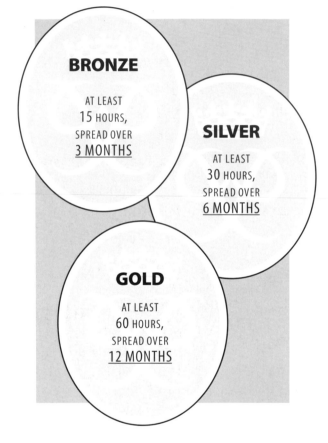

BRONZE

AT LEAST
15 HOURS,
SPREAD OVER
3 MONTHS

SILVER

AT LEAST
30 HOURS,
SPREAD OVER
6 MONTHS

GOLD

AT LEAST
60 HOURS,
SPREAD OVER
12 MONTHS

- Diary

- Three Counselling Sessions

- Account for Assessment

- Study Topic at Gold

GROUP TWO (Service requiring specialised training) and

GROUP THREE (Service leading to a specific qualification)

BRONZE
- Complete a course of specialised training and reach the required standard.
- Undertake related practical service.
- **Timescale:** at least 8 weeks involvement.

SILVER
- Complete a course of specialised training and reach the required standard.
- Undertake related practical service.
- **Timescale:** at least 16 weeks involvement.

GOLD
- Complete a course of specialised training and reach the required standard.
- Undertake 40 hours of related practical service.
- **Timescale:** at least 12 months involvement.

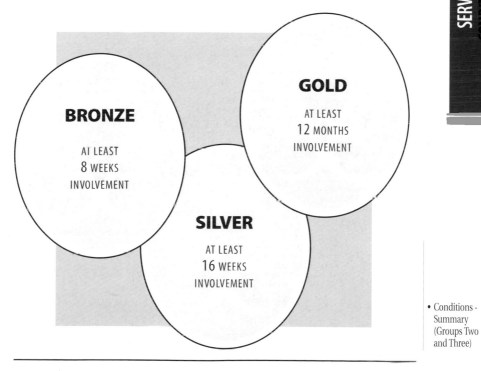

BRONZE

AT LEAST
8 WEEKS
INVOLVEMENT

GOLD

AT LEAST
12 MONTHS
INVOLVEMENT

SILVER

AT LEAST
16 WEEKS
INVOLVEMENT

- Conditions -
  Summary
  (Groups Two
  and Three)

59

Conditions in Detail – Group One

OVERVIEW

Group One comprises Service activities in which there is a substantial element of practical involvement. The Service should be appropriate to the level of Award and reflect the interests and abilities of the participants and fulfil a need within the community.

For this practical service to be most effective, it is important that participants receive any relevant skills training, information or advice in order that the Service may be carried out with sufficient competence, confidence and safety and that they are adequately briefed on the needs of those they are seeking to serve or the objective of the project they propose to undertake.

It is also important that a full record of practical service is kept by each participant and that there are regular meetings between participant and Assessor during the period of Service to discuss progress and resolve any problems. It is essential that appropriate briefing and training is given at all stages and that supervision and/or monitoring is maintained.

CONDITIONS IN DETAIL

1. Briefing

Briefing should help the participant to confirm that they have made the right choice of Service and clarify the commitment. Through discussion and negotiation between the participant and the Award Leader and/or Supervisor, the initial briefing should cover the following areas:

- Establish the nature of the Service to be undertaken, i.e:
    - the practical task
    - the commitment required.
- Define and understand the purpose of the Service:
    - the purpose of the actual task
    - the benefits to the individual, organisation and community.
- Identify the potential benefits to the participant.
- Define the role of the participant by:
    - discussing and agreeing an individual programme of practical service
    - agreeing targets and discussing expectations.

- Provide necessary training, such as:
  - health and safety, legal factors
  - appropriate skills training
  - relevant awareness training.
- Establish a system for supervision and monitoring and agree the process for evaluation and assessment.
- Discuss completion of the diary and the format of the account and, at Gold, the study topic.
- Establish contact with the Supervisor and Assessor as appropriate before commencing practical service.
- Arrange the date and time of the first counselling session and suggest possible dates for the following two sessions.

2. The Practical Service

The Requirement

BRONZE: at least 15 hours, spread over 3 months

SILVER: at least 30 hours, spread over 6 months

GOLD: at least 60 hours, spread over 12 months

Forms of Service

The Group One Service programme is intended to be broad-based and there is no one nationally recognised Governing Body to cover all the different types of Service likely to be undertaken. For convenience, and to provide a framework for the diverse activities, the forms of Service have been divided into the following groups:

Children

Elderly People

People with Special Needs

Other People in Need

The Environment

Fundraising

- Group One: Conditions in Detail
  Briefing
  - The Practical Service

General guidelines for each of these groups are given on pages 72-81, followed by a list of practical service opportunities and contacts. These are not exhaustive but they should assist Leaders and participants to discover a local source of help; otherwise they may wish to consult their Operating Authority for further guidance.

The choice of Service should be appropriate to participants' maturity; reflect their personal interest and comply with the spirit of giving Service to the community. Whilst the initial reason for offering Service is to gain an Award, in the final analysis participants should feel that they have given of themselves to the benefit of others. It is important they feel they have a specific role and a contribution to make. The experience should motivate and encourage young people to continue giving Service after completing their Award.

Many forms of Group One Service will be undertaken by working with/alongside experienced adults in their professional or voluntary capacity who, by their example, will provide on-the-job training and help to build up the confidence of younger participants. Some tasks may be undertaken as part of a team either on a rota basis, e.g. hospital tea bar, or on a 'one-off' basis, e.g. a conservation project. More mature participants will show greater independence but their work will still need to be supported. At the Gold stage, participants should be sufficiently mature and motivated to identify community needs and make a choice to which they are prepared to commit themselves wholeheartedly. Thorough briefing and appropriate choice of study topic will reduce the need for direct supervision but access to supervisory support should be available as required. Counselling sessions will have greater depth.

Some Service opportunities demand a concentration of hours of involvement, such as assisting in a holiday play scheme, but it is important that participants also give a personal commitment over the required timescale and this may be achieved by some other community involvement, preferably of a similar nature.

• Group One: Conditions in Detail - The Practical Service

In choosing a form of Service, it is important to anticipate the implications of withdrawing the participant's help at the end of the required period; it can be very distressing for a vulnerable person in need if a young person's support ends abruptly.

Minimum age restrictions and legal and insurance requirements may apply to some practical service opportunities and must always be observed. In some cases, it may be necessary to inform the parents or guardians of participants under the age of 18 regarding the nature of Service being undertaken.

The form of practical service may be changed if circumstances make continuation of the original choice impracticable or inappropriate.

3. Counselling

At least three counselling sessions with the Supervisor and/or Assessor are to be arranged during the period of practical service. The purpose of the counselling sessions is to:

- Discuss the progress of the project.
- Clarify and provide guidance if the young person is concerned about the value of their contribution.
- Support participants in resolving problems.
- Help participants learn from their experiences.
- Agree targets and discuss expectations for the next phase of practical service; review the choice of Service if necessary.
- Review the progress of the diary, the study topic (at Gold) and, towards the end of the period of Service, discuss the form of account for assessment.

The time which elapses between the preliminary briefing and further counselling sessions will be governed by the nature and type of practical service.

4. Diary, Account and Study Topic

Diary

During the period of practical service a diary should be kept to build up a detailed record of the Service undertaken and provide a good basis for the preparation of the account. It may be written or presented in some other inventive way. The first entry should detail the initial briefing session. It should be presented at counselling sessions and for assessment.

• Group One:
  Conditions in
  Detail
  - Counselling
  - Diary,
    Account and
    Study Topic

Account

An account should be compiled for assessment which may take the form of an oral debrief or be written, pictorial, taped or presented in some other imaginative way. It should be a reflective report of the Service, providing an opportunity to review what has been achieved. It should highlight the need for the Service and the benefits to the organisation concerned and/or the wider community, as well as enabling the participant to identify what they have gained from the experience.

Study Topic (Gold Award only)

At Gold level, a study must be completed over a twelve-month period which should illustrate a broad knowledge of some related social, environmental or cultural aspect of the Service being offered, rather than recounting details of the specific practical involvement which will be included in the account. The format may be written, taped, slide, video or photographic. It may include a collection of information and resource material, e.g. leaflets, press cuttings, sketches. Participants are encouraged to find other inventive ways of presenting their investigations.

5.   Supervision and Assessment

Supervision, briefing, counselling and assessment are to be carried out by an appropriately qualified or experienced person nominated and approved by the Operating Authority and/or the appropriate Governing Body/Service Agency.

Assessment should ensure participants understand the significance of the Service given. The process should review and discuss:

- The practical service undertaken, with attention to reliability, competence, relationships and attitudes.
- The diary.
- The account.
- The study topic at Gold.
- Completion of the *Record Book*.

At Bronze and Silver, the Assessor will normally be the person who has been involved in supervising or checking the practical service. The signature of this person should appear in the *Record Book*.

• Group One:
  Conditions in
  Detail
  - Diary,
    Account and
    Study Topic
  - Supervision
    and
    Assessment

SERVICE
CONDITIONS

At Gold, assessment must take place in conjunction with an independent Assessor who should be a senior official of the organisation through which the practical service was given or, failing this, by a person who is knowledgeable in the needs of the local community, such as a doctor, minister or social worker. The signature of this person should appear in the *Record Book*.

Conditions in Detail – Groups Two and Three

OVERVIEW

Groups Two and Three comprise those forms of Service which require courses of training and the completion of related practical service. Group Two involves courses of specialised training, whilst Group Three courses lead to the attainment of a nationally recognised qualification; both should be followed by a period of practical service.

CONDITIONS IN DETAIL

1. Training

Participants should enrol on a course of specialised training and inform the Instructor that they will be pursuing it as part of their Award programme. On satisfactory completion of the course and, in the case of Group Three, attainment of the relevant qualification, Course Instructors or Examiners should sign the participant's *Record Book*.

For Group Two, the structure and format of training courses will vary depending on the agency or organisation involved and the resources available. The course should have an emphasis on practical sessions and the methods used could include discussion, case studies, group work, brainstorming and questioning. For Group Three the structure and length of the course will usually be pre-determined by the agency offering the qualification.

2. Practical Service

The practical service in each case should relate wherever possible to the training undertaken, so that young people have the opportunity to apply the knowledge gained on the course to practical situations. It should include a Service to the community, not a project-based study, and may be undertaken either as a group or on an individual basis.

At Bronze and Silver, a period of practical service should be undertaken. At Gold, participants must complete at least 40 hours practical service.

Participants must receive adequate **briefing** before giving practical service. This should include an understanding of the purpose of the task, relevant health and safety guidelines and a clarification of roles and responsibilities.

Counselling and reviewing sessions should be arranged during the period of practical service as appropriate, with at least three sessions at Gold. The purpose of these is to discuss progress, deal with problems, review targets and help participants to learn from their experiences.

Participants will need to keep a **diary** or detailed record of the practical service undertaken, which should be presented as evidence for assessment.

3. Timescale
The combined period of training and practical service must be:

BRONZE:	**at least 8 weeks**
SILVER:	**at least 16 weeks**
GOLD:	**at least 12 months**

Notes: The following times are given as <u>advice only</u> to assist organisations in planning Groups Two and Three courses with related practical training.

At Bronze the combined period of training and practical service should be at least 15 hours including approximately 8 hours of training.

At Silver the combined period of training and practical service should be at least 30 hours including approximately 12 hours of training.

At Gold the combined period of training and practical service should be at least 60 hours including approximately 20 hours of training.

• Groups Two and Three: Conditions in Detail
- Practical Service
- Timescale

4. Instruction and Assessment

For any form of Service in Groups Two and Three, it is essential that both the Instructor and the Assessor are qualified people approved by the appropriate Governing Body/Service Agency and the Operating Authority. At Gold level, instruction and assessment should not be undertaken by the same person.

The completion of the course or training must be certified in the *Record Book* by the Instructor or Examiner from the Governing Body. Only when this and the required practical service have been completed should the Assessor sign the *Record Book*.

The assessment of practical service for Groups Two and Three should confirm that participants have applied the knowledge learnt during the period of training and have shown reliability, competence and an understanding of the need for the Service given.

SERVICE CONDITIONS

• Groups Two and Three: Conditions in Detail
- Instruction and Assessment

Record Books

The *Record Book* represents the experiences and achievements of a young person and remarks should be personalised, positive and encouraging. It should always record success and achievement rather than failure.

In the event of a young person not satisfying the Assessor, he or she should be informed of the reason and no entry made in the *Record Book* until the conditions have been fulfilled.

Dates of starting and successful assessment are to be entered on the appropriate page in the *Record Books*. Assessors should ensure that the date entered is the actual date on which the assessment was carried out and state clearly that any safety requirements have been met.

SERVICE
RECORD BOOKS

Bronze

SERVICE (Groups Two & Three)

TITLE OF SERVICE GIVEN *LIFESAVING*

DATES STARTED *1/10/92* COMPLETED *31/3/93*

TRAINING GIVEN BY *B. McPHERSON*

FORM OF TRAINING COMPLETED (GROUP TWO)

OR
QUALIFICATION GAINED (GROUP THREE) *AWARD OF MERIT*

PRACTICAL SERVICE UNDERTAKEN *Life support programme & Water Safety Project in the Community*

Assessor's report:

Patrick was eager to learn and gained a well deserved Award of Merit. He helped with a water safety project where he was involved in teaching young children life support, including resuscitation. He also worked with people with disabilities with whom he communicated well and he has made many friends in the group to such an extent that he is going to continue his involvement.

SIGNED *A. Fuller* DATE *31 . 3 . 93*

QUALIFICATION *RLSS UK EXAMINER*

26

Silver

SERVICE (Group One)

TITLE OF SERVICE GIVEN *Working with elderly people*

DATES STARTED *19/1/93* COMPLETED *26/1/94*

BRIEFING SESSIONS GIVEN BY *E. JONES* ON *19/1/93*

COUNSELLING SESSIONS HELD ON (1) *2/3/93* (2) *20/6/93* (3) *17/9/93*

FORM OF PRACTICAL SERVICE *Helping at Beech House Residential Care Home*

Assessor's report: *of practical service*

Ivan performed many useful tasks helping to decorate the common room and running the gardening club. Over the year he visited on a regular basis, became totally involved in the life of the home and developed warm relationships with many of the residents.

of participant's diary and account of the service

Ivan kept a regular diary which was a good record of his service from which he compiled an interesting account of his time at Beech House.

of study

A very perceptive study comprising photographs of the residents, their life histories and current attitudes to the concept of caring for the elderly.

SIGNED *M. Woodward.* DATE *26/1/94*

QUALIFICATION / POSITION *Officer-in-Charge, Beech House, Residential Care Home.*

11

Gold

GROUP ONE: GENERAL GUIDELINES AND USEFUL ORGANISATIONS

Children

Introduction

It is expected that the children being assisted will have particular needs and that participants will add to the quality of their life or help them to learn or practise new skills. The Service should provide something extra over and above normal provision.

Briefing

The content of the briefing should be sensitive and relevant to the age and ability of the participant. Prior to undertaking Service with children, participants should:

- Have an appropriate understanding of the needs and background of the children they are helping.
- Have knowledge of the aims and functions of the organisation or establishment with whom the Service will be given.
- Be sufficiently and appropriately briefed or trained to carry out the Service safely and effectively. Where any equipment is used, relevant training must be given and safety procedures followed. Participants must not attempt to carry out tasks for which they are not appropriately trained.
- Have an understanding of the purpose of their role.
- Know whom to contact if immediate help is needed.
- Have a background knowledge where appropriate of child development and the difficulties facing those children who are deprived, in care or in need.
- Know about the support Services and organisations available to children, e.g. Social Services, Childline.
- With the assistance of the Supervisor, ensure that the children being assisted understand the period of time Service is to be given and the implications when it comes to an end.
- Know where to seek support if they experience difficulties or become distressed as a result of giving Service.

The British Red Cross Babysitters' Training programme forms an ideal briefing for participants working with children. Babysitting in itself is not an acceptable form of Service.

• Children

Due regard must be made to the responsibilities for the approval of staff and others in regular contact with children as outlined in the Children Act 1989. Advice should be obtained from the Operating Authority.

Participants should be encouraged to continue their involvement with children after they have completed the Award requirements.

Examples of Service

- Visiting a children's home, the children's ward at a local hospital or school and working with children in need by providing supportive learning, e.g. playing games, talking, music, reading.
- Providing additional support for children with special needs, such as looking after disadvantaged children on holiday, befriending schemes, literary schemes.
- Assisting with children at risk, e.g. escorting them on outings such as sports fixtures or going shopping.
- Assisting children in need at day centres, in crèche facilities, on play schemes or at jigsaw and toy libraries.

Useful Contacts

- Social and Probation Services.
- Local Education and Health Authorities.
- National Organisations, such as National Society for Prevention of Cruelty to Children, National Children's Homes, Riding for the Disabled, PHAB, The Children's Society, Save the Children Fund.
- Local Voluntary Organisations.

• Children

Elderly People

Introduction
Participants are expected to assist elderly people who have particular needs by giving Service which will improve their quality of life.

Briefing
The content of the briefing should be sensitive and relevant to the age and ability of the participant. Prior to undertaking Service with elderly people, participants should:

- Have an appropriate knowledge of the needs and background of the elderly person/people they are helping.
- Have knowledge of the aims and functions of the organisation or establishment with whom the Service will be given.
- Be sufficiently briefed to carry out the Service safely and effectively. Where any equipment is used, relevant training must be given and safety procedures followed. Participants must not attempt to carry out work for which they are not appropriately trained.
- Have an understanding of the purpose of their role.
- Know whom to contact if immediate help is needed.
- Have a general background knowledge relating to the difficulties facing some elderly people, e.g. deteriorating health, illness, loneliness, and appreciate the effects these have on lifestyle.
- Know about the support services and organisations available to elderly people, particularly in the local community, e.g. Social Services, Women's Royal Voluntary Service, Help the Aged.
- With the assistance of the Supervisor, ensure that the person/people being assisted understand the period of time Service is to be given and the implications when it comes to an end.
- Know where to seek support if they experience difficulties or become distressed as a result of giving Service.

Participants should be encouraged to continue their involvement after they have completed their Award requirements.

Examples of Service
- Regularly visiting an elderly person to provide company, conversation, assistance with correspondence and reading. This may be in sheltered accommodation, a home for elderly people, a hospital or in the person's own home.

- Assisting an elderly person with odd jobs in the home, such as gardening, decorating or shopping.
- Helping with the work of an organisation concerned with the care of elderly people.
- Helping in other venues, such as old people's clubs or day centres.

Useful Contacts
- Charities concerned with the welfare of elderly people such as Help the Aged, Age Concern, Women's Royal Voluntary Service or The Royal British Legion.
- Homes for elderly people, nursing homes, day centres, hospitals, etc.
- Community Nurses and local Health Centres.
- Local Church or other religious groups.
- Other Community groups, such as the Women's Institute.

People with Special Needs

Introduction
Participants are expected to assist people with special needs by undertaking a task or project which will lead to improving their quality of life. The emphasis must always be on working with those they are assisting, not for them.

Briefing
The content of the briefing should be sensitive and relevant to the age and ability of the participant. Prior to undertaking Service, participants should:
- Have an appropriate understanding of the needs and background of the people they are assisting.
- Have knowledge of the aims and functions of the organisation, establishment or project with whom the Service will be given.
- Be sufficiently briefed or trained to carry out the Service safely and effectively. Where any equipment is used, relevant training must be given and safety procedures followed. Relevant training must be provided for specific skills, e.g. sign language.
- Understand the purpose of their role.
- Know whom to contact if immediate help is needed.

SERVICE
GROUP ONE - GUIDELINES

- Elderly People
- People with Special Needs

- Have a relevant background knowledge of the differing needs and lifestyles of people with, for example, learning or physical disabilities.
- Know about the relevant support Services and organisations available, particularly in the local community.

- With the assistance of the Supervisor, ensure that the person/people being assisted understand the period of time Service is to be given and the implications when it comes to an end.
- Know where to seek support if they experience difficulties or become distressed as a result of giving Service.

The National Federation of Gateway Clubs' *Distance Learning Pack* would form a good briefing session for participants working with people with learning difficulties.

Participants should be encouraged to continue their involvement after they have completed the Award requirements.

Examples of Service
- Helping to compile talking newspapers for the blind.
- Developing 'sympathetic ear' facilities.
- Helping at day centres, special schools, residential homes, leisure centres, etc.
- Assisting people in the local community, e.g. befriending schemes.
- Developing local opportunities in the community for people with special needs.

Useful Contacts
- Organisations such as Crossroads, FYD, MENCAP, National Federation of Gateway Clubs, PHAB, Royal National Institute for the Blind, Royal National Institute for the Deaf, RNID, Scope.
- Local 'special' schools, residential homes, day centres, etc.
- Social Services.

• People with
  Special Needs

Other People in Need

Introduction

Participants will be expected to undertake some work which will improve the quality of life of an individual or group in need.

Briefing

The content of the briefing should be sensitive and relevant to the age and ability of the participant. Prior to undertaking Service with people in need, participants should:

- Have an appropriate understanding of the needs and background of the people they are helping.
- Have knowledge of the aims and functions of the organisation or establishment with whom the Service will be given.
- Be sufficiently briefed or trained to carry out the Service safely and effectively. Service in this group may be confidential and participants must not attempt to carry out tasks for which they are not trained or qualified. Where equipment is used, relevant training must be given and safety procedures followed.
- Understand the purpose of their role.
- Know whom to contact if help is needed.
- Have a relevant background knowledge relating to the difficulties facing the particular person/people in need and appreciate the effects these have on lifestyle.
- Know about the relevant support Services and organisations available, particularly in the local community.
- With the assistance of the Supervisor, ensure that the person/people being helped understand the period of time the Service is to be given and the implications when it comes to an end.
- Know where to seek support if they experience difficulties or become distressed as a result of giving Service.

Participants should be encouraged to continue their involvement after they have completed the Award requirements.

Examples of Service

- Hospital visiting, hospital hostess schemes or escorting patients to Sunday Services in the hospital Chapel.
- Working with hospital radio or in hospital libraries.
- Working with homeless people, e.g. in soup kitchens, hostels.
- Helping at day centres or on trips or excursions.

• Other People in Need

- Assisting at local support centres, such as drugs support units.
- Working with local support groups, e.g. bereavement groups, victim support groups.
- Assisting with telephone or face-to-face counselling Services.

Useful Contacts
- Organisations such as Alcoholics Anonymous, Action in Smoking Health, Crossroads, Council for Local Voluntary Services, National Association for Mental Health, Royal British Legion, Samaritans, Salvation Army, Shelter, Terrence Higgins Trust, Women's Royal Voluntary Service.
- Local hospitals, 'Friends' of local hospitals, St. John Ambulance or British Red Cross Hospital Libraries.
- Cheshire Homes, Nursing Homes, Church groups or Citizen's Advice Bureaux.
- Other support groups, local counselling Services and voluntary care groups.

The Environment

Introduction
Service through the environment offers a wide range of opportunities, from straight-forward conservation projects through to local education and awareness projects. Working on environmental projects should be of benefit to the community at large and to our heritage. It may also provide participants with the opportunity to become involved with environmental issues at a practical, social or political level.

Briefing
The content of the briefing should be sensitive and relevant to the age and ability of the participant. Prior to undertaking Service, participants should:
- Have a clear understanding of the purpose of the project and the aims and functions of the organisation or group involved.
- Have an understanding of the purpose of their role.
- Be sufficiently briefed or trained and have a relevant practical knowledge to carry out the Service safely and effectively; they must not attempt to carry out tasks for which they are not appropriately trained. Where any machinery or tools are used, relevant training and safety procedures must be followed and protective clothing worn.

- Know whom to contact if immediate help is needed.
- Have an understanding of the importance of caring for the environment.
- Develop an understanding of environmental issues, particularly in relation to the local community.

Having completed the Award requirements, participants should be encouraged to promote environmental awareness and an understanding of sustainable development, particularly in their local community.

Examples of Service

- Campaigning for improved cycle routes.
- Helping with the construction and repair of footpaths, stiles, fences, stone walls.
- Assisting with checking rights of way and sign posting.
- Helping with urban conservation projects such as improving derelict areas or organising litter collections.
- Improving natural habitats and encouraging the increase of specific types of flora and fauna.
- Assisting with and raising awareness about recycling and waste collection projects.
- Working on projects of local historical interest such as steam railways, canals and locks, cycle ways, public and other buildings, working museums, etc.
- Undertaking watches or surveys of wild life and plants in conjunction with a conservation group or trust, e.g. Badger Watch, Bats, Barn Owls.
- Involvement with local community projects such as community woodlands projects, best kept village or 'Britain in Bloom'.

If the emphasis of the practical activity is learning or developing a particular technique, then the activity may be more appropriate to the Skills Section, rather than the Service Section.

Useful Contacts

British Trust for Conservation Volunteers, Civic Trust, Council for Environmental Education, Council for Protection of Rural England,

• The Environment

Countryside Commission, English Heritage, English Nature, Field Studies Council, Forestry Authority, Friends of the Earth, Groundwork Foundation, Heritage Coast Wardens, National Parks, National Rivers Authority, National Trust, Royal Society for the Protection of Birds, Royal Society for the Prevention of Cruelty to Animals, Rural Development Commission, Scottish Conservation Projects Trust, Scottish Natural Heritage, Tidy Britain Group, Woodland Trust, World Wide Fund for Nature, Young People's Trust for the Environment and Nature Conservation, Youth Hostels Association.

For a comprehensive list of useful contacts look in *Who's Who in the Environment* available free from the Environmental Council.

GROUP ONE - GUIDELINES

SERVICE

Fundraising

Introduction

Participants should be involved in raising funds for local or national charities, disadvantaged groups or individuals, or for worthwhile community projects. (Participants raising funds for their own Award Unit or to aid their own participation in the Award may not count this as Service.) The choice of charity or cause should be the young person's, but it is vital that he/she develops an understanding of the context in which fundraising takes place and the background needs of the recipients.

Through fundraising, participants should have the opportunity to gain practical experience in planning, publicising, organising, administering, staffing and managing a fundraising event.

It is strongly recommended that participants contact the charity in order to seek guidance and information before undertaking any fundraising activities.

Briefing

The content of the briefing should be sensitive and relevant to the age and ability of the participant. Prior to undertaking fundraising activities for charity, participants should:

- Contact a local branch or meet with an officer of the charity.
- Have a clear understanding of the aims and functions of the charity and the issues that Jie behind its work.

• The Environment
• Fundraising

- Have knowledge of how funds raised will be used and the subsequent effects on the lives of the recipients. Where opportunities exist, a visit to the recipients is recommended.
- Decide on the method of fundraising and properly plan any fundraising activities. The effort, thought and preparation is more important than the amount raised.
- Have or seek advice to ensure that all legal requirements are met, e.g. public liability insurance, licensing.
- Decide on the procedure for collecting funds and plan how any fundraising activities should be concluded, i.e. the presentation of a cheque to the charity.
- Publicise events as appropriate. At some events a display could be set up illustrating the role of the charity and how monies will be spent.

Participants should be encouraged to continue to support the work of the charity or remain involved in fundraising activities after they have completed the requirements of the Award.

Examples of Service

- Organising fundraising activities such as:
  - a sponsored event, e.g. walk, ride, swim
  - sales of work/produce
  - a jumble sale, car boot sale, book sale, bring and buy
  - an event, e.g. dinner, disco, fashion show, sporting event.
- Helping in a charity shop, stall or office.
- Co-ordinating a series of fundraising events.

Useful Contacts

- Local, National and International Charities.
- Local children's homes, homes for elderly people, hospitals and health trusts.
- Local radio, newspaper and television appeals.

For useful contacts refer to the *Voluntary Agencies Directory* published by the National Council for Voluntary Organisations which is also available in libraries. A reading list on fundraising is available from the National Youth Agency. Information and publications are also available from a number of charities.

SERVICE
GROUP ONE - GUIDELINES

• Fundraising

GROUP TWO:
SERVICE REQUIRING SPECIALISED TRAINING

Group Two comprises courses of specialised training, followed by related practical service. A section on ideas for practical service is included at the end of each programme.

Animal Welfare

CARE FOR ANIMALS

Aim: To appreciate the inter-relationship between animals and the community.

The following courses should involve as many practical demonstrations and visits to suitable venues and as much practical work and participation as possible.

BRONZE
Pets and pet-ownership
Participants should have knowledge of the following:
1. Reasons for keeping pets, animals available, owner's responsibility.
2. Caring for and keeping large pet mammals, e.g. dogs, cats.
3. Caring for and keeping small pet mammals, e.g. rabbits, hamsters, mice.
4. Caring for and keeping non-mammal pets, e.g. birds, tortoises, snakes.
5. Animal Services, e.g. veterinary surgeons, animal societies, police, guide dogs.
6. Other activities with animals, e.g. pet shops, shows, clubs.

The course should be organised by a suitably experienced person such as a veterinary surgeon, a senior officer of an animal welfare society, or a biology teacher. A veterinary surgeon should tutor at least two sessions. The course organiser may invite other experts to tutor other sessions.

Course assessment – this should be by oral examination conducted by the course organiser and the veterinary surgeon.

SILVER

The importance of animals to the community and vice versa

Note: Participants who have not followed the Bronze course should cover the content of the first session.

Participants should have knowledge of the following:

1. The role of animals in sport, work, as providers of food etc.
2. Horses – various roles; principles of care and keep.
3. Cattle – providers of milk, meat, leather.
4. Sheep – providers of wool, meat.
5. Pigs – providers of meat.
6. Poultry – providers of meat, eggs.
7. Methods of husbandry – collection and uses of end-products of the above.
8. Domestication of animals and the role of the community in safeguarding their welfare.

The course should be organised by a veterinary surgeon, a senior officer of an animal welfare society or a biology teacher. A veterinary surgeon should tutor at least two sessions. The course organiser may invite other experts to tutor other sessions.

Course assessment – this should be by oral examination conducted by the course organiser and the veterinary surgeon.

GOLD

Wider inter-relationships of society and animals

Note: Direct entrants to the Gold Award should cover the content of the first sessions of both the Bronze and Silver programmes.

Participants should have knowledge of:

1. Native wild animals – zoos, wild-life parks, conservation.
2. Experimental and laboratory animals and the varying social views related to this subject.
3. Important diseases such as rabies, tuberculosis, brucellosis, etc.
4. The role of the veterinary profession and other animal-orientated organisations, and their deployment, integration and significance in the community.

The course should be organised by a Veterinary Surgeon who may invite other experts to tutor other sessions.

Course assessment – this should be by oral examination conducted by the course organiser/veterinary surgeon and a second examiner who is similarly associated with animals, such as a senior officer of an animal welfare society or a biology teacher.

• Animal
 Welfare
 - Care for
 Animals

GROUP TWO - PROGRAMMES

SERVICE

Practical Service

Some suggestions for practical service are outlined below:

- Helping in animal shelters or sanctuaries.
- Fundraising for or helping an animal charity.
- Assisting at a veterinary surgeon's as a volunteer.
- Volunteering for organisations such as Guide Dogs for the Blind.
- Helping a neighbour in need, such as a disabled person or someone who is ill, to look after a pet.
- Helping at a local stables, such as Riding for the Disabled.
- Caring for school pets during weekends and holidays.

Assessment of practical service – a written report or oral presentation should be made on the findings and experiences of the practical service.

Resource material can be obtained by writing to the Pedigree Petfoods Education Centre (see Useful Addresses).

Emergency Services

AMBULANCE SERVICE

The following programme for Bronze, Silver and Gold levels outlines the main areas to be covered in an Ambulance Service Course. A more detailed syllabus is available from Award Headquarters on request.

Instruction and assessment is at the discretion of Chief Ambulance Officers in their respective services to whom application should be directed.

BRONZE

Participants should attend sessions on the following:

1. *Introduction* – welcome, outline of course content and objectives. History of the Ambulance Service, primary responsibilities of the Service and its relationship to the National Health Service.
2. *The Ambulance Service* – its organisation and rank structure.
3. *Ambulance Stations* – tour of the Ambulance Station and accident and emergency vehicles, including the equipment carried.

4. *Calls and Routine Requests* – making 999 calls, ordering routine patient transport, what to do whilst awaiting the arrival of the Ambulance Service.
5. *Emergency Resuscitation* – CPR – recovery position/ examination of the unconscious patient.
6. *The Role and Training of Ambulance Staff* – Ambulance personnel, their role in the Service, grades and training.
7. *First Aid Kits* – their content and purpose.
8. *Emergency Aid Procedures* – priorities of treatment and First Aid.

Course assessment – a written or oral assessment should take place in order to determine whether a satisfactory level of knowledge and practical skill has been achieved during the period of training.

SILVER

Participants should attend sessions on the following:

1. *Introduction* – welcome, outline of course content and objectives. History of the Ambulance Service, primary responsibilities of the Service and its relationship to the NHS.
2. *The Ambulance Service* – its organisation and rank structure. Mobilisation of vehicle and types of incidents.
3. *Ambulance Stations* – tour of the Ambulance Station, types of vehicles and their uses, the range of equipment carried, its use and storage.
4. *Calls and Routine Requests* – Ambulance Service response to major incidents, arrangements for ordering routine patient transport and the essentials of immediate action.
5. *Emergency Resuscitation* – CCPR (more advanced), examination and care of the unconscious patient.
6. *Day Hospitals and Out-Patient Clinics* – day hospitals and out-patient facilities, their purpose and Ambulance Service provision. Include a visit.
7. *Mechanical Resuscitations* – different types of resuscitators, their use and application.
8. *Ambulance Control Centre* – the role and function of Control Centres. Include a visit.

Course assessment – a written or oral assessment should take place in order to determine whether a satisfactory level of knowledge and practical skill has been achieved during the period of training.

• Emergency
Services
- Ambulance
Service

GOLD

Note: Direct entrants to the Gold Award should cover briefly the following subjects from the Silver course before commencing the Gold programme:

- Ambulance Service organisation and management arrangements.
- The purpose of day hospital and out-patient departments including visits.
- Ambulance Service communications and control centres.

Participants should attend sessions on the following:

1. *Introduction* – welcome, outline of course content and objectives. Background to the Ambulance Service, primary responsibilities and its relationship to the NHS.
2. *Ambulance Stations* – different types of ambulances, including front line ambulances, the type of equipment carried, its use and maintenance and storage on the vehicle.
3. *The Scene of an Incident* – information required by ambulance crews at the scene of an incident, i.e. monitoring of patients' vital signs, the history of the incident and when the incident happened.
4. *Law and the Ambulance Service* – the law and how it affects the Service, including exemptions with regard to speed limits, lighting regulations, traffic signs, patients' personal property, certification of death and the Coroners' Court.
5. *Emergency Resuscitation* – necessary skills to teach emergency resuscitation and care of the unconscious casualty. (Participants are encouraged to participate in a public training programme).
6. *Regional Ambulance Training Centre* – the role and function of Regional Ambulance Training Centres and the training and development of Ambulance Personnel. Where possible, include a visit or overnight stay.
7. *Diversity* – the diversity of the Ambulance Service. Other activities with which the Service is involved, such as operational and management Services to the Local District Health Authority, District Bed Bureaux.
8. *Support Services* – back-up facilities within the Ambulance Service. Administration, fleet management and workshops.

• Emergency Services
- Ambulance Service

9. *Innovation in First Aid* – improvisation and use of local available resources in the treatment of an injury where First Aid equipment is not readily available.
10. *Accident and Emergency Unit* – the organisation and work of a Unit. Include a visit.
11. *Major Incidents* – the role of the Ambulance Service in responding to major incidents.
12. *External Influences on the Ambulance Service* – problems facing the Ambulance Service, demands, categorisation of patients, escorts, abortive journeys and hoax calls.
13. *Specialist Vehicles* – specialist response vehicles and equipment, their use and purpose.
14. *The Paramedic Service* – development of the Service, its role and responsibilities, additional equipment carried by crews.

Course assessment – a written or oral assessment should take place in order to determine whether a satisfactory level of knowledge and practical skill has been achieved during the period of training. Assessment should not be made by the Course Instructor.

Practical Service

Some suggestions for practical service are outlined below:
- Assisting with station duties.
- Assisting with station open days.
- Assisting with education programmes.
- At Gold, assisting with Bronze Ambulance Service courses.

Assessment of practical service – a written report or oral presentation should be made on the findings and experiences of the practical service.

CIVIL AID

Civil Aid, a registered charity formed in 1968, provides Service opportunities at Bronze, Silver and Gold levels. Participants must follow a registered course of specialised training.

Following this, a variety of work in the community is on offer. Course Registration Forms are available on request (please send a stamp to cover postage) from Civil Aid (see Useful Addresses).

Trainers and Assessors for the courses must be one of the following:
- A registered Civil Aid Instructor.

• Emergency
Services
- Ambulance
Service
- Civil Aid

- An Instructor or Trainer from another voluntary emergency organisation (a photocopy of the current certificate must be held by Civil Aid).
- An Instructor or Trainer from a full-time emergency Service. (A photocopy of a current qualification must be held by Civil Aid.)
- A qualified teacher/holder of a Further & Adult Education Teacher's Certificate who holds a Civil Aid proficiency certificate.
- A Local Authority-appointed Instructor, registered with Civil Aid.

For a copy of the full syllabus send a stamped, self-addressed envelope to Award Headquarters in Windsor.

FIRE SERVICE

The following syllabus for Bronze, Silver and Gold levels outlines the main areas to be covered in a Fire Service Course. The structure and length of the course will vary depending upon the individual Brigade's organisation and availability of resources and manpower.

Instruction and assessment is at the discretion of Chief Fire Officers of County or Metropolitan Brigades in England and Wales, or the Firemaster for Scottish Brigades, to whom application should be made for training courses.

BRONZE

Participants should attend sessions on the following:

1. *Introduction* – talk given by senior officer to include welcome, outline of course content and objectives.
2. *The Fire Service* – its organisation and rank structure, history and tradition.
3. *How to act if a fire occurs* – the various methods and correct procedures for calling the Fire Service, e.g. use of exchange telephone. The process from lifting receiver to acceptance of call at a fire station.
4. *What to do while awaiting the arrival of the Fire Brigade* – save lives; shut doors and windows; meet fire brigade on arrival; inform officer in charge what has been observed of fire; persons reported in building; position of fire; intensity; point out nearest water supply if known.

• Emergency Services
- Civil Aid
- Fire Service

5. *The Fire Station* – tour of the fire station and vehicles, including appliances and equipment carried.

6. *Fire* – the process of combustion by means of a triangle, causes of fire, how fire spreads, emphasis on the toxic effects of smoke produced by modern furniture and fittings, the dangers of entering smoke and how to act if caught in smoke.

7. *Methods of Rescue* – types of rescue methods, including crawling with an unconscious person.

8. *Fireman's Lift* – the technique. Participants should not attempt to lift persons heavier than themselves.

9. *Knots and Lines* – see Fire Service Drill Book.

10. *Methods of extinguishing small fires* – buckets, mats for beating or smothering, soda water syphon, chemical extinguishers, hand pumps and garden hoses. Demonstrate the operation of a hand pump.

11. *Hose Drills* – running out length of hose, connecting to a hydrant and shipping a branch.

12. *Fire Prevention* – dangers and precautions in the home relating to domestic heating, the airing of linen, cleaning materials, petrol, coal fires, electric irons, wiring, fuses, meters and switches, gas, oil stoves, storage of materials, decorations, fireworks, candles, bonfires, smoking, doors and windows.

Course assessment – a written and/or oral assessment should take place in order to determine whether a satisfactory level of knowledge and skill has been achieved during the period of training. Where possible, include tests of practical ability to apply the instruction given on the course.

SILVER

Note: Direct entrants to the Silver Award should cover the Bronze training, which may be compressed into four sessions, in addition to the syllabus below.

Participants should attend sessions on the following:

1. *Introduction* – talk given by senior officer to include welcome, outline of course content and objectives.

2. *The Fire Service* – its organisation, structure and functions, including peacetime structure, powers under the Fire Services

Act 1947, mobilising first attendances, type of incidents involved, e.g. special services, communications. Include a visit to a control room.

3. *Water Supplies* – description of the nearest town's mains, hose reels, hydrants, private hydrants, open water, water relay.

4. *Fire Prevention and Means of Escape in Places of Public Entertainment and Large Buildings* – sprinklers, drenchers, automatic fire alarms, fire telephones, dry and wet risers, fire resisting doors.

5. *Hand Appliances* – water, foam, CO2, Halon and powder extinguishers, how to identify and activate, and for which purpose each is suited.

6. *Methods of Rescue* – resumé of Bronze Award, explanation and demonstration of 2, 3 and 4-handed carrying seats and blanket removal method.

Course assessment – a written and/or oral assessment should take place in order to determine whether a satisfactory level of knowledge and skill has been achieved during the period of training. Where possible, include tests of practical ability to apply the instruction given on the course.

GOLD

Note: It is expected that participants intending to follow the Fire Service Gold Award course will already have completed the Silver course. If they are Direct entrants at Gold level, however, they will be expected to cover, in addition to the Gold course, whatever basic training in the Bronze and Silver course is considered necessary and desirable by the Course Instructor.

Participants should attend sessions on the following:

1. *Introduction* – talk given by senior officer to include welcome, outline of course content and objectives, safety aspects and a tour of the station and fire appliances.

2. *What is Fire and Putting it Out* – revision of Silver syllabus, triangle of combustion, fire spread, effects of heat and smoke, how to act in smoke, the causes of fire and methods of extinguishing them. If possible, this session should include a demonstration of various fire extinguishers likely to be found in premises.

3. *Mobilising Fire Service Resources* – command and control procedure and the turn out system at Fire Stations. This session may also include methods of rescue and practical knot tying.

• Emergency Services
- Fire Service

4. *Fire Service Organisation* – cover all aspects of Brigade Management Services, support and administration, such as Brigade Command and Control, Brigade Headquarters, Brigade Workshops, Fleet Management, Brigade Training School, Staff and Career Development and Public Relations. A visit to each department is expected. Course members are encouraged to organise these themselves.

5. *Fire Prevention* – the history of fire prevention legislation and its implementation leading up to the Fire Precautions Act 1971. Issue of literature on fire safety, fire investigation principles and arson prevention. (This session should be covered by a Fire Safety Officer).

6. *Fire Protection* – to include fire protection principles in public premises and places of work, focusing on emergency lighting, fire doors, automatic fire detection systems, fire drills and fire fighting equipment. A practical demonstration should be included, if possible.

7. *Fire Safety (practical exercise)* – participants should produce a single line plan drawing of either their home, workplace, youth club or school to assist in their understanding of an effective system for fire safety.

8. *Community Links* – the work of the Brigade in the community and how it tries to educate the public on matters of fire safety through initiatives such as poster campaigns, smoke detector campaigns, school visits, 'Welephant', national fire safety quiz, fire safety week campaigns and Brigade exhibitions. The role of the Fire Safety Department, Publicity and Education Department and Schools Liaison Officer.

9. *Practical Service* – discussion and planning of practical service.

Course assessment – a written and/or oral assessment should take place to determine whether a satisfactory level of knowledge and skill has been achieved during the period of training. Where possible, include tests of practical ability to apply the instruction given on the course. Assessment should not be made by the Course Instructor.

Practical Service

Some suggestions for practical service are outlined below:

- Assisting with Fire Station Open Days.
- Assisting with Fire Safety campaigns, targeting youth clubs, children's homes, schools, homes for elderly people or private households.

• Emergency Services
  - Fire Service

- Detailed investigation into areas such as potential causes of fire in the home or public places, fire precautions or fire prevention.
- At Gold, assisting with Bronze Fire Service courses.

Assessment of Practical Service – a written report or oral presentation should be made on the findings and experiences of the Practical Service.

POLICE SERVICE

The following syllabus for the Bronze, Silver and Gold levels outlines the main areas to be covered in a Police Service Course, the aim of which is to introduce participants to the roles of the Police Service.

All officers involved in running these courses will be aware of the National Youth Bureau Policy on enfranchisement of young people. Whilst the subject of the course is the Police Service, the addressing of values and attitudes will be consistent with that Policy.

BRONZE

Participants should attend sessions on the following:

1. *Introduction* – welcome by a senior officer to the Police staff, outline of course content and objectives. The work of the Police, the Police Service Statement of Common Purpose and Values.
2. *The Police Service* – its organisation and rank structure, policies on equal opportunities and quality of Service, appointment, probation, training, promotion, Police Staff College and discipline regulations.
3. *The Magistrate's Court* – organisation and functions of the court, discussion of the procedures which are followed in court. Include a visit.
4. *Police Communications* –
   a. Public systems: telephone, telex, facsimile, portable telephones.
   b. Control rooms: 999 system, graded response, command and control system and Police national computer.
   c. TV and radio assistance.
5. *Road Accidents* – what to do at the scene of a road accident, First Aid, safety of people, security of property, safety of other road users (traffic control), trapped people, fire and dangerous substances. (Course organisers may wish to set up

• Emergency Services
- Police Service

a mock road accident or a demonstration of dealing with injured people by St. John Ambulance).

6. *Road Safety* – the importance of road safety, education of the public, the old and the young, the Highway Code and maintenance of cycles.

7. *Major Incidents* – a brief resumé of the kind of major incidents which have occurred over recent years. This will include crashed aircraft, railway incidents, football disorders/incidents, terrorist bombs, cross Channel ferries etc. The session will then examine the role of the police in co-ordinating the emergency Services and the sort of problems that need to be addressed, e.g. public control, care of victims, care of property, evidence for enquiries.

8. *Identification Systems* – witness observations and recognition of suspects, personal description, edicon, identification parades, fingerprint evidence and DNA identification. (A practical exercise for this session may include questions about a part of the town/city familiar to participants to illustrate how they actually see).

9. *Specialist Roles* – Drug Squad, Intelligence Systems, Detectives, Traffic Department and Mounted Section/Police Dogs. Include a visit to one of these units or invite an officer to attend this session and assist by answering questions.

Course assessment – a written or oral assessment should take place in order to determine whether a satisfactory level of knowledge and practical skill has been achieved during the period of training.

SILVER

Note: Direct entrants to the Silver Award should cover the following subjects from the Bronze course: Welcome to the Course, Organisation of the Police Service, Road Accidents.

Participants should attend sessions on the following:

1. *Departments of the Service* – Uniform Patrol, Priority Policing Team, Area Response Group, Traffic Department, Criminal Investigation Department, Regional Crime Squad, Major Crime Support Unit, Plain Clothes Department, Mounted and Dog Section, Fraud Squad, Special Branch, Community Services, Scenes of Crime Unit, Scientific Support, Family Support Units, Training, Underwater Search Unit, Found Property, Control Rooms, Administration, Station Enquiries and Support Services.

• Emergency
Services
- Police
Service

2. *Police Stations* – role and functions of:
   a. The Enquiry Office – the range of enquiries made by the public.
   b. The Custody Suite – the role of the custody officer and duties in relation to the conditions of detention of arrested persons.
   c. The Control Room – the communications processes in the Service. Include a visit(s).
3. *Crime Prevention* – Neighbourhood Watch Schemes, Juvenile Crime Prevention Panels, safeguarding property, National Crime Intelligence System, Criminal Investigation Department and the Police National Computer.
4. *Safety of Motor Vehicles* –
   a. Safety of the vehicle, covering some basic faults, how to correct them and the Vehicle Defect Rectification Scheme.
   b. Safe driving, covering the training of Police drivers.
   c. Police Pursuits Policy and the implications of mistakes. (Where possible, this session should be conducted by a Traffic Officer with, 'a.' being covered practically).
5. *Identification Methods* – closed circuit television, fingerprints and automatic fingerprint retrieval, identification parades, edicon, Crimestoppers and practical fingerprinting and its difficulties.
6. *The Courts* – procedures and workings of the courts. The session may take place in a court which is not open to the public. An enactment of a trial could be organised.
7. *Police Responsibilities in Relation to Property* – the legal aspects of finding property, the duties placed upon Police in relation to recording lost and found property, together with methods to store, return and dispose of property. Also include motor vehicles and animals which come into police possession.

Course assessment – a written or oral assessment should take place to determine whether a satisfactory level of knowledge and practical skill has been achieved during the period of training.

GOLD

Note: Direct entrants to the Gold Award should cover all elements of the Silver course, together with the programme below. Both the

• Emergency Services - Police Service

training and practical service requirements can be fulfilled, if the participant is over 18 and a half years of age, by joining the Special Constabulary for at least one year.

Participants should attend sessions on the following:

1. *A Simple Case* – conduct an investigation and complete a file of evidence in relation to a simple offence of theft.
2. *The Courts* – procedures and workings of the courts. The session may take place in a court which is not open to the public. An enactment of a trial could be organised.
3. *Court Visit* – visit a Magistrates' or Crown Court to see the proceedings in a contested case.
4. *Care and Treatment of Children and Young People* – this session could be run as a discussion with participation by Probation Officers, NSPCC Inspectors or Social Workers covering subjects such as children's homes, remand centres, prisons, places of safety, attendance centres, community service.
5. *Optional Visit (over 18 years only)* – visit to a community home, detention or attendance centre.

Course assessment – a written or oral assessment should take place to determine whether a satisfactory level of knowledge and practical skill has been achieved during the period of training. Assessment should not be made by the Course Instructor.

Practical Service

Some suggestions for practical service are outlined below:

- Assisting with and setting up Cycling Proficiency Tests.
- Cycle marking.
- Assisting in station duties (where possible).
- Assisting with Intermediate Treatment or the Probation Service.
- Helping out in night shelters, community homes, probation hostels or with 'at risk' groups.
- Neighbourhood Watch or School Watch Schemes.
- Junior Crime Prevention Panels.
- Other forms of community and crime prevention work such as School Community Action Teams.
- At Gold, assisting with Bronze Police Service courses or special constabulary duties.

Assessment of Practical Service – a written report or oral presentation should be made on the findings and experiences of the practical service.

• Emergency
  Services
  - Police
  Service

Leadership in the Community

AWARD SCHEME LEADERSHIP (Gold Only)

This programme is designed to provide an understanding of the aim, content and conditions of The Duke of Edinburgh's Award and training for active leadership within an Award Unit.

Before embarking on this Service programme, it is important that the Leader of the Unit discuss with the participant the commitment of taking on a role of responsibility within the Unit. The number of young people participating in this programme at any one time should be carefully considered, in order that sufficient support and training can be given to a trainee young leader.

It is hoped that participants will continue in a leadership capacity within a Unit beyond the period required for the completion of their Gold Service.

All Award Leadership programmes must include:
1.   A training course.
2.   On-going practical service within an Award Unit.
3.   A leadership development exercise of the participant's choice.

Training Course

Mature participants should be encouraged to attend an Adult Award Leadership Course organised by their Operating Authority. It may be more appropriate for others to attend a locally organised training course for potential young leaders in their own age group. This should reflect the experience and practical service responsibilities of the individual participants.

In exceptional circumstances, where it is impractical to organise a group training course, a personal training programme may be drawn up by the Leader and the participant. This must be approved by the Operating Authority.

The course of training for all participants must be of at least 20 hours duration and may take the form of single sessions, or be combined with residential weekend and one day courses. The *Over to You* training pack may provide useful resources for the course.

SERVICE

GROUP TWO - PROGRAMMES

• Leadership
  in the
  Community
  - Award
    Scheme
    Leadership

Outside speakers should be introduced throughout the course in order to broaden the participants' knowledge of the operation of the Award in their area and help them to make contacts. A variety of participative training methods should be used, including role play, simulation exercises, discussion and practical involvement.

Topics to be covered include:
- The aim and philosophy of the Award.
- Framework and conditions.
- The details of each Section, including the personal value of participation.
- The support structure of the Award – Award Officers, Operating Authorities, Award Committees, Award Centres and Assisting Organisations.
- Management and organisation within a Unit and the concept of teamwork.
- Operational and promotional literature and videos.
- An introduction to the groupwork skills of working with young people, including listening and counselling skills and instructing.
- The world of young people – using the Award programme to meet the individual needs of young people.
- Targeting particular groups, such as young offenders, young people with special needs and ethnic minority groups.

Participants should also be encouraged to:
1. Acquire specific skills which they can employ within their Unit, e.g. mountain walking or physical recreation qualifications.
2. Visit an Award Unit within another Operating Authority, in order to broaden their experience.

Practical Service

Participants should be involved in a leadership capacity within their Award Unit for at least 12 months under the supervision of an experienced Leader. If there are insufficient genuine opportunities to give practical service within their own Unit then they should be encouraged to support another local Unit to which they are introduced by their Operating Authority.

Participants' roles, responsibilities and expectations should be agreed in advance and should reflect their age and experience. Possible roles include:

• Leadership in the Community - Award Scheme Leadership

- Arranging and supervising a course or courses in a specific Section of the Award, e.g. Bronze Service opportunities.
- After appropriate training, instructing in a specific activity, e.g. campcraft, navigation, or Physical Achievement tests.
- Offering leadership to and co-ordinating the activities of a Bronze group.
- With appropriate training and experience, acting as an Assessor for a particular activity, e.g. a Skill or Physical Activity at which they are proficient.

There is an expectation of regular attendance throughout the period of Service and participants should also be encouraged to attend Unit staff meetings in order that they can plan their future commitment to the Unit within a framework of teamwork.

The Leadership Development Exercise

With the continuing support of the Unit Leader the participant should undertake a specific project to demonstrate organisational and leadership skills. This should be the participant's own choice but should also meet the needs of the Unit. Examples include:

- Organising an Expedition training programme leading to Assessment for a Bronze group.
- Giving an introductory talk to a group of potential participants and guiding them in their choice of Award activities.
- Drawing up a training programme for a participant or group of participants in one of the Sections of the Award, indicating time, cost, arrangements for instruction and assessment etc.
- With the agreement of the Leader, review the administrative arrangements of the Unit including enrolment, consent forms, monitoring progress, issuing Awards etc.
- Arrange a social event or fundraising event for the Unit.
- Conduct an audit of Unit equipment and review the loan procedures.
- Organise a course for participants, e.g. Fire Service, Life Skills. Monitor their progress and arrange for assessment.

• Leadership in the Community - Award Scheme Leadership

Assessment

All participants must work with the support and supervision of an appropriately qualified and experienced Leader approved by the Operating Authority.

Assessment, which should be ongoing and take into account an appraisal by the Unit Leader, should be undertaken by the Award Officer of the Operating Authority or their nominee.

For assessment purposes participants should keep notes along with a diary, showing dates and details of practical service together with a report on the Leadership Development Exercise. Assessment should include an understanding of the philosophical values and personal benefits of each Section of the Award.

SERVICE THROUGH RELIGIOUS EDUCATION

Service involving work with young people or children may be given in the context of religious education and spiritual development. This would entail working with a religious-based or inter-faith group in an educative way in order to create opportunities for personal and spiritual development. Working in a Sunday School or Chedar, or with a religious-based youth group are ideal situations for this type of work.

Before commencing, participants must receive suitable training which will include aspects of group work and leadership, as well as a relevance to the chosen religion. A period of practical service will then follow, which should be properly supervised and organised. Participants are advised to seek advice from their Operating Authority or Regional or Territorial Office on the suitabilitiy of the practical service before commencing; certain activities which are considered to contribute to a form of worship, such as being a server, choir member, cantor or kirdeen jedha, are not acceptable in the Service Section. In all cases, the practical service undertaken must involve a contribution to the local community.

Training Resources

Training resources and formal programmes which are available are detailed below:

- **Christian** - Many churches and related organisations recognise and deliver appropriate training programmes. For further details, contact should be made with the local church, church headquarters or organisation's central office. Some useful addresses are included at the back of this book. Two resources which are particularly recommended are:

>*Kaleidoscope* – basic training material for those wishing to work with children in the church. *Spectrum* - an inter-church training programme for those wishing to become church youth workers and work with young people in the church.

Courses should be organised which are appropriate to the level of Award using these resources.

- **Jewish** – For a copy of the Bronze, Silver or Gold programmes, contact the Jewish Lads' and Girls' Brigade.

Participants wishing to pursue this option with another religious tradition, such as Hindu, Muslim or Sikh, or an inter-denominational or inter-faith organisation, should draw up a programme with an appropriate member of their faith community or organisation. In order to do this, they may wish to seek the advice of their Operating Authority or Regional Office. If the nature of the work to be undertaken is essentially that of working with youth groups, the programme for youth work may be useful. The programme should be submitted to Award Headquarters for approval prior to commencing.

YOUTH WORK

Many National Voluntary Youth Organisations, e.g. NABC, Youth Clubs UK and Local Authority Youth Services organise comprehensive packages of training which provide ideal opportunities for young people to undertake this option. In such cases, this syllabus will assist participants and Leaders in selecting an appropriate course. It will also indicate the requirements for each level of Award to those organisations who do not arrange their own training scheme.

In order to enable individual participants to make a significant contribution within the youth organisation and to learn from their experiences, the three strands of the syllabus are:

• Leadership in the Community - Service Through Religious Education - Youth Work

- Training programme and a project.
- Active leadership and participation in a group/club.
- Personal development of the participant.

The training programme may be given as a series of single training sessions, be combined with or given entirely at a residential course, or a series of individual tutorials, provided that the minimum hours are undertaken.

Participants should build up a portfolio to help them record and evaluate their work and show evidence of personal development. It should contain information gathered during the training programme and project, a diary and record of the period of active leadership together with any photographs, letters or publicity material.

Course assessment – This should be based on attendance, participation and discussion of the portfolio showing evidence or improved personal awareness and understanding. At Gold, it should be undertaken at Borough/County level.

BRONZE
Participants should attend sessions on the following:

1. *Background Knowledge* – basic information about the group/club, what it provides, other local youth provision.
2. *Membership* – a profile of the membership, age range, background, the balance of members in terms of gender, race and ability and their reasons for attending the group or club.
3. *Programme and Activities* – discussing the purpose of youth work in providing social education opportunities. Participate in the organisation and running of an activity or event for peers or a younger age group and record the learning outcomes.
4. *Personal Skills* – identifying personal skills and qualities, how to develop them in a youth club setting.
5. *Project* – working alongside another youth worker, planning and carrying out a project with a purpose such as publicising an event or organising, under close supervision, an activity in a junior club.

The Course work should be a minimum of 8 hours.

Practical Service

Active leadership – Assisting with specific supervised activities in a junior club over a three month period. Participants should be given regular guidance and feedback on their performance.

SILVER

Participants should attend sessions on the following:

1. *Background Knowledge* – the aims of the club/organisation, provisions of the local Youth Service, profile of the local community.
2. *Principles and Practice* – the basic principles of good youth work practice, concept of groups, improving participation; an introduction to issues such as equal opportunities, racism, and deprivation in urban and rural areas.
3. *Programmes and Activities* – exploring the purpose of youth work in assisting young people in the transition towards adulthood and the issues affecting young people in today's society. Organising an activity or event for peers or a younger age group and recording the learning outcomes.
4. *Personal Skills* – identifying personal strengths, using them in the club/group, making decisions, taking initiative. Concept of teamwork, introduction to styles of leadership.
5. *Project* – Organising and evaluating an activity with a purpose for a small group of young people with the support of a youth worker.

The Course work should be a minimum of 15 hours.

Practical Service

Active leadership – Adopt a leadership role in a small group with the support of a youth worker over a period of 6 months. Participants should receive regular review and counselling sessions

GOLD

Participants should attend sessions on the following:

1. *Background Knowledge* – the purpose of youth work and its educational role. The aims of the club/organisation; an evaluation of its success, the local provision for young people and the issues affecting them.
2. *The Youth Work Curriculum* – exploring the concept of informal education and delivery of the youth work curriculum which is educational, participative, empowering and seeks to

• Leadership in the Community - Youth Work

promote equal opportunities; the issues confronting young people in the transition towards mature and responsible adulthood and those affecting young people in today's society.

3. *Programmes and Activities* – designing and implementing a programme taking account of the needs of young people and their different stages of development; recording the preparation including the objectives and method and evaluating the outcomes.

4. *Leadership* – discussing styles and function of leadership, relationships between youth workers and young people, decision-making processes, committee work and methods of evaluation.

5. *Personal Skills* – assessing personal strengths and weaknesses, devising a programme for personal development.

6. *Project* – undertaking and evaluating a practical project with a purpose which is related to the course work, such as: organisation of a junior club or organisations, a project integrating those with special needs, planning an Open Award night, organising an arts event.

The Course work should be a minimum of 20 hours.

Practical Service

Active leadership – Adopt a leadership role in a group/club with the guidance of a youth worker for a minimum of 12 months. Participants should receive regular review and counselling sessions.

Rescue

CAVE RESCUE
(Minimum Age: 18 years and at Gold level only)

Aim: To train participants to become full members of a recognised cave rescue team.

Cave Rescue is only open to participants over 18 years and at Gold level only.

Participants are expected to join a recognised Cave Rescue team either in a probationary capacity or as a full member. To be eligible, they must be able to demonstrate that they have sufficient caving skills and experience to be accepted for team membership

• Leadership in the Community - Youth Work
• Rescue - Cave Rescue

and they must also be able to comply with any other normal team requirements for membership.

Cave rescue is a potentially very dangerous activity and Operating Authorities must ensure that participants have adequate insurance cover. They will not be insured unless they are probationary or full members of a recognised team.

GOLD

Participants should (under each main heading) know the following:

1. Surface Organisation:
   a. Call-out procedure.
   b. Responsibility for own correct personal clothing and equipment.
   c. Procedure on arrival at an accident.
   d. Surface organisation of the team and responsibilities within it.
   e. Role of other emergency services, supporting organisations and volunteers.
2. Underground Organisation:
   a. Underground organisation and responsibilities within the team.
   b. Personal responsibilities as a team member.
   c. Knowledge of the role of specialists, e.g. cave divers.
3. Personal Skills:
   a. Safe application of those single rope techniques and ladder techniques commonly used by cavers.
   b. Reasonable familiarity with the caves and mines within the team area.
4. Rescue Skills:
   a. General knowledge of (and skill in using) all normal rescue equipment and rescue techniques used by the team.
   b. Loading and use of the type(s) of cave rescue stretcher(s) held by the team.
   c. Use of the team communications equipment and correct radio procedures.

• Rescue
- Cave Rescue

5. First Aid:
    Either
    a. Hold a current First Aid Certificate issued by a recognised body (e.g. St. John Ambulance).
        or
    b. Have the ability to diagnose and assist in the treatment of those injuries and conditions most commonly encountered underground including hypothermia, fractures and dislocations, bleeding, shock, crush and head injuries.

Practical Service

After satisfying the above conditions, participants will be expected to give at least 40 further hours as a probationary or full member of the rescue team.

COASTGUARD SERVICE

HM Coastguard is the UK authority for the co-ordination and conduct of search and rescue at sea in the waters surrounding the United Kingdom and 1,000 miles out into the Atlantic. They operate a comprehensive communications system based on 21 Maritime Rescue Centres situated around the coast. A continuous 24-hour radio watch on the VHF distress frequency is maintained at all of these centres through some 84 remote radio transmitting and receiving sites around our coast.

In addition to this radio watch, 999 emergency telephone calls from coastal areas are handled and advice on safety can be provided at any time, day or night. The centres have direct radio or landline links with the coast radio stations, rescue helicopters, lifeboats, coastguard stations and patrol vehicles in their districts and the facilities necessary for co-ordinating all forms of maritime rescue whether they be at sea or on the coastline.

HM Coastguard also performs a number of other duties in connection with the beaches and foreshores. In addition to the rescue centres there are coastguard stations which are manned during periods of bad weather or high casualty risk. These stations are in the charge of a regular coastguard officer assisted by volunteers enrolled in the Coastguard Auxiliary Service. The Auxiliary Coastguard also supply the personnel required for coastal search and cliff rescue teams and many assist the regular

• Rescue
  - Cave Rescue
  - Coastguard
    Service

Coastguard at the rescue centres or as reporting members. There is ample scope for challenging and active work for young people with an interest in the sea with particular emphasis on communications and giving direct assistance to the general public.

Operating Authorities that wish to arrange training for this type of Service should contact the appropriate Regional Controller, HM Coastguard. In coastal districts the address of the nearest Maritime Rescue Co-ordination Centre or Maritime Rescue Sub Centre will be found in the telephone directory.

When the participants are ready for assessment, the Operating Authority should approach the nearest Regional Controller, HM Coastguard, and ask for a convenient date and place for the assessment to be held. A list of the names of participants should accompany the request.

The Regional Controller, HM Coastguard, will delegate to a senior officer the task of making the assessments and recording the results in individual *Record Books.*

For a copy of the full syllabus, send a stamped, self-addressed envelope to Award Headquarters in Windsor.

LIFEBOAT SERVICE

The RNLI is a voluntary organisation for saving life at sea supported entirely by voluntary contributions and administered by a Committee of Management. The British Isles are divided into six Divisions each controlled by an Inspector, assisted by a Deputy Inspector; they are responsible to the Committee of Management through the Director. There are 125 all-weather lifeboats and 148 inshore lifeboats stationed around our coastline and manned as required by volunteer crews. Training for this volunteer service will be arranged at certain suitable stations where Instructors are available, and application should be made to the Inspector of the area concerned through the Royal National Lifeboat Institution. Each group under training must be limited to a maximum of six. **Participants must wear secure lifejackets, which will be provided, when afloat.**

• Rescue
 - Coastguard Service
 - Lifeboat Service

When a group is ready for assessment, the Inspector will be informed and the necessary arrangements made. The results will be entered in the participant's *Record Book. Volume II Admiralty Manual of Seamanship* will cover most of the syllabus.

It may be possible for participants to accompany the lifeboat crew on exercise. In order to do this each participant must be covered by personal insurance. All participants must be able to swim 50 yards fully clothed.

For a copy of the full syllabus send a stamped, self-addressed envelope to Award Headquarters in Windsor.

MOUNTAIN RESCUE
(Minimum Age: 18 years and at Gold level only)

Young people choosing to undertake Mountain Rescue must join a Mountain Rescue Team recognised by the Mountain Rescue Council as a bona fide probationary member. Most teams are unable to offer training to participants who do not plan to continue as team members after completing their Award requirements.

Mountain Rescue is potentially a dangerous activity and Operating Authorities must ensure that participants have adequate insurance cover.

Participants must be 18+ years of age and live and/or work within the Team's normal recruiting area. Most Teams will require that probationers, before they join the Team, have some mountaineering experience and are able to move safely over difficult country in varying weather conditions. Many Teams also require some previous First Aid training.

Participants should have read the *Mountain and Cave Rescue Handbook* and be familiar with its contents. They should also be thoroughly familiar with the BMC Booklet *Safety on Mountains*.

GOLD

In all areas covered by the programme, participants will be required to follow the operating procedures of the Rescue Team they join.

• Rescue
  - Lifeboat
    Service
  - Mountain
    Rescue

Participants should also:

1. Know the call-out procedure, be aware of their personal responsibility to turn out with correct clothing, footwear and equipment, and know the procedures on arrival.

2. Demonstrate an ability to use a 1:25 000 and 1:50 000 Ordnance Survey map and a compass by day and night to reach a six-figure grid reference and navigate in bad visibility (cloud and mist) in featureless country.

3. Have a good knowledge of the mountain area within which the Team operates.

4. Be conversant with those aspects of mountaineering which are peculiar to the area in which the Team operates. If this includes steep ground or climbing crags, familiarity with movement on steep ground and attention to personal and group safety with and without the use of a rope should be demonstrated. This will be required as a minimum, some Teams may require considerably more crag and climbing expertise. In any case, participants must satisfy the requirements of the Rescue Team.

5. Know the common knots, belaying techniques and rope management used by climbers. Know methods of management used by the Team for stretcher lowering ropes.

6. Know the principles of rope care and storage, and equipment storage arrangements in the Team headquarters or other areas.

7. Have a knowledge of First Aid as required by the local Team. Most Teams require members to hold a full First Aid qualification. Some will require knowledge of the application and use of their splints and other specialised equipment.

8. Know how to assemble, load and carry the Team's mountain rescue stretcher(s).

9. Know standard radio procedures including the phonetic alphabet.

10. Be able to use a field radio set.

11. Know standard procedures and safety precautions used when operating with helicopters.

12. Know the hazards relating to winter conditions in the mountains.

13. Be aware of the hazards in other situations such as crashed aircraft, particularly military aircraft.

• Rescue
  - Mountain
    Rescue

14. Be aware of all that is involved, and have participated in training operations, in the organisation, search, rescue and evacuation for a person missing in difficult country.
15. Be aware of all that is involved and have participated in training operations for the rescue and evacuation of a casualty from a crag face.

Practical Service

Participants are reminded that, following a period of training, at least 40 hours practical service must be completed as a probationary or full member of a Rescue Team.

Safety

CYCLIST TRAINING INSTRUCTION

Aim: To encourage a greater awareness of the problems of cycling on the road and to train or help train other cyclists or Cycle Training Instructors.

Service should be arranged in collaboration with Local Authorities operating Cyclist Training Schemes and in particular with their Road Safety Officers. Advice and information is available from the Royal Society for Prevention of Accidents (RoSPA) from whom specialists' certificates may also be obtained.

BRONZE

Aim: To assist an Instructor with cycle training.

Training: Before a participant qualifies for the Bronze Award he or she must have obtained a Cyclist Training Certificate awarded by RoSPA or a Local Authority alternative.

Practical Service

Participants must assist a qualified Instructor for a minimum of two training courses for child cyclists in a Cyclist Training Scheme. This will require Service of not less than 15 hours over a minimum period of three months.

SILVER

Note: Direct entrants to the Silver Award must hold a Cyclist Training Certificate.
Aim: To carry out cycle training as an Instructor.

Training as a Cyclist Training Tutor or Instructor will require participants to have a knowledge of the following:
a. The Highway Code.
b. The fundamental principles of cycle training for young cyclists.
c. Training of young cyclists as potential vehicle drivers.
d. Equipment and literature for use at indoor and outdoor training periods.
e. Use of visual materials in conjunction with Instructor's notes, if appropriate.
f. Practical demonstrations of safe cycling.

Practical Service

Participants must serve as an Instructor for a minimum of three training courses for child cyclists in a Cyclist Training Scheme. This should involve the organisation of both indoor and outdoor sessions, including time for preparation, e.g. setting up training equipment, marking registers, assisting with the checking of bicycles – and for conclusion of each period, e.g. the clearing away of equipment. This will require Service of not less than 30 hours over a minimum period of six months.

GOLD

Note: Direct entrants to the Gold Award must hold a Cyclist Training Certificate and be proficient and experienced cyclists.
Aim: To organise and instruct advanced cycle training and/or to train other cycling Instructors.

Participants are required to undergo a period of training in:
Either:
a. Instructing children at an advanced level, such as RoSPA's Advanced Cycle Test programme
or:
b. Training Cycling Instructors

Practical Service

Participants will be expected to either:
a. Instruct children for the Advanced Cycling Test or equivalent in the following subjects:
    i. *Practical Roadcraft* – including stopping and starting in traffic; turning right and left; vehicle parking;

SERVICE
GROUP TWO - PROGRAMMES

• Safety
- Cyclist
  Training
  Instruction

commonsense and courtesy; traffic signs; road markings; lights on vehicles.

ii.   *The Highway Code* – for all road users.

iii.   *Finding the Way* – map reading; direction and information signs, assessing hazards from maps, choosing the best routes.

iv.   *Practical Cycling Maintenance* – emergency repairs, adjustment for safety, knowledge of cycle maintenance.

or:

b.   Undertake the training of other CycleTraining Instructors.

HOME ACCIDENT PREVENTION

Leaders are advised to seek expert help from Instructors and Qualified Assessors.

Course Tutors are advised to obtain a Tutors' training pack available from the Royal Society for the Prevention of Accidents.

Material and help can usually be obtained from local Environmental Health Departments, Health Education Departments, Trading Standards, Fire Brigades, suppliers of all fuels, gas, water and electricity, accident prevention groups and other recognised bodies.

BRONZE

Aim: To teach participants about the basic aspects of home safety, how common causes of accidents are identified and the appropriate preventative action.

Participants should:

1.   Demonstrate an understanding of the general aspects of home safety and how statistics are used to identify and categorise the more common types of home accidents.

2.   Identify the major fire hazards in the home, how they can be properly managed and the correct action to take in the event of a fire in the home.

3.   State the correct actions to be taken in order to identify and prevent possible accidents outdoors.

• Safety
 - Cyclist
   Training
   Instruction
 - Home
   Accident
   Prevention

4. Identify how children are at risk from accidents in the home, the most common categories of accidents involving children and how these risks can be limited.

5. Demonstrate knowledge and understanding of how accidents involving older people occur in relation to falls, burns, incorrect storage of household items and accidents involving medicines and poisons.

On completion of the course participants should compile a project, such as a survey, on one of the following topics (it may be undertaken on either an individual or group basis):

- General safety in the home.
- Child safety equipment.
- Fire in the home.

The format should to be decided by the participant but the project should show:

- Identification of the areas of hazard in the topic area.
- Identification of the risks in each area.
- Suggestions for appropriate action to prevent or limit accidents caused by the risks.

Advice on projects can be obtained from *The RoSPA Guide to projects in Home Safety.*

Course assessment – participants will be expected to answer either written or oral questions, as appropriate, on all aspects of the course. They should also present their project for assessment.

Practical Service

Participants are encouraged to give practical service following the course. This may include:

- Presenting the project results and findings to the organisation or group benefiting from its compilation.
- Giving talks or presentations on Home Accident Prevention to groups such as youth groups or school children.
- Assisting with a presentation or display on Home Accident Prevention at a suitable venue such as a school.
- Distributing information on Home Accident Prevention such as leaflets and posters.

• Safety
  - Home
    Accident
    Prevention

SILVER

Aim: To develop knowledge and awareness of the hazards and risks in and around the home and to develop an increasing sense of responsibility towards the safety of the family in general.

Participants should:
1. Be able to identify how statistics are gathered in relation to home accidents and the cost implications to the Health Service and the family.
2. Identify how accidents in the home can affect the entire family and the correct actions to take when an accident occurs.
3. Be able to demonstrate how home surveys are carried out and checklists generated.
4. Conduct home surveys in:
   a. Kitchen, laundry and bathroom.
   b. Living and sleeping areas.
   c. Outdoors, garage and gardens.
5. Identify the hazards associated with household appliances and demonstrate knowledge of how to wire a 13 amp plug and correct size of fuse for various appliances.

On completion of the course participants should compile a project, such as a survey, on one of the following topics (it may be undertaken on either an individual or group basis):
- Planning a room for safety.
- Designing safe appliances or toys.
- Safety management in DIY or gardening.

The format should be decided by the participant, but the project should show that the participant has:
- Conducted appropriate research.
- Identified suitable subject areas.
- Made suitable suggestions which are correct and likely to prevent accidents.

Course assessment – participants will be expected to answer either written or oral questions, as appropriate, on all aspects of the course. They should also present their project for assessment.

Practical Service

Participants are expected to give practical service following the course. This may include:

- Presenting the project results and findings to the organisation benefiting from its compilation.
- Giving talks or presentations on Home Accident Prevention to other groups, such as youth groups or school children.
- Setting up a presentation or display on Home Accident Prevention at a suitable venue, such as a school.
- Distributing information on Home Accident Prevention such as leaflets and posters.

GOLD

Aim: To build on the information covered by the Bronze and Silver courses.

Participants should:
1. Have an understanding of the information contained in the Bronze and Silver courses.
2. Demonstrate understanding of how emergency plans are formulated – and how evacuation procedures can save time in an emergency.
3. Detail the correct action to be taken in emergency situations involving water, electricity and gas.
4. Identify how safety is considered during house design and how it affects room layout; also how warnings and advice are given by means of signs, symbols and labels on all household appliances and furnishings.
5. Identify opportunities in the community to promote home safety by means of local groups or organisations.

On completion of the course participants should complete a project. This should involve the design and compilation of a training pack on the subject 'Basic Home Accident Prevention'. It may be undertaken on either an individual or group basis.

Course assessment – participants will be expected to answer either written or oral questions, as appropriate, on all aspects of the course. They should also present their project supported by a 15-20 minute presentation. The presentation should be given to an audience outside the group and should demonstrate:
- Preparation and planning.
- Identification and recognition of audience.
- Understanding of topic.
- Communication skills.

• Safety
 - Home
   Accident
   Prevention

Practical Service

Participants are required to give 40 hours of practical service spread over 12 months. This may include:

- Presenting the project results and findings to the organisation benefiting from its compilation.
- Giving talks or presentations on Home Accident Prevention to other groups, such as youth groups or school children.
- Organising displays on Home Accident Prevention at suitable venues, such as conferences and open days.
- Assisting in the organisation of Home Accident Prevention courses for Bronze participants.

ROAD SAFETY

Aim: To encourage a greater awareness of the problems facing road users and issues relating to road safety.

Service should be arranged by, or in collaboration with, the Road Safety Officer of the Local Authority. Most Police Forces have an Accident Prevention Officer or equivalent who may also be able to assist with some sessions. Alternatively, instruction may be undertaken by a teacher, youth leader or driving instructor who is experienced in all aspects of road safety and who should work closely with the Road Safety Officer.

The Instructor must refer to the latest edition of the Highway Code for guidance and an outline of the requirements of the law. Road Safety Officers should be able to provide a range of resources to assist with the delivery of the course.

Site visits and practical road training sessions must be properly planned and supervised and younger participants should be briefed on appropriate safe practices to ensure all reasonable precautions are taken. Instructors must have regard to Health and Safety at Work regulations.

• Safety
  - Home
    Accident
    Prevention
  - Road Safety

BRONZE

Aim: To develop an understanding of issues relating to road safety and the nature of road accidents, particularly in the context of the participant's own local environment and age group.

Participants should:

1. Investigate the way in which accident data is collected, how it is stored, and how it may be used.
2. Assess the relative contributions to accidents of:
   a. Human error (e.g. alcohol, speed, inexperience).
   b. Environment (e.g. weather, road surface condition, visibility).
   c. Vehicle (e.g. defective tyres, faulty brakes).
   (A variety of sources should be used, such as press cuttings, case studies and other data.)
3. Select a geographical area and put together a profile of the road accidents within that area. This should refer to factors such as age, male/female ratios, time, circumstances, cause, location and types of road users, e.g. car, cyclist, motorcyclist, pedestrian. Include research methods such as questioning friends and peers as well as using data.
4. Undertake a travel survey such as a study of travel patterns of people within a particular age group, e.g. the participant's own. Examine factors such as the use of public transport and reasons for journeying, e.g. to school, college, work. Outline problem areas and suggest improvements.
5. Examine road safety issues through an appropriate project, i.e. select a familiar section of street or road in a town or village and identify possible dangers. Bear in mind the needs of groups such as elderly or disabled people.
6. Learn about and establish the principles of vehicle safety maintenance. Select a vehicle and draw up a priority list of features requiring special attention. Be able to identify and correct defective parts for checking by an expert.
7. Understand the properties of reflective and fluorescent materials and their safety application to vulnerable road users in particular. Obtain samples and test for effectiveness and customer acceptability. Compile a list of appropriate items, their cost and where they can be obtained.

Course assessment: a course assessment must take place followed by a period of practical service.

SERVICE
GROUP TWO - PROGRAMMES

• Safety
  - Road Safety

SILVER

Note: Direct entrants to the Silver Award should become familiar with the contents of the Bronze programme.

Aim
1. To gain an understanding of issues relating to road safety education and the nature of road accidents, particularly in the context of the participant's local environment and age group.
2. To prepare participants for vehicle ownership and individual responsibilities.

Participants should:
1. Investigate the risks faced by different age groups from road traffic accidents and make comparisons to other types of accident, e.g. at work, in the home. Examine the costs and consequences of road accidents.
2. Become familiar with procedures at the scene of road accidents. Learn emergency aid skills, e.g. CPR, recovery position, dealing with severe bleeding. A qualified First Aid Instructor should deliver this session.
3. Understand the effects of alcohol and drugs and the requirements of the law. Undertake related research such as a survey of either public awareness or the availability of educational literature on this subject.
4. Understand the contribution of seat restraints to casualty reduction. Become familiar with current legislation. Prepare a consumer report on availability, pricing and the fitting of child seat restraints.
5. Find out about the availability of local training courses for cyclists, motorcyclists, horse-riders and car drivers (including those for disabled people). Visit one of these organisations and familiarise yourself with the training techniques used.
6. Research the costs involved in vehicle ownership, the documentation necessary and the safety advantages and disadvantages of the chosen mode of transport. Obtain insurance premium quotations. Give a talk to a group of teenagers in a school, college or youth organisation on vehicle ownership, the costs, advantages and disadvantages.

Course assessment: a course assessment must take place followed by a period of practical service.

• Safety
  - Road Safety

GOLD

Note: Direct entrants to the Gold Award should become familiar with the Silver programme.

Aim
1. To develop an awareness of the more complex issues relating to road safety, such as the perspectives of different pressure groups, road safety legislation, the contribution of public transport, road safety as an environmental issue and the level of provision for vulnerable groups.
2. To assess how a local street environment succeeds or fails in incorporating fair and effective safety design.
3. To embark upon an extended programme of road safety Service.

Participants must discuss their proposed course of training and practical service with a Road Safety Officer or practitioner before commencing.

Participants should:
1. Study a site that was improved by low-cost engineering treatment. Analyse the previous accident record, the reasons for treatment and the post-treatment record. Close involvement with a Road Safety Officer and engineering colleagues is necessary.
2. Select a local site and record road user movements, user opinions and the perceived and actual danger or conflict. Make use of a range of methods and materials, where available, such as photography, video filming or tape recordings. Present recommendations to the Engineering Department.
3. Make contact with a road user or lobby group, e.g. a group involved with the needs of disabled road users or citizens with English as a second language, or one concerned with the protection of rural areas. Research the views of the different parties involved and communicate their problems to the general public.
4. Choose and research another aspect of road use and road safety.

Course assessment: a course assessment must take place followed by a period of practical service.

• Safety
 - Road Safety

Practical Service

Some examples of practical service for Bronze, Silver or Gold level are outlined below:

- Assisting with road safety education programmes, e.g. helping a play group leader or Road Safety Officer at a local play group.
- Promoting the use of road safety materials such as reflective materials, helmets and seat restraints to a group of people such as parents at a pre-school group or members of a youth club. This may be either through a promotional talk or by publishing the findings of a survey on this subject in a local magazine or newsletter.
- Helping with a publicity campaign relating to a group of road users, such as the disabled.
- Representing the interests of the participant's age-group on a local road safety group or committee.
- Training or assisting with the training of road users, whether pedestrians, cyclists, motorcyclists or horse riders.
- Assisting in the training of Bronze road safety scheme participants.

GROUP THREE:
SERVICE REQUIRING A SPECIFIC QUALIFICATION

Care in the Community

CHILD CARE, FIRST AID AND HOME NURSING

BRONZE

St. John Ambulance	Essentials of First Aid
	Caring for the Sick Preliminary Level
	Caring for the Child Preliminary Certificate
British Red Cross	Youth First Aid Certificate
	Youth Nursing Certificate
	Youth Infant and Child Care Certificate
St. Andrew's Ambulance	Junior First Aid Certificate
	Junior Nursing Certificate
	Junior Child Care Certificate
Order of Malta	Cadet First Aid Voucher
Ambulance Corps	Cadet Nursing Certificate
National Association for Maternal & Child Welfare	Alternate Modular

SILVER

St. John Ambulance	Lifesaver Plus (formerly Public First Aid Certificate) or Community First Aid (Wales)
	Caring for the Sick Level 1
British Red Cross	Adult Standard First Aid Certificate
	Adult Standard Nursing Certificate
St. Andrew's Ambulance	Standard First Aid Certificate
	Emergency First Aid Certificate (with examination)
	Standard Nursing Certificate (Caring for the Sick)
	Adult Child Care Certificate
Order of Malta	Adult First Aid Certificate
Ambulance Corps	Adult Home Nursing Certificate
National Association for Maternal & Child Welfare	Level 1

• Care in the
  Community
  - Child Care,
  First Aid and
  Home
  Nursing

GOLD

St. John Ambulance	Lifesaver Plus (formerly Public First Aid Certificate) or Community First Aid (Wales)*
	Caring for the Sick Level 1*
	Caring for the Sick Level 2
British Red Cross	Adult Standard First Aid Certificate*
	Adult Standard Nursing Certificate*
St. Andrew's Ambulance	Standard First Aid Certificate*
	Second Standard First Aid Certificate
	Standard Nursing Certificate*
	Higher Nursing Certificate
	Adult Child Care Certificate*
Order of Malta Ambulance Corps	Adult First Aid Certificate*
	Advanced First Aid Certificate (OMAC members only)
	Adult Home Nursing Certificate*
National Association for Maternal & Child Welfare	Level II

These courses may only be undertaken for Gold if they have not been undertaken for Silver.

Instruction and Assessment must be carried out by approved instructors and examiners of the voluntary aid societies listed above, to whom all applications should be made and whose regulations must be followed.

Note: First Aid at Work – in exceptional circumstances, and with the approval of the Operating Authority, a First Aid at Work certificate may be completed. However, the course must be undertaken on a voluntary basis and there must be a genuine commitment of the participant's leisure time. This option is not available at Gold if First Aid training was undertaken for the Silver level.

• Care in the Community - Child Care, First Aid and Home Nursing

Leadership in the Community

DANCE LEADERSHIP

Dance Leaders in the Community Award
16+ years – Gold level or for those over the age of 16 years who are undertaking Silver or Bronze.

Recognised and funded by the Arts and Sports Councils and endorsed by the Community Dance and Mime Foundation, this basic course is aimed at those people working through dance within the community, wishing to extend their knowledge of movement and dance and to acquire confidence in working in a dance context with groups or individuals within the community. Further information is available from the Yorkshire Dance Centre (see Useful Addresses).

EXPEDITION AND MOUNTAIN LEADERSHIP

Basic Expedition Training Award (BETA)
18+ years – Gold level or for those over the age of 18 years who are undertaking Silver or Bronze.

BETA is for those who wish to lead groups outdoors and focuses on the skills of leadership, caring for the countryside and living out of doors. Details are available from the CCPR.
Note: Participants must be 18 years old before they can qualify for BETA, but training can commence at 17 years.

Mountain Leader Training
18+ years – Gold level or for those over the age of 18 years who are undertaking Silver or Bronze.

Registration on the Mountain Leader Training Scheme is for those with a genuine interest in hillwalking and party leadership, who have a minimum of one year's mountain experience. This scheme trains and assesses participants in their ability to lead a walking group anywhere in the UK. Details are available from the Mountain Leader Training Board.

SERVICE
GROUP THREE - PROGRAMMES

• Leadership in the Community
 - Dance Leadership
 - Expedition and Mountain Leadership

SPORTS LEADERSHIP

Junior Sports Leaders Award (JSLA)

14+ years – Bronze level only

The JSLA is intended for young people between the ages of 14 and 16 years working within a youth organisation or the school environment. The training and practical work is designed to give participants an appreciation of the skills required to lead sporting activities. Details are available from the CCPR.

Community Sports Leaders Award (CSLA)

16+ years – Gold level or for those over the age of 16 years who are undertaking Silver or Bronze.

The CSLA is a preliminary Sports Leaders' Award providing the ideal introduction and foundation for those young people wishing to assist in the voluntary activities of a club or youth organisation and lead groups in sporting or recreational activity. It aims to develop self-confidence, leadership skills and organisational skills relating to sport and is an ideal preparation for those wishing to pursue a National Governing Body Coaching qualification. Details are available from the CCPR.

Hanson/Higher Award

18+ years – Gold level or for those over the age of 18 years who are undertaking Silver or Bronze.

The Hanson Leadership Award is for those who wish to enhance their leadership skills and develop not only an interest in sport but also in sports administration and areas of special needs. It also includes a National Governing Body Coaching, Officiating or Leadership Award and 30 hours of voluntary sports leadership.

Note: Participants must be 18 years old before they can qualify for the Hanson Award, but training can commence at 17 years. Details are available from the CCPR.

• Leadership in the Community - Sports Leadership

YOUTH LEADERSHIP WITH UNIFORMED ORGANISATIONS

A number of National Voluntary Youth Organisations, who have their own Leadership Training Programmes, are able to count some of these as Service training for the Award. **Such training may be undertaken for Silver and Gold Awards only. It is not acceptable to undertake Youth Service at Silver and Gold as Community Service, i.e. in Group One.** The Community Service Programme may be used for Service within Voluntary Youth Organisations at **Bronze level only.** This Service should include supervised assistance with specific aspects or subjects such as music, craft and badgework.

For Silver and Gold level the following adult leadership training course must be followed and details of requirements should be obtained from the organisation concerned. Training courses should be followed by a period of practical service and, at Gold level, this must be at least 20 hours which, together with training, is to be spread over 12 months.

Army Cadet Force Association
SILVER
Cadets:
Attend and successfully complete a Junior Instructors' Cadre.
Complete the 3 Star syllabus for a Cadet and the Community.
Know the history of the ACF and organisations in the detachment, area and County. Study the history of the Regiment or Corps of the cap badge worn. (The standard expected will be well above that demanded at 2 Star level).
Assessment – Area or County level.

GOLD
Cadets:
Attend and perform satisfactorily at a Senior Cadet Instructors Cadre or, for a Cadet who has not used the ACF Service Syllabus at Silver, successfully complete a Junior Instructors' Cadre.
Give a minimum of 40 hours of Service to the detachment.
Hold the rank of Corporal for a period of not less than 12 months or, where there is no NCO vacancy, be a 3 Star Cadet.

• Leadership in the Community - Youth Leadership with Uniformed Organisations

Adults:
Complete 20 hours minimum training which may include MOD or The Duke of Edinburgh's Award courses. Instruct or supervise cadet activities for a minimum period of 40 hours.
Assessment – County or National Level.

Air Training Corps
SILVER
Cadet Corporal for 6 months minimum.
Assessment – Squadron Commander or Training Officer.

GOLD
Cadet Sergeant for 12 months minimum or to have been qualified as Staff Cadet for 12 months.
Assessment – Squadron Commander or Training Officer.

Boys' Brigade
SILVER
6 months Service in a leadership role within any section of the Company.
Course: Brigade Leadership or any specialised Brigade or external training course appropriate to the work undertaken.
Assessment – Company Captain plus Battalion /District/National Training Centre.

GOLD
12 months Service in a Leadership role within any section of the Company.
Course: KGVI/Officer Basic Training or any specialised Brigade or external training course appropriate to the work undertaken.
Assessment – Company Captain plus Battalion/District/National Training Centre.

Campaigners
SILVER
Phase 1 Training.
Assessment – Chief Regional Trainer.

GOLD
Phase 2 Training (in addition to Phase 1).
Assessment – Chief Regional Trainer.

• Leadership in the Community - Youth Leadership with Uniformed Organisations

Church Lads' and Church Girls' Brigade

SILVER

NCO Proficiency Certificate plus a minimum of 20 hours Service over 6 months under supervision of Formation Training Officer. List of projects available from HQ.

Assessment – Formation Training Officer in consultation with NHQ.

GOLD

Junior Leaders' Training Course including King George VI Leadership Training Course.

Assessment – NHQ.

Combined Cadet Force

SILVER

Hold the rank of Corporal for at least six months or pass the Proficiency Certificate.

Attend Central Camp and attend two Field Days.

Know the history of the CCF and study the history of the Service. In the case of Army Sections the history of the Regiment/Corps/School whose cap badge is worn.

Assessment – Section Commander/Contingent Commander

GOLD

Attain the minimum rank of Sergeant/Petty Officer and hold the rank for at least 12 months.

Attend a Methods of Instruction or Special to Arms Cadre or Service equivalent and give at least 20 periods of instruction, or pass the Advanced Standard of the APC and complete at least 40 hours Service for the contingent (e.g. staff cadet, storeman, office clerk, armourer).

Assessment – Section Commander/Contingent Commander.

Girls' Brigade England and Wales

SILVER

Grade III Young Leader.

Assessment – Commissioner (Division) or Commandant (Unattached District).

- Leadership in the Community
  - Youth Leadership with Uniformed Organisations

GOLD
Warrant Officer Grade or Commissioned Rank.

Assessment – Commissioner (Division) or Commandant (Unattached District).

Girls' Brigade Scotland
SILVER
Preparation for Leadership Part 1 and 2.

Assessment – Regional Commissioner.

GOLD
Warrant Officer Training or Basic Officer Training.

Assessment – Regional/National Training Committee.

Girls' Brigade Northern Ireland
SILVER
Sub Officer Rank.

GOLD
Sub Officer or Commissioned Officer Rank.

Assessment – District Commandant and/or Headquarters Training Officer.

Girls' Venture Corps Air Cadets
SILVER
Staff Cadet Award.

Assessment – Regional Senior Officers.

GOLD
Either:

Staff Cadet Award (if not gained for Silver).

or:

Adult Leadership Award.

Assessment – Regional Senior Officers.

The Guide Association
Note: The following is available to members of The Guide Association only. Non-members of The Guide Association cannot help at Unit meetings for any Section of the Award, i.e. Bronze, Silver or Gold.

• Leadership in the Community - Youth Leadership with Uniformed Organisations

SILVER

Either:

Basic Leadership Certificate (Making it Count).

or:

Senior Section Camp Permit endorsed for leadership.

GOLD

Either:

Basic Leadership Certificate (Making it Count), if not gained for Silver.

or:

Senior Section Camp Permit endorsed for Leadership, if not gained for Silver.

or:

Stages 1 and 2 of The Guide Association Leadership Scheme.

or, if holding a Warrant:

Quartermaster's Certificate.

or:

Camper's Licence.

or:

Pack Holiday Licence.

Note: Participants may pursue an activity in the Leadership Octant part of the 'Look Wider' programme but they must first ensure that it is listed in The Duke of Edinburgh's Award Handbook.

The Scout Association

Note: Under the rules of The Scout Association participants under the age of 16 who are not Members of the Association cannot assist with helping a Pack or a Colony.

SILVER

Helpers' Course for those over the age of 16 years.

Assessment – Section Leader in conjuction with the Course Director.

Initial Training for those over the age of 17 years.

Assessment – Assistant District Commissioner (Leader Training).

GOLD

Introductory Training for those over the age of 17 years

or:

Leadership I or Leadership II.

• Leadership
in the
Community
- Youth
Leadership
with
Uniformed
Organisations

Assessment – Assistant District Commissioner (Leader Training), Personal Training Advisor, Approved Course Director.

Note: Those below the minimum ages should follow the Gold Youth Service programme (Group 2).

Sea Cadet Corps

SILVER
Leading Rate/Corporal including 6 months Service.
Assessment – Certified District Officer or Commanding Officer.

GOLD
Either:
Cadet Petty Officer/Sergeant **plus** further 6 months Service for minimum 12 months total.
or:
Adult Petty Officer/Sergeant or authorised civilian instructor for minimum period of 12 months.
Assessment – Certified District Officer or Commanding Officer.

St. John Ambulance

SILVER
Cadet NCO Training plus Cadet Corporal for 6 months.

GOLD
Cadet: NCO Training, plus Cadet Sergeant or Cadet Leader for 12 months.
Adult: Youth Leader Training Phase I and II plus 40 hours Service to Division/Set over at least 12 months.

• Leadership
in the
Community
- Youth
Leadership
with
Uniformed
Organisations

Life Saving

LIFE SAVING (RLSS UK)

Obtain one of the following RLSS Awards:

BRONZE

Rookie Star Grade 4 Level 4.
Rookie Star Grade 4 Summary Award.
Lifesaving 3.
Bronze Medallion.

SILVER

Bronze Medallion*.
Award of Merit.

GOLD

Award of Merit*.
Distinction.
National Beach Lifeguard qualification.
National Pool Lifeguard qualification.
Teacher's Certificate.
These Awards may be undertaken if they have not been completed for a previous Award, i.e. Bronze or Silver.

SURF LIFE SAVING

Obtain one of the following from the Surf Life Saving Association:

BRONZE

Surf Competence plus Intermediate Resuscitation.

SILVER

Surf Competence plus Intermediate Resuscitation*
or:
Surf Lifeguard Medallion.

GOLD

Surf Lifeguard Medallion*
or:
Advanced Resuscitation.
These Awards may be undertaken if they have not been completed for a previous Award, i.e. Bronze or Silver.

• Life Saving
  - Life Saving
    (RLSS UK)
  - Surf Life
    Saving

SERVICE

GROUP THREE - PROGRAMMES

CANOE LIFEGUARD

Obtain one of the following from the British Canoe Union:

BRONZE
Canoe Safety Test.

SILVER
Rescue Test or Assistant Lifeguard Award.

GOLD
Lifeguard.

RESCUE COXSWAIN

Obtain an Award from the Royal Yachting Association:

BRONZE
Club Rescue Coxwain.

SILVER
Fleet Rescue Coxwain.

GOLD
Fleet Rescue Coxswain*
This may be undertaken if it has not been completed for a previous Award, i.e. Bronze or Silver.

Service Section Index

SERVICE INDEX

• Index

133

Expeditions

SECTION

David Noton/National Trust

Expeditions

S E C T I O N

CONTENTS

Aim of the Expeditions Section

To encourage a spirit of adventure and discovery.

The Principles

All ventures involve self-reliant journeying in the countryside, on waterways or at sea, conceived with a purpose and undertaken on foot, by cycle, on horseback or in canoes or boats by participants' own physical effort and without motorised assistance. The venture must present the participants with an appropriate challenge in terms of purpose and achievement with the minimum of Leader intervention.

The venture demands:
- Enterprise and imagination in concept.
- Forethought, careful attention to detail and organisational ability in preparation.
- Preparatory training, both theoretical and practical, leading to the ability to journey safely in the chosen environment.
- Shared responsibility for the venture, leadership from within the group, self-reliance and co-operation among those taking part.
- Determination in execution.
- A reflective report related to the purpose of the venture

Benefits to Young People

Although the challenges are expressed in terms of physical demands by travelling for a given number of kilometres, miles or hours, the Award is concerned with the development of the individual and the social interaction of the group.

The Expeditions Section should provide opportunities to:
- **demonstrate enterprise** – by encouraging different modes of travel and an unlimited choice of purposes for the ventures, the Award provides the opportunity for young people to demonstrate the greatest possible enterprise and imagination,

- **work as a member of a team** – the Expeditions Section differs from the other Sections insofar as it is a group effort and all must work together as members of a team to ensure a successful outcome of the venture,
- **respond to a challenge** – the initial level of challenge is determined by the group but the weather and the demanding surroundings in which ventures take place always necessitate the group responding to a series of unforeseen challenges,
- **develop self-reliance** – a progressive programme of training with diminishing external Leader involvement enables the young people to become more self-reliant until the group is able to carry out the qualifying venture unaccompanied,
- **develop leadership skills** – members of the group have the opportunity to exercise the role of leader during different aspects of the venture so that everyone has a chance to develop their own style of leadership and the ability to communicate their intentions to others,
- **recognise the needs and strengths of others** – the whole group must work together to complete the venture, so it is essential that each member recognises the strengths and weaknesses of others and all are involved in mutual support,
- **make decisions and accept the consequences** – outdoor ventures in the countryside and on water demand total commitment and groups have to learn to make decisions affecting their well-being and accept the consequences of their actions,
- **plan and execute a task** – each group has to plan and execute a venture with a clearly defined purpose related to its members' interests and abilities. This follows a training programme from which they acquire the necessary experience so that they can complete the task by their own effort,
- **reflect on personal performance** – to increase the effectiveness of the training and the memorable experiences of their venture, the participants should have opportunities to reflect on personal performance and review their progress as a team,
- **enjoy and appreciate the countryside** – the conditions of the Expeditions Section preclude the use of towns, and villages where practical, so that young people have the opportunity to enjoy and appreciate the countryside. The Section encourages positive responses to the natural world and growing environmental awareness.

Types of Venture

There are three types of venture:

- **Expeditions** which have journeying as their principal component.
- **Explorations** which involve less journeying and a greater proportion of time spent on approved, first hand investigations or other specified activities. Explorations must take the form of a journey and involve a minimum of ten hours travelling time.
- **Other Adventurous Projects** which are of an equally or more demanding nature but which depart from the specified conditions.

Requirements

All ventures must take place in the context of a journey.

- At **BRONZE** participants are required to undertake an Expedition.
- At **SILVER** they may choose to undertake either an Expedition or an Exploration.
- At **GOLD** they may choose an Expedition, an Exploration or an Other Adventurous Project.

The following are requirements for all types of venture:

- All qualifying ventures must have a clearly defined purpose.
- After completing the venture participants must produce a report related to this purpose.
- Ventures should take place between the end of March and the end of October.
- Ventures should involve joint planning and preparation by all members of the group.
- Groups must consist of between four and seven young people.
- Accommodation will be by camping and all equipment must be suitable for the activity and environment in which the venture is to take place.
- Participants must be trained in the necessary skills by experienced Instructors.
- Participants must undertake practice journeys to ensure that they are able to journey safely and independently in their chosen environment.

- All ventures must be supervised and assessed by suitably experienced adults.

Summary of Conditions

QUALIFYING EXPEDITION REQUIREMENTS

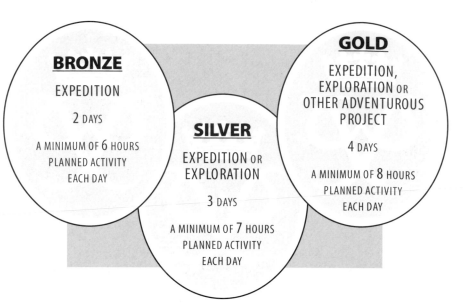

BRONZE
EXPEDITION
2 DAYS
A MINIMUM OF 6 HOURS PLANNED ACTIVITY EACH DAY

SILVER
EXPEDITION OR EXPLORATION
3 DAYS
A MINIMUM OF 7 HOURS PLANNED ACTIVITY EACH DAY

GOLD
EXPEDITION, EXPLORATION OR OTHER ADVENTUROUS PROJECT
4 DAYS
A MINIMUM OF 8 HOURS PLANNED ACTIVITY EACH DAY

	BRONZE	SILVER	GOLD
Walking	15 miles 24 kilometres	30 miles 48 kilometres	50 miles 80 kilometres
Cycling (1 unsurfaced = 2 surfaced)	70 miles 113 kilometres	120 miles 193 kilometres	170 miles 274 kilometres
Horse Riding	4 hours per day	5 hours per day	6 hours per day
Canoeing	4 hours per day on water	5 hours per day on water	6 hours per day on water
Rowing	4 hours per day on water	5 hours per day on water	6 hours per day on water
Sailing	12 hours over the 2 days	21 hours over the 3 days	32 hours over the 4 days

Conditions which apply to all Ventures and all Modes of Travel

PURPOSE

All ventures must have a clearly defined and pre-conceived purpose which provides a focus for the venture.

The range of purposes include:
- Practical first hand observations, investigation or study.
- Aesthetic appreciation.
- Literary or historic journeys.
- The completion of a physically demanding journey.

A wealth of ideas for Expedition and Exploration purposes can be found in the *Exploration Resource Pack*. The purpose of the venture should receive early consideration when the venture is being planned and be related to the interests and abilities of those taking part.

REPORTS

Summarising the experiences of the venture and sharing them with others is an important and enjoyable part of the overall process.

A report must be submitted after all ventures and it is the responsibility of the participants to decide on the form and nature of the report. It may be written, oral, photographic, audio or video, tape/slide or any other acceptable form, or combination of forms.

The report should be related to the purpose of the venture.

It may be an individual submission from each of the participants or a joint project.

To emphasise the purpose of the venture and the subsequent report, the participants may submit the report to any adult who has been actively involved in the venture, or in its preparation, such as the Assessor, Supervisor, Instructor, or Mentor in the case of an Exploration. The person to whom the report is submitted must be sufficiently familiar with all the participants to be able to assess their submission or contribution, in relation to their age aptitude and ability, but must not be related to any of the participants in the group.

• Conditions which apply to all Ventures and Modes of Travel
- Purpose
- Reports

EXPEDITIONS
CONDITIONS

This provides scope for imaginative reports and presentations using slides and other audio/visual displays to let participants share their experiences with colleagues, parents and others and receive greater attention and recognition for their endeavours.

Reports should be based on first-hand observations and recordings and not be concerned with mundane details such as food lists and menus. It is much more important to include feelings, relationships, and reactions to the environment, each other and the venture.

Models, sketch maps, diagrams and photographs can be used to enhance reports where the purpose is of a practical nature. Similarly the use of sketches, paintings, collages, embroideries and weavings can be used to illustrate a purpose involving aesthetic appreciation, and drama may be an excellent method of reporting on a literary theme. If the purpose of the venture is to complete a physically demanding journey then the report should include systematic recordings of physical capabilities or personal thoughts and feelings at various stages of the venture.

Oral reports may be presented to the Assessor at the end of the venture, by prior arrangement, as this involves a considerable time commitment. Suitable provision must be made for the presentation of the report which must be separate from the debriefing carried out by the Assessor immediately at the end of the venture.

NUMBERS

The minimum number in a group at all levels of Award and for all modes of travel will be four and the maximum seven.

It is not necessary for all the group to be undertaking the Award or to be under assessment. It is, however, necessary for all to be trained and properly equipped to the same standard as the participants. Ideally all members of the group should be of a similar age and level of experience and, for the qualifying venture, must be within the age range of the Award being undertaken.

Young people who have already qualified in the Expeditions Section at the same or a higher level of the Award must not be included in the qualifying venture.

• Conditions
which apply to
all Ventures
and Modes of
Travel
- Reports
- Numbers

Participants being assessed for different levels of Award must not be in the same group – i.e. a group under assessment cannot consist of Silver and Gold or Bronze and Silver participants.

ACCOMMODATION

Accommodation will be by camping. In exceptional circumstances the use of barns, bothies or mountain huts may be allowed. If accommodation other than camping is used, then permission must be given in writing from the highest level within the Operating Authority, and not at Unit level.

A different camp site must be used each night for Expeditions but, for Explorations, the same camp site may be used on more than one night if the needs of the Exploration necessitate this.

EQUIPMENT

Clothing, footwear and equipment should be suitable for the activity and the environment in which it is to be used and generally conform to current accepted practice. The equipment must be capable of resisting the worst weather since, in the event of a serious deterioration in conditions, safety may well depend on it being able to withstand the prevailing conditions.

Details of the personal emergency equipment which must be carried is listed under the requirements of the Bronze, Silver and Gold levels of the Award. The essential personal emergency equipment is practically the same irrespective of the mode of travel.

All equipment and food to be used during the venture must be carried by the group. In exceptional circumstances, however, with written permission from the highest level within their Operating Authority, and not at Unit level, certain individuals within a group may have some camping equipment and food pre-positioned at camp sites. They must always carry the listed emergency equipment and their own sleeping bag. These individuals will, normally, still be expected to carry equipment to about a quarter of their own bodyweight, as will other members of the group. Groups must always carry at least one tent, cooking equipment and some food so that they always have the shelter of a camp to fall back on if they should fail to reach their destination.

- Conditions which apply to all Ventures and Modes of Travel
  - Numbers
  - Accommodation
  - Equipment

TRAINING

Training in safety procedures, First Aid, navigation, campcraft, Country Code and purpose work must take place in addition to the skills required by the method of journeying and the environment in which the venture is taking place.

Training should be provided by those who have the necessary skills and experience in the mode of travel and the environment in which the venture is going to take place. No specific qualifications are stipulated by the Award except in the case of preliminary First Aid training, when instruction should only be given by one of the following:

1. An Instructor in First Aid recognised by one of the voluntary aid societies, the Armed Services or the Health and Safety Executive.
2. A qualified teacher or youth leader who holds a valid First Aid Certificate.
3. A State Registered Nurse or Health Visitor.
4. An Instructor approved by the Operating Authority

Whilst it is acceptable for some aspects of training to take place within school or work time when these subjects already form part of the curriculum, for both practice and qualifying ventures participants are expected to show adequate evidence of voluntary effort and a substantial contribution of leisure time.

Before the qualifying venture, Instructors must certify in the *Record Book* that participants have undergone training in the required skills and have reached a level of competence appropriate to the enterprise being undertaken.

PRACTICE JOURNEYS

Following initial training, prior to the qualifying venture, all participants are required to carry out practice journeys, which may or may not be accompanied by adults. The final practice journey before the qualifying venture should be unaccompanied.

Practice journeys must not be over the same route or in the same vicinity of the route to be used for the assessed venture. The

• Conditions which apply to all Ventures and Modes of Travel
- Training
- Practice Journeys

conditions should be as similar as possible to those anticipated for the qualifying venture and in terrain which is equally demanding. Practice journeys should include one or more nights' camping at Bronze level and two or more nights' camping at Silver and Gold levels. Instructors must certify in the *Record Books* that the necessary practice journeys have been completed.

Unaccompanied practice journeys must be supervised and, if in Wild Country, the appropriate Wild Country Panel informed using the standard *Expedition Notification Form* available from Operating Authorities.

Practice journeys provide an excellent opportunity for testing and selecting clothing and equipment for personal and group needs and for developing an idea for the purpose of the qualifying venture. They also facilitate team building and help participants appreciate the level of skills and physical fitness required for the qualifying venture.

It is not advisable to undertake practice journeys immediately prior to the qualifying venture as this can make unreasonable demands on the participants.

EXPEDITION SEASON

The Expedition Season is between the end of March and the end of October and, although specific dates are not prescribed, this period coincides approximately with British Summer Time. The resulting extended daylight may have a significant influence on the well-being of the participants and the peace of mind of the adults involved. Even so, care should be taken with both early and late season ventures to enable groups to journey the required distances within sufficient hours of daylight.

For very experienced older participants, approval may be given for out of season Expeditions, but permission must be given in writing by the highest level within the Operating Authority, and not at Unit level. If the venture takes place in Wild Country the plans must be agreed by the relevant Wild Country Panel and the Supervisor must hold the Scottish Winter Mountain Leader Award or have equivalent experience. For details see the *Expedition Guide.*

• Conditions which apply to all Ventures and Modes of Travel
 - Practice Journeys
 - Expedition Season

AN OUTLINE PROGRAMME FOR PARTICIPANTS

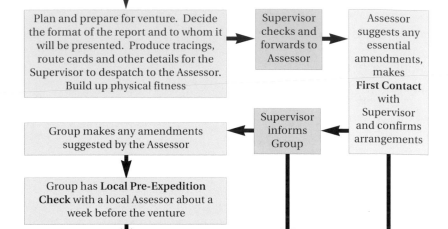

Form a group of between 4 and 7 young people

Decide on a purpose for the venture, a location, and the mode of travel

Undertake training in the common syllabus, skills related to the mode of travel and purpose of the venture

Assemble equipment and complete practice journeys

Plan and prepare for venture. Decide the format of the report and to whom it will be presented. Produce tracings, route cards and other details for the Supervisor to despatch to the Assessor. Build up physical fitness

Supervisor checks and forwards to Assessor

Assessor suggests any essential amendments, makes **First Contact** with Supervisor and confirms arrangements

Group makes any amendments suggested by the Assessor

Supervisor informs Group

Group has **Local Pre-Expedition Check** with a local Assessor about a week before the venture

The First Meeting - Participants and Supervisor meet with Assessor the day before setting out on their journey (in the venture area)

Participants undertake the venture

The Debriefing – At the final destination the Group meets the Assessor for an oral Debriefing. The Assessor confirms the arrangements for the presentation of reports and signs the appropriate page in the *Record Book*

Reports - Participants complete reports and present them to the designated person, and ensure the *Record Books* are signed to complete Expeditions Section. Oral reports may be presented to the Assessor in the venture area if prior arrangements have been made

• Conditions which apply to all Ventures and Modes of Travel - Outline Programme for Participants

PLANNING AND PREPARING FOR THE QUALIFYING VENTURE

The planning and organisation of the venture must be a joint undertaking by the group. They must share responsibility for choosing a purpose for the venture, finding an environment suitable for the purpose, selecting suitable routes, locating camp sites a suitable distance apart and preparing route cards and plans. The plans should be submitted through the Supervisor, to the Assessor for approval. The plans should indicate details of the route, distances, check points, timings and, in Wild Country Areas, alternative foul weather routes and escape routes, as well as rations to be carried by the group. The Assessor should also be informed of the purpose of the venture, the form and nature of the report and to whom it is to be submitted. Groups must ensure that their plans allow sufficient time at the end of the qualifying venture for the Assessor to carry out a debriefing.

THE EXPEDITION GUIDE

The *Award Handbook* only deals with the conditions and the syllabus. Further guidance on the conditions, supervision and assessment is to be found in the *Expedition Guide* which covers all aspects in greater detail.

Participants, Instructors, Supervisors and Assessors should use the *Expedition Guide* and other relevant Award literature such as the *Exploration Resource Pack, Land Navigation - Route Finding Map and Compass* and *Playback – A Guide to Reviewing Activities* as source materials and as a basis for their training programmes.

Record Books

The *Record Book* represents the experiences and achievements of a young person and remarks should be personalised, positive and encouraging. It should always record success and achievement rather than failure. In the event of a young person not satisfying the Assessor, he or she should be informed of the reason and no entry made in the *Record Book* until the conditions have been fulfilled. Before assessing the qualifying venture, the Assessor should ensure that the preliminary training and practice journeys have been completed and correctly entered as such in the *Record Book*.

EXPEDITIONS

Qualifying Venture

TYPE OF VENTURE: Canoe Exploration

AREA: Leeds / Liverpool Canal

DATES STARTED: 12/7/94   COMPLETED: 14/7/94

PURPOSE: To study structures on a 30 mile section

Assessor's report *of expedition / exploration and debrief:*

Jane participated in a most successful Exploration. The venture was ideally located mainly in the splendid isolation of the summit level. The group was very well prepared and equipped and Jane was a particularly competent canoeist who was able to cope with the very demanding schedule which the group had set for itself. Her enthusiasm was most apparent in the

30

Silver

EXPEDITIONS

debriefing session which explored each members contribution.

The report of the venture will be assessed

by Brian King - Instructor

SIGNED: John Longbottom   DATE: 14/7/94

ASSESSOR: B.C.U Senior Instructor

Review of participant's report:

Excellent preparation + background study ensured the success of this exploration, which concentrated on the construction and architecture of the locks and bridges. It was made even more interesting by the comparison with the Rochdale Narrow Canal near to Jane's home. Jane's photography was of an excellent quality and her pen and pencil sketches of architectural features, and her numerous cartoons of her companions, further enhanced the quality of her outstanding report.

SIGNED: B. King   DATE: 27.8.'94

ASSESSOR/SUPERVISOR/INSTRUCTOR*

*delete as appropriate: BRIAN KING, BA - ATD, NND, SENIOR LECTURER (ART)

31

Qualifying Expedition

TYPE OF EXPEDITION/~~EXPLORATION/OTHER ADVENTUROUS PROJECT~~

FOOT EXPEDITION

EXPEDITION NOTIFICATION No. 54/204/94/A/9 OAP REF NO:

AREA   CUMBRIA – CENTRAL AND EASTERN FELLS

DATES STARTED: 2/8/94   COMPLETED: 5/8/94

PURPOSE Meteorological observations on Lakeland Fells

Assessor's Report of Venture and Debrief:

David was a member of a fit and well trained group. Their equipment was excellent and both their navigation and campcraft was of a high standard. They were always on time in spite of their demanding programme of observations. It was most apparent at the debriefing that David was instrumental in pulling the team together and kept spirits high in spite of the wet weather and high winds. The group clearly enjoyed their venture and were well able to meet all the challenges involved.

17

Gold

EXPEDITIONS

The report of the venture will be assessed
by   BETHAN HAKSTEEG

SIGNED *Bethan Haksteeg.*   DATE 6/8/94.
ASSESSOR Cumbria Panel Assessor.

Review of Participant's Report:

The purpose of the expedition was to compare wind speed and temperature at "people height" on the windward and leeward side of Lakeland fells. They used a mixture of tailor-made and home made equipment. David was very proud of his home-made collapsible thermometer screen. The observations, recordings and combined report was excellent

SIGNED *Bethan Haksteeg.*   DATE 10/9/94.
ASSESSOR/~~SUPERVISOR/INSTRUCTOR~~
* delete as appropriate

18

• Record Books

The Bronze Expedition

REQUIREMENTS

The venture must be an Expedition.

CONDITIONS

Age
Participants must be between their 14th and 25th birthdays. Some discretion is given to Operating Authorities to permit a few who would be just too young to enter but who are part of a larger group over this age, to make a start with their friends.

Practice Journeys
All participants must complete at least one practice journey which should correspond as closely as possible to the qualifying (assessed) Expedition and must utilise the same mode of travel.

Duration
Two days with one overnight camp.

A minimum of six hours planned activity must take place each day. The planned activity time will include journeying, navigation, setting up and striking camp and on tasks related to the purpose of the Expedition.

At least one substantial meal should be cooked under camp conditions each day.

Land Ventures
Distance
The following minimum distances are mandatory:

On foot	24 km	15 miles
Cycling	113 km	70 miles

Each kilometre/mile cycled on an unsurfaced lane, track or bridleway counts as two kilometres/miles towards the total.

Horse Riding
Expeditions must involve travelling for a minimum of 4 hours each day in addition to other planned activity.

The Land Environment

All Bronze Expeditions should take place in normal rural country which is unfamiliar to the participants.

On Foot

Routes should make as little use of roads as possible and every effort should be made to avoid villages.

Cycling

Routes should involve minor roads, lanes, tracks and bridleways. Cycling on footpaths is illegal. Villages must be avoided if possible but, because of the distance involved, routes may have to pass through villages. The distance cycled from home to the venture area must not be included in the qualifying mileage.

Horse Riding

Routes should involve lanes, tracks and bridleways. Villages should be avoided where possible.

Water Ventures
Distance

No fixed distance is laid down for Expeditions on water but the following minimum number of hours must be spent travelling in addition to other planned activity:

Canoeing:	Four hours of paddling time each day.
Rowing:	Four hours of rowing time each day.
Sailing:	Twelve hours planned activity over the two days, averaging six hours each day. Sailing dinghies must be used.

Numbers

There must be a minimum of two craft involved in the venture to render mutual support except for pulling boats, such as gigs and cutters, which are able to accommodate the whole group.

The Water Environment

Rivers, canals, lakes and other inland waters.

EXPEDITIONS BRONZE

Note: Although Bronze Expeditions on land and water in more demanding surroundings are not expressly forbidden, all participants must be trained and equipped to a standard sufficient to enable them to meet any hazards which they may encounter. The requirements and syllabus of the Silver and Gold levels, as appropriate, must be utilised if the venture takes place in a more demanding environment. If the venture takes place in Wild Country, the appropriate Wild Country Panel must be informed using the standard Expedition Notification Form available from Operating Authorities.

Personal Emergency Equipment

The following equipment must be carried irrespective of the mode of travel:

- Map(s).
- Watch.
- Torch.
- First Aid kit.
- Whistle.
- Coins/card for telephone.
- Notebook and pencil.
- Spare jumper/sweatshirt.
- Waterproof jacket or coat.

The list is a suitable basis for Expeditions on water but additional items are required according to the mode of travel.

Common Training Syllabus for all Bronze Expeditions on either Land or Water
Safety and Emergency Procedures

- Choosing suitable clothing, footwear and emergency equipment and knowing how to use it.
- Expedition fitness.
- Skills associated with the mode of travel.
- Keeping together.
- Telling people where you are going – route cards.
- Knowing what to do in the case of an accident or emergency.
- Summoning help – what people need to know, telephoning for help, written message.
- Fetching help, self-help and waiting for help to arrive, keeping safe and warm, helping people to find you.

- Weather forecasts – knowing how, where and when to obtain weather forecasts, relating weather forecasts to observed conditions, looking for signs which will indicate changes in the weather.

Basic First Aid

Training based on the current edition of the Authorised Manual of St. John Ambulance, St. Andrew's Ambulance Association, The British Red Cross.
- Action in an emergency – resuscitation, airway, breathing and circulation.
- The treatment of wounds and bleeding, treatment for shock.
- The treatment of blisters, cuts, abrasions, minor burns and scalds, headaches, insect bites, sunburn, splinters.
- The recognition of more serious conditions such as sprains, dislocations and broken limbs.

Navigation

At Bronze level in normal rural country, all route finding should be based on the map alone. Using a compass in rural country devoted to agriculture, with its hedges, meadows and fields under crop, is inappropriate and unnecessary. It causes ill-feeling with the farmers, hinders young people in developing a 'sense of direction' and retards their map reading skills. The 1:25 000 scale *Pathfinder* maps, available for the whole of England, Scotland, Wales and parts of Northern Ireland, should be used wherever possible as it makes instruction and learning easier. They show the field boundaries, making it easier to locate precisely the footpaths, tracks and lanes used for travel in this type of country, so helping to reduce friction with landowners. Participants should also be familiar with the 1:50 000 *Landranger* maps.

Bronze groups who undertake expeditions in large areas of woodland or forested areas may wish to use the full compass syllabus of the Gold level of the Award.

The Preparatory Map Skills
- The nature of maps.
- The use of 1:25 000 *Pathfinder*, 1:50 000 *Landranger* or the relevant maps in Northern Ireland and abroad.
- Map direction.
- Scale and distance, measuring distance, distance and time.
- Conventional signs.

• Conditions
  - Common
    Training
    Syllabus

- Marginal information.
- Grid references.
- A simple introduction to contours and gradient.
- The ability to give a verbal description of a route linking two places from the map.

The Practical Map Skills
- Setting the map by inspection (two methods).
- Locating position from the map.
- Determining geographical direction and direction of travel from the map. Checking the direction of paths using the set map.
- Identifying features in the countryside by using the map.
- Locating features marked on the map in the countryside.
- Planning a route, preparing a simple route card.
- Following a planned route.

Compass Skills
The introduction of the compass at Bronze level should only be at a basic level. It should not be introduced until the participants have mastered the techniques of finding their way using the map alone.
- The care of the compass.
- Direction from the compass in terms of the cardinal and the four intercardinal points. Setting the map by the compass where magnetic variation may be ignored.

Camp Craft
- Choosing and caring for camping gear.
- Packing a rucksack, waterproofing the contents, always keeping the weight down to a minimum, and about a quarter of the body weight when walking.
- Choosing a camp site, arrangements for water, cooking and sanitation, refuse disposal, fire precautions. Pitching and striking tents.
- Cooking and the use of stoves, safety procedures and precautions which must be observed when using stoves and handling fuels. Cooking simple meals under camp conditions.

Country, Highway and Water Sports Codes
- Understanding the spirit and content of the Country Code. The avoidance of noise and disturbance to rural communities.

- A thorough knowledge of the content of the Highway Code with special emphasis on specific modes of travel such as horse riding or cycling if they are to be utilised during the venture.
- If undertaking a water venture, a thorough knowledge of the Water Sports Code.

Purpose Work
- Choosing a purpose.
- Researching relevant information.
- Developing observation skills and different methods of recording information.
- Skills relevant to the method of presentation of the report.

Team Building
The Expeditions Section involves participants working as a team in order to complete their venture. Team building should permeate all Expedition training and can be enhanced through team building exercises and regular reviews so that when the group sets out on the qualifying venture, participants are able to work together as an effective and cohesive unit.

Additional Training for Cycling and Horse Riding Expeditions
Cycling
Training to the standard of the National Cycling Proficiency Scheme and the Right Track Awareness Programme as appropriate. Maintenance and repair of the cycle. Loading a cycle with equipment and handling a loaded cycle. The skills associated with off-road cycling as appropriate.

Horse Riding
Training to Pony Club 'C' standard. A knowledge of tethering or picketing. All must be competent in ensuring the well-being of the horse for the duration of the Expedition. Recognition of dangerous going and the action to be taken in the event of an accident to horse or rider.

Additional Training for Expeditions on Water
Training should be directed towards the completion of a journey on water and not restricted to the skills of handling the craft. It must be concerned with any potential hazards associated with the

- Conditions
  - Additional Training

water on which the venture will take place, as well as infections or health concerns related to any possible water pollution.

For all Expeditions on water, participants must be able to swim a distance of **at least 25 metres in light clothing without any buoyancy aid** and be competent and confident in the relevant capsize and recovery drill and man overboard drill.

All participants must:
- Wear appropriate buoyancy aids or life-jackets. Exceptions may be made, with the approval of the Operating Authority, for rowing ventures on canals and rivers, and for sculling craft where traditionally, by custom and practice, life jackets are not usually worn, except on the instruction of the cox.
- Wear suitable clothing and footwear.
- Be able to recognise and treat hypothermia.
- Understand the Water Sports Code.

All craft must have adequate buoyancy and be sound, suitable and fitted out for the conditions in which they are to be used. A suitable repair kit must be carried and participants should be trained in its use.

Canoeing
All participants must be adequately trained to:
- Satisfy the Assessor as to their competence.
- Demonstrate that their equipment is waterproofed.
- Satisfy the Assessor that their kayak or canoe, and equipment and clothing is suitable for the venture.

Kayakists must be to the standard of the BCU 3 Star or Proficiency Test.

Open canoeists must be to at least the standard of the BCU 1 Star.

Rowing
All participants must undergo training based on the syllabus for 'Boatwork' in the *Expedition Guide* or the training schemes of the Sea Cadets, Scouts and Guides.

Sailing
All participants must attain proficiency to the standard of the RYA National Dinghy Certificate Level 2.

• Conditions
- Additional
  Training

The Silver Expedition

REQUIREMENTS
The venture may be an Expedition or an Exploration.

CONDITIONS

Age
Participants must be between their 15th and 25th birthdays.

Practice Journeys
All participants must complete a minimum of two practice journeys which should correspond as closely as possible to the qualifying (assessed) venture and must use the same mode of travel. Practice journeys should include two nights camping.

Participants who have completed their Bronze Award using the same mode of travel are exempt from one practice journey.

Duration
Three days with two overnight camps.

A minimum of seven hours of planned activity must take place each day. The planned activity time will include journeying, navigation, setting up and striking camp and on tasks related to the purpose of the Expedition/Exploration.

At least one substantial meal should be cooked under camp conditions each day.

Land Ventures
Distance
The following minimum Expedition distances are mandatory:

On foot	48 km	30 miles
Cycling	193 km	120 miles

Each kilometre/mile cycled on an unsurfaced lane, track or bridleway counts as two kilometres/mile towards the total.

Horse Riding
Expeditions must involve travelling for a minimum of 5 hours each day in addition to other planned activity.

The Land Environment

Silver ventures should take place in normal rural or open country which is unfamiliar to the participants. The environment should make more demands on the participants than that used at Bronze level and should represent an intermediate stage between the normal rural environment and Wild Country. Areas of open country should be used, or included, where possible.

Note: Although Silver ventures in more demanding surroundings are not expressly forbidden, all participants must be trained and equipped to a standard sufficient to enable them to meet any hazards which they may encounter. The requirements and syllabus of the Gold level must be utilised if the venture takes place in Wild Country. The appropriate Wild Country Panel must be informed using the standard Expedition Notification Form, available from Operating Authorities.

On Foot

Routes should make as little use of roads as possible and every effort should be made to avoid villages.

Cycling

Routes should involve minor roads, lanes, tracks and bridleways. Cycling on footpaths is illegal. Villages must be avoided where possible but because of the distances involved routes may occasionally have to pass through villages. The distance cycled from home to the venture area must not be included in the qualifying mileage.

Horse Riding

Routes should involve lanes, tracks and bridleways. Every effort should be made to avoid villages.

Water Ventures
Distance

No fixed distances are laid down for Expeditions on water, but the following minimum number of hours must be spent in travelling, in addition to other planned activity:

Canoeing: Five hours of paddling time each day.
Rowing: Five hours of rowing time each day.
Sailing: Twenty one hours of planned activity over the three days averaging seven hours each day.

• Conditions
 - Land
   Ventures
 - Water
   Ventures

Numbers

There must be a minimum of two craft involved in the venture to render mutual support except for pulling boats, such as gigs and cutters, which are able to accommodate the whole group.

The Water Environment

The qualifying venture must take place in surroundings which present an appropriate challenge and are unfamiliar to the participants.

| Canoeing and Rowing: | Canals, rivers or other inland waterways and lakes in rural areas. |
| Sailing: | Inland waters, estuaries or sheltered coastal waters. |

Supervision of Ventures in Estuaries and Sheltered Coastal Waters

Canoeing, Rowing and Sailing: The Supervisor should be suitably experienced in the mode of travel, familiar with the area in which the venture takes place, and accompany the venture in a safety boat.

Contact should not be made with the group during the journey except for the needs of assessment and supervision. In estuaries and sheltered coastal waters the safety boat must be sufficiently remote from the participants to avoid destroying the group's sense of remoteness and self-reliance and yet be able to render assistance in an emergency within a reasonable period of time.

It is more in keeping with the philosophy of the Expeditions Section for participants to choose waters and craft where they can venture with relatively remote supervision rather than undertake a journey which, for safety reasons, requires immediate supervision.

Personal Emergency Equipment

The following equipment must be carried irrespective of the mode of travel:

- Map(s).
- Watch.
- Torch.
- First Aid kit.
- Whistle.
- Coins/card for telephone.
- Notebook and pencil.
- Spare jumper/sweatshirt.
- Waterproof jacket or coat.
- Bivvy bag/large poly bag and waterproof trousers should be carried if appropriate.

The list is a suitable basis for ventures on water but additional items may be required according to the mode of travel.

Explorations

Further information on Explorations can be found on page 180.

Common Training Syllabus for
Silver Expeditions or Explorations on Land or Water
Safety and Emergency Procedures

- Choosing suitable clothing, footwear and emergency equipment and knowing how to use it.
- Expedition fitness.
- Skills associated with the mode of travel.
- Keeping together.
- Telling people where you are going – route cards.
- Knowing what to do in the case of an accident or emergency.
- Summoning help – what people need to know, telephoning for help, the written message.
- Fetching help, self-help and waiting for help to arrive, keeping safe and warm, helping people to find you.
- Weather forecasts – knowing how , where and when to obtain weather forecasts, relating weather forecasts to observed conditions, looking for signs which will indicate changes in the weather.

• Conditions
 - Common
 Training
 Syllabus

Basic First Aid

Training based on the current edition of the Authorised Manual of St. John Ambulance, St. Andrew's Ambulance Association, The British Red Cross.

- Action in an emergency – resuscitation, airway, breathing and circulation.
- The treatment of wounds and bleeding. Treatment for shock.
- The recognition of more serious conditions, sprains, dislocations and broken limbs.
- Be able to recognise and treat hypothermia.
- The treatment of blisters, cuts, abrasions, minor burns and scalds, headaches, insect bites, sunburn, splinters.

Navigation

At Silver level in normal or open country, most route finding should be based on the map alone. Using a compass in rural country devoted to agriculture with its hedges, meadows and fields under crop, is inappropriate and unnecessary. It causes ill-feeling with the farmers, hinders the young people in developing a 'sense of direction' and retards their map reading skills. The 1:25 000 scale *Pathfinder* maps, available for the whole of England, Scotland, Wales and parts of Northern Ireland, should be used wherever possible as it makes instruction and learning easier. They show the field boundaries, making it easier to locate precisely the footpaths, tracks and lanes used for travel in this type of country, so helping reduce friction with landowners. Participants should also be familiar with the 1:50 000 *Landranger* maps.

Silver groups who use large woodland or forested areas for their ventures may wish to use the full compass syllabus of the Gold level of the Award.

The Preparatory Map Skills

- The nature of maps.
- The use of the 1:25 000 Pathfinder, 1:50 000 Landranger or the relevant maps in Northern Ireland and abroad.
- Map direction.
- Scale and distance, measuring distance, distance and time.
- Conventional signs.
- Marginal information.
- Grid references.

• Conditions
 - Common
 Training
 Syllabus

- Understanding contours, recognition of major land forms such as hills, valleys, ridges etc., slope and gradients, determination of height.
- The ability to give a verbal description of a route linking two places from the map.

The Practical Map Skills
- Setting the map by inspection (two methods).
- Relating the map to the ground. Locating position from the map.
- Determining geographical direction and direction of travel from the map. Checking the direction of paths using the set map.
- Identifying features in the countryside by using the map.
- Locating features marked on the map in the countryside.
- Relating the map to the ground and estimating speed of travel and arrival times.
- Planning a route, preparing a simple route card. Estimating speed of travel and arrival times. (ETA – Estimated Time of Arrival).
- Following a planned route.

Compass Skills
The compass should not be introduced until the participants have mastered the techniques of finding their way using the map alone.
- The care of the compass.
- Direction from the compass in terms of the cardinal and inter-cardinal points.
- Measuring direction in degrees.
- Setting the map by compass where magnetic variation may be ignored.
- Determining the direction of footpaths or direction of travel.
- Travelling on a bearing. Obtaining a grid bearing from the map, allowing for magnetic variation where appropriate.
- The influence of ferrous objects and electro magnetic fields.
- Magnetic variation and the relationship between True, Magnetic and Grid Norths.

• Conditions
 - Common
   Training
   Syllabus

Camp Craft

- Choosing and caring for camping gear.
- Packing a rucksack, waterproofing the contents, always keeping the weight down to a minimum and about a quarter of the body weight when walking.
- Choosing a camp site, arrangements for water, cooking and sanitation, refuse disposal, fire precautions. Pitching and striking tents.
- Cooking and the use of stoves, safety procedures and precautions which must be observed when using stoves and handling fuels.
- Using dehydrated foods under Expedition conditions. Cooking substantial meals under camp conditions.

Country, Highway and Water Sports Codes

- Understanding the spirit and content of the Country Code. The avoidance of noise and disturbance to rural communities.
- A thorough knowledge of the content of the Highway Code with special emphasis on specific modes of travel such as horse riding or cycling, if they are to be utilised during the venture.
- If undertaking a water venture, a thorough knowledge of the Water Sports Code.

Purpose Work

- Choosing a purpose.
- Researching relevant information.
- Developing observation skills and different methods of recording information.
- Skills relevant to the method of presentation of the report.

Team Building

The Expeditions Section involves participants working together as a team in order to complete their venture. Team building should permeate all Expedition training and can be enhanced through team building exercises and regular reviews so that when the group sets out on the qualifying venture, participants are able to work together as an effective and cohesive unit.

- Conditions
  - Common Training Syllabus

Additional Training for Cycling and Horse Riding Ventures
Cycling
Training to the standard of the National Cycle Proficiency Scheme and the Right Track Awareness Programme as appropriate. Maintenance and repair of the cycle. Loading a cycle with Expedition equipment and handling a loaded cycle. The skills associated with off-road cycling as appropriate.

Horse Riding
Training to Pony Club 'C' or 'C plus' standard. A knowledge of tethering or picketing. All must be competent in ensuring the well-being of the horse for the duration of the venture.

Recognition of dangerous going and the action to be taken in the event of an accident to horse or rider.

Additional Training for Expeditions on Water
Training should be directed towards the completion of a journey on water and not restricted to the skills of handling the craft. It must be concerned with any potential hazards associated with the water on which the venture will take place, as well as infections or health concerns related to any possible water pollution.

For all ventures on water, participants must be able to swim a distance of at least **25 metres in light clothing, without a buoyancy aid** and be competent and confident in the relevant capsize and recovery drill and man overboard drill.

All participants must:
- Wear appropriate buoyancy aids or life jackets. Exceptions may be made with the approval of the Operating Authority for rowing ventures on rivers, and for sculling craft where traditionally, by custom and practice, life jackets are not usually worn, except on the instruction of the cox.
- Wear suitable clothing and footwear.
- Be able to recognise and treat hypothermia.
- Understand the Water Sports Code.

All craft must have adequate buoyancy and be sound, suitable and fitted out for the conditions in which they are to be used. A suitable repair kit must be carried and participants should be trained in its use.

• Conditions
 - Additional
  Training

Canoeing

All participants must be adequately trained to:

- Satisfy the Assessor as to their competence.
- Demonstrate that their equipment is waterproofed.
- Satisfy the Assessor that their kayak or canoe, and equipment and clothing is suitable for the venture.

Kayakists must be at least to the standard of the BCU 3 Star or Proficiency Test.

Open canoeists must be to at least the standard of the BCU 2 Star.

Rowing

All participants must undergo training based on the Award's syllabus for 'Boatwork' in the *Expedition Guide* or the training schemes of the Sea Cadets, Scouts and Guides.

Sailing

Sailing dinghies or keelboats.

All participants must attain proficiency to the standard of the RYA National Dinghy Certificate Level 3 or the RYA National Keelboat Certificate Level 3.

EXPEDITIONS
SILVER

• Conditions
  - Additional
    Training

The Gold Expedition

REQUIREMENTS

The venture may be an Expedition, an Exploration or an Other Adventurous Project.

CONDITIONS

Age

Participants must be between their 16th and 25th birthdays. Those who have completed the Bronze or Silver Expeditions Sections must undertake the required training and practice journeys for Gold level beyond the age of sixteen.

Practice Journeys

All participants must complete a minimum of three practice journeys which should correspond as closely as possible to the qualifying (assessed) venture and must use the same mode of travel. Practice journeys should include at least two nights camping.

Participants who have completed their Bronze Award using the same mode of travel are exempt from one practice journey. Participants who have a completed their Bronze and Silver Awards or their Silver Award only, using the same mode of travel, are exempt from two practice journeys.

Duration

Four days with three overnight camps.

A minimum of eight hours of planned activity must take place each day. The planned activity time will include journeying time, navigation, setting up and striking camp and on tasks related to the purpose of the venture.

At least one substantial meal should be cooked under camp conditions each day.

Land Ventures
Distance
The following minimum Expedition distances are mandatory:

On foot	80 km	50 miles

Cycling	274 km	170 miles

Each kilometre/mile cycled on an unsurfaced lane, track or bridleway counts as two kilometres/miles towards the total.

Horse Riding
Expeditions must involve travelling for a minimum of 6 hours each day in addition to other planned activity.

The Land Environment
The environment must be appropriate to the purpose of the venture and the route and the surrounding area must be unfamiliar to the participants.

On Foot
All Expeditions must be in Wild Country, remote from habitation with the use of roads limited to that necessary to move between areas of Wild Country. Routes should make as little use of roads as possible and every effort should be made to avoid villages. Explorations may take place in open country as defined on page 181.

Cycling
All Expeditions must be in Wild Country. Routes should involve minor roads, lanes, tracks and bridleways in upland and unpopulated areas of Wild Country. Cycling on footpaths is illegal. Villages must be avoided if possible but because of the distance involved routes may occasionally have to pass through villages. Explorations may take place in open country as defined on page 181. The distance cycled from home to the venture area must not be included in the qualifying mileage.

Horse Riding
All Expeditions must take place in Wild or open country. Routes should involve lanes, tracks and bridleways. Every effort must be made to avoid villages.

Wild Country

Wild Country is defined as being areas remote from habitation in which all ventures, for reasons of safety, must be completely self-sufficient.

Journeys should be through rather than over Wild Country. i.e. solitude not altitude.

The areas defined as Wild Country in the United Kingdom are shown on the map below.

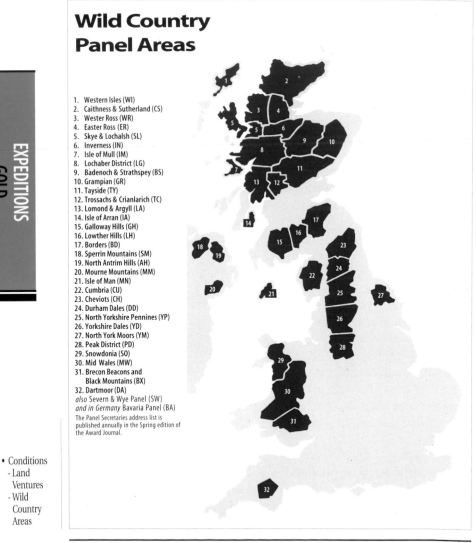

Wild Country Panel Areas

1. Western Isles (WI)
2. Caithness & Sutherland (CS)
3. Wester Ross (WR)
4. Easter Ross (ER)
5. Skye & Lochalsh (SL)
6. Inverness (IN)
7. Isle of Mull (IM)
8. Lochaber District (LG)
9. Badenoch & Strathspey (BS)
10. Grampian (GR)
11. Tayside (TY)
12. Trossachs & Crianlarich (TC)
13. Lomond & Argyll (LA)
14. Isle of Arran (IA)
15. Galloway Hills (GH)
16. Lowther Hills (LH)
17. Borders (BD)
18. Sperrin Mountains (SM)
19. North Antrim Hills (AH)
20. Mourne Mountains (MM)
21. Isle of Man (MN)
22. Cumbria (CU)
23. Cheviots (CH)
24. Durham Dales (DD)
25. North Yorkshire Pennines (YP)
26. Yorkshire Dales (YD)
27. North York Moors (YM)
28. Peak District (PD)
29. Snowdonia (SO)
30. Mid Wales (MW)
31. Brecon Beacons and
    Black Mountains (BX)
32. Dartmoor (DA)
also Severn & Wye Panel (SW)
and in Germany Bavaria Panel (BA)

The Panel Secretaries address list is published annually in the Spring edition of the Award Journal.

• Conditions
- Land
Ventures
- Wild
Country
Areas

In each area there is a voluntary Wild Country Expedition Panel to advise on ventures being undertaken in their area. Names and addresses of all the Panel Secretaries are published in the Directory which is in the Spring edition of *Award Journal.*

Advance notice, in duplicate, on the standard *Expedition Notification Form,* which is available from Operating Authorities, must be given of all ventures in Wild Country Areas, including unaccompanied practice journeys. This notice, addressed to the appropriate Panel Secretary, must be given at least **six weeks in advance** (or four weeks in advance if an Assessor is not required). A Notification Reference Number will be allocated to each qualifying venture which should be entered into the participants' *Record Books* following the successful completion of the venture.

For ventures outside the United Kingdom notice must be given to the Operating Authority at least twelve weeks in advance using the standard *Notification Form for Ventures Abroad.* When the information has been received from the Operation Authority a Notification Reference Number will be allocated by the Territorial/Regional Office which should be entered in the participants' *Record Books* following the successful completion of the venture. There is, however, a Wild Country Panel in Bavaria for which the standard (green) *Expedition Notification Form* should be used.

Familiarisation

In order to adapt to the Wild Country environment, adjust to the routine of camp life and prepare themselves and their equipment, it is advisable for participants to spend forty eight hours in the area prior to the start of the qualifying venture.

Participants should always arrive in the Wild Country Area the day before the venture to facilitate the initial meeting between the participants, the Supervisor and the Assessor. If camping, the base camp site should not be used by the groups as a camp site during the venture.

• Conditions
  - Wild Country Areas
  - Familiarisation

Water Ventures
Distance
No fixed distances are laid down for Expeditions on water but the following minimum number of hours must be spent travelling in addition to other planned activity:

Canoeing: Six hours of paddling time each day.
Rowing: Six hours of rowing time each day.
Sailing: Thirty two hours planned activity over the four days, averaging eight hours each day.

Numbers
There must be a minimum of two craft involved in the venture to render mutual support except for keelboats and pulling boats, such as gigs and cutters, which are able to accommodate the whole of the group.

The Water Environment
The water must present an appropriate challenge to the participants and must be unfamiliar to them.

Canoeing and   Rivers, certain inland waterways and lakes.
Rowing: Sheltered coastal waters and estuaries
                  may be used.
Sailing: Inland waters, lochs, estuaries or sheltered
                  coastal waters. Yachts and keelboats may use
                  open sea areas.

Supervision of Ventures in Estuaries, Sheltered Coastal Waters and Open Sea Areas
Canoeing, Rowing and Sailing: The Supervisor should be suitably experienced in the mode of travel, familiar with the area in which the venture takes place, and accompany the venture in a safety boat.

Contact should not be made with the group during the journey except for the needs of assessment and supervision. In estuaries and sheltered coastal waters the safety boat must be sufficiently remote from the participants to avoid destroying the group's sense of remoteness and self-reliance and yet be able to render assistance in an emergency within a reasonable period of time.

It is more in keeping with the philosophy of the Expeditions Section for participants to choose waters and craft where they can venture with relatively remote supervision rather than undertake a journey which, for safety reasons, requires immediate supervision.

Yachts and Keelboats: In open sea areas, the Supervisor should be aboard and hold the RYA/DTp Yachtmaster Offshore Certificate. The Supervisor should not be involved in the skippering, crewing, navigation, control or management of the boat except for reasons of safety.

Personal Emergency Equipment
The following equipment must be carried irrespective of the mode of travel:
- Map(s).
- Compass.
- Watch.
- Torch with spare bulb and batteries.
- First Aid kit.
- Whistle.
- Coins/card for telephone.
- Notebook and pencil.
- Spare jumper/sweatshirt.
- Extra warm clothing including head gear and gloves.
- Bivvy bag/large poly bag.
- Matches.
- Emergency rations.
- Waterproof jacket or coat and trousers.

The list is a suitable basis for ventures on water but additional items are required according to the mode of travel.

Common Training Syllabus
for all Gold Expeditions, Explorations
or Other Adventurous Projects on Land or Water
Safety and Emergency Procedures
- Choosing suitable clothing, footwear and emergency equipment and knowing how to use it.
- Expedition fitness.

- Skills associated with the mode of travel.
- Keeping together.
- Telling people where you are going – route cards.
- Knowing what to do in the case of an accident or emergency.
- Summoning help – what people need to know, telephoning for help, the written message.
- Fetching help, self-help and waiting for help to arrive.
- Keeping safe and warm, helping people to find you.
- Weather forecasts – knowing how, where and when to obtain weather forecasts, relating weather forecasts to observed conditions, looking for signs which will indicate changes in the weather.

Basic First Aid

Training based on the current edition of the Authorised Manual of St. John Ambulance, St. Andrew's Ambulance Association, The British Red Cross.
- Action in an emergency – resuscitation, airway, breathing and circulation.
- The treatment of wounds and bleeding. Treatment for shock.
- The recognition and the immediate treatment of more serious conditions, sprains, dislocations and broken limbs.
- The emergency transport of casualties.
- The recognition, treatment and prevention of hypothermia.
- The treatment of blisters, cuts, abrasions, minor burns and scalds, headaches, insect bites, sunburn and splinters.

Navigation

The use of the 1:25 000 *Outdoor Leisure* or *Pathfinder* maps, available for the whole of England, Scotland and Wales and parts of Northern Ireland, should be used wherever possible as it makes instruction and learning easier. They show the field boundaries, making it easier to locate precisely the footpaths, tracks and lanes used for travel in this type of country, so helping to reduce friction with landowners. Participants must also be familiar with the 1:50 000 Landranger maps and/or any foreign maps of the area in which the venture is to take place.

The Preparatory Map Skills
- The nature of maps.
- Map direction.
- Scale and distance, measuring distance, distance and time.
- Conventional signs.
- Marginal information.
- Grid references.
- Understanding contours, recognition of major land forms such as hills, valleys, ridges, spurs. Interpretation of contours into mountain land forms and relief, slope and gradients and the determination of height.
- The ability to give a verbal description of route linking two places from the map.

The Practical Map Skills
- Setting the map by inspection (two methods).
- Relating the map to the ground. Locating position using the map.
- Determining geographical direction, and direction of travel from the map. Checking the direction of paths using the set map.
- Identifying and locating features in the country by using the map.
- Locating features marked on the map in the countryside.
- Relating the map and contours to the ground. Estimating journey times in Wild Country..
- Planning a route, preparing a route card. Estimating speed of travel and arrival times. (ETA – Estimated Time of Arrival).
- Following a planned route.
- Navigation in restricted visibility. Action to be taken in the event of being lost.

Compass Skills
The compass should not be introduced until the participants have mastered the techniques of finding their way using the map alone.
- Care of the compass.
- The influence of ferrous objects and electromagnetic fields.
- Magnetic variation and the relationship between True, Magnetic and Grid Norths.
- Direction from the compass in terms of the cardinal and inter-cardinal points.

- Conditions
  - Common
    Training
    Syllabus

- Measuring direction in degrees.
- Setting the map by the compass where magnetic variation may be ignored.
- Determining the direction of footpaths or direction of travel.
- Travelling on a bearing. Obtaining a grid bearing from the map, allowing for magnetic variation where appropriate and travelling on a bearing.

Practically all the understanding and techniques listed above are equally important for ventures on land or on water, but instruction should be modified as necessary for water ventures and charts substituted.

Camp Craft

- Choosing and caring for camping gear.
- Packing a rucksack, waterproofing the contents, keeping the weight down to a minimum and about a quarter of the body weight when walking.
- Choosing camp sites, arrangements for water, cooking and sanitation, refuse disposal and fire precautions. Pitching and striking tents.
- Cooking and the use of stoves, safety procedures and precautions which must be observed when using stoves and handling fuels.
- Using dehydrated foods under Expedition conditions.
- Cooking substantial meals under camp conditions.

Country, Highway and Water Sports Codes

- Understanding the spirit and content of the Country Code. The avoidance of noise and disturbance to rural communities.
- A thorough knowledge of the content of the Highway Code with special emphasis on specific modes of travel such as horse riding or cycling if they are to be utilised during the venture.
- If undertaking a water venture, a thorough knowledge of the Water Sports Code.

Purpose Work

- Choosing a purpose.
- Researching relevant information and useful contacts.
- Developing observation skills and different methods of recording information.
- Skills relevant to the method of presentation of the report.

Team Building

The Expeditions Section involves participants working together as a team in order to complete the venture. Team building should permeate all Expedition training and can be enhanced through team building exercises and regular reviews so that when the group sets out on the qualifying venture, participants are able to work together as an effective and cohesive unit.

Additional Training for Cycling and Horse Riding Ventures

Cycling

Training to the standard of the National Cycle Proficiency Scheme and the Right Track Awareness Programme as appropriate. Maintenance and repair of the cycle. Loading a cycle with Expedition equipment. Handling a loaded cycle. The skills associated with off road cycling as appropriate.

Horse Riding

Training to Pony Club 'B' standard. A knowledge of tethering or picketing. All must be competent in ensuring the well-being of the horse for the duration of the venture.

Recognition of dangerous going and the action to be taken in the event of an accident to horse or rider.

Additional Training for Water Ventures

Training should be directed towards the completion of a journey on water and not restricted to the skills of handling the craft. It must be concerned with any potential hazards associated with the water on which the venture will take place, as well as infections or health concerns related to any possible water pollution.

For all ventures on water, participants must be able to swim a distance of at least **25 metres in light clothing, without a buoyancy aid** and be confident and competent in the relevant capsize and recovery drill and man overboard drill.

All participants must:

- Wear appropriate buoyancy aids or lifejackets. Exceptions may be made, with the approval of the Operating Authority, for rowing ventures on rivers, and for sculling craft where traditionally, by custom and practice, lifejackets are not usually worn, except on the instruction of the cox.

- Wear suitable clothing and footwear.
- Be able to recognise and treat hypothermia.
- Understand the Water Sports Code.

All craft must have adequate buoyancy and be sound, suitable and fitted for the conditions in which they are to be used. All craft must carry a suitable repair kit.

Canoeing

All participants must be adequately trained to:

- Satisfy the Assessor as to their competence.
- Demonstrate that their equipment is waterproofed.
- Satisfy the Assessor that their kayak or canoe, and equipment and clothing is suitable for the venture.

Kayakists must be at least to the standard of the BCU 3 Star or Proficiency Test.

Open canoeists must be to at least the standard of the BCU 2 Star, plus recovery of capsized canoe.

Rowing

All participants must undergo training based on the Award's programme for 'Boatwork' in the *Expedition Guide* or the training schemes of the Sea Cadets, Scouts and Guides.

Sailing

Sailing dinghies or keelboats.

All participants must attain proficiency to the standard of the RYA National Dinghy Certificate Level 5, with the exception of certain aspects such as the use of spinnakers or rudderless sailing. For yachts/keelboats the RYA Day Skipper Shore-based and Practical Certificates as appropriate to the type of boat. For off-shore ventures it is mandatory to hold the appropriate award.

For Expeditions in yachts involving overnight passages in open sea areas, at least one crew member must hold the RYA/DTp Coastal Skipper Certificate of Competence.

• Conditions
  - Additional
    Training

Open Golds

Many Operating Authorities and Wild Country Panels organise Open Gold opportunities to enable independent participants, and those unable to form a viable group, to complete their qualifying venture. These opportunities last at least six days which includes a familiarisation and planning period followed by a supervised and assessed qualifying Expedition. All the necessary training and practice journeys must be undertaken before a participant can take part.

Many 'Open Gold' weeks are advertised in *Award Journal* and they frequently prove to be an exciting and challenging climax to Award participation.

• Open Golds

Explorations

At both Silver and Gold levels of the Award, the concept of 'expeditioning' is extended by the introduction of the Exploration which enables participants to place greater emphasis on the 'discovery' element by reducing the 'journeying' element in the venture.

The aim of the Expeditions Section is to encourage a spirit of adventure and discovery. A physically demanding journey is not an end in itself, it is part of a process. Although, for many, the journey is the most significant element, it is only part of the overall 'expedition experience'. All ventures must have a clearly defined and pre-conceived purpose which should be related to the interests and abilities of those taking part. After completion of the venture, participants must present their findings to others in an appropriate and imaginative way.

The difference between the Expedition and Exploration options is one of emphasis between journeying and purpose work. Both types of venture must embrace both elements but the balance spent on each may vary. The choice of venture should depend on the ability, interests and preference of the young people involved.

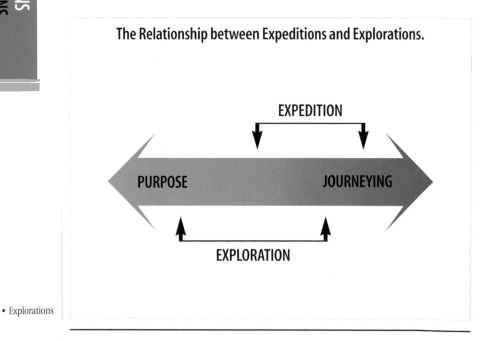

The Relationship between Expeditions and Explorations.

EXPEDITION

PURPOSE   JOURNEYING

EXPLORATION

• Explorations

The Conditions and Criteria for Explorations

All Explorations must take place within the context of an Expedition and must involve a minimum of 10 hours journeying time. All modes of travel used in Expeditions may be used for Explorations.

Participants are required to complete the same preparation and training, including practice journeys, as if they were undertaking an Expedition at either Silver or Gold level. The same requirements and conditions apply to Explorations as to Expeditions except those which relate to distance or travelling time.

The same camp site may be used on more than one night if the needs of the Exploration necessitate this.

The Exploration Environment for Silver Ventures

Normal rural or open country should be used and the environment must be appropriate for the venture and unfamiliar to the participants. Roads must be avoided as much as possible and every effort made to avoid villages. The site(s) of the Exploration and the camp site(s) should be remote to the extent that the group should feel the need to be self-reliant and dependent on its own resources.

The Exploration Environment for Gold Ventures

Wild Country, open country or coastal areas which are isolated and remote from habitation should be used. The environment must be appropriate for the venture and be unfamiliar to the participants. Roads must be avoided as much as possible and both the site(s) of the Exploration and the camp site(s) should be remote to the extent that the group should feel the need to be self-reliant and dependent on their own resources.

Ensuring Success

The *Exploration Resource Pack* provides a wealth of information and guidance on the planning, preparation and execution of Explorations.

At an early stage it is useful to find someone who is knowledgeable and experienced in the chosen field of interest and is willing to become the group's 'Mentor'. This should be someone who combines the function of advisor, guide and friend and helps to derive the best value from the venture.

To ensure a successful outcome to an Exploration, participants and Leaders should read the above conditions, understand the Expedition requirements at the relevant level and ensure that the Exploration complies with the conditions. All Explorations

should use the following criteria at all stages of the planning and preparation to ensure success:

1. The Exploration must be located in an area where it is safe for the participants to work by themselves, taking into account their training, preparation and experience.
2. The venture area should be sufficiently remote from habitation for the group to be self-reliant and dependent upon its own resources.
3. The venture must take the form of a journey with an appropriate balance between project work and journeying (minimum 10 hours) during the qualifying period.
4. The Exploration should be suited to the aptitudes and abilities of the participants.
5. The purpose of the Exploration should be limited and properly focused.
6. It should be possible to fulfil the purpose of the Exploration in the time available.
7. Fulfilment of the purpose should depend upon the journeying element. If it could be completed by visiting a library or museum, it is not suitable for an Award Exploration.
8. The Exploration must be based on the participants' first-hand observations, experience or study.
9. The recording techniques and equipment should be appropriate to the study.
10. The fieldwork during the Exploration should be based on previous study or activity.
11. It is useful if someone with specialist knowledge (a Mentor) is involved from the early planning stage of the venture.
12. The format of the report must be agreed beforehand.
13. The group should be aware of conservation issues and should not harm that which it is studying.

14. If the Exploration involves a more hazardous pursuit, such as a water-based activity, climbing or caving, the participants must have the necessary skills and, above all, the experience to cope with situations which may arise.
15. The Supervisor should ensure that the participants are aware of any potential hazards which the Exploration may present.
16. The responsibilities of the Mentor, Supervisor and Assessor should be agreed beforehand and adequate lines of communication should be established prior to the venture.

Other Adventurous Projects

Other Adventurous Projects are of an equally or more demanding nature than the normal Gold Expedition or Exploration but depart from some of the specified conditions of the Expeditions Section. They provide participants with even greater scope for imagination and enterprise for their venture and many distinguished enterprises have taken place. Though there is great scope for innovation, Other Adventurous Projects must still comply with the spirit and philosophy of the Expeditions Section – an unaccompanied journey which has been planned and prepared by the participants and where the participants are self-reliant and sufficiently remote from habitation to be dependent on their own resources.

The Panel which considers Other Adventurous Projects offers the following advice to assist participants to submit a successful application:

Choice   The essential simplicity of the traditional Expedition/ Exploration and its role in personal and group development is such that any departure from this format should not be undertaken without careful consideration.

Age   Other Adventurous Projects are best suited to young adult participants in the Award – those between the ages of 18 and 25 and who are not in loco parentis

Initiative   Other Adventurous Projects should be initiated by the participants themselves and be their 'brainchild'. The concept should be distinguished by a boldness,

• Other Adventurous Projects

imagination and enterprise. As in all ventures in the Expeditions Section, the planning and preparation should be carried out by the participants themselves. A project which only modestly exceeds the expectations of a Gold Expedition, but which is entirely conceived and executed by the participants, is preferable to a much more ambitious venture which has been initiated and planned by Adult Leaders.

Conditions Other Adventurous Projects must take place in the context of an Expedition. Reading the conditions in the Expeditions Section in this Handbook must always be a first step and those conditions which define the environment for an Expedition, i.e. Wild Country, isolation, remoteness from habitation and the need for dependency on one's own resources, are particularly important ingredients for a successful project.

Appropriate training for the mode of travel and thorough preparation are essential for Other Adventurous Projects whether in the UK or abroad. Involvement in the customs, culture and life of overseas countries is vital in any visit and time should be set aside for this, but always before or after the Adventurous Project itself.

Skills The participants themselves must have the necessary level of skills and techniques to be able to cope with any demands made upon them rather than their safety being dependent upon adult intervention. All the training requirements and practice journeys must be fulfilled.

Joint Initiative Operating Authorities and Youth Organisations run events to all parts of the world involving many young people. It is acceptable for Award participants to plan and carry out a traditional Expedition within the context of these major events. Providing it is properly supervised and assessed, it does not matter whether the venture is on foot in the Pyrenees or by dug-out canoe in the Amazon Basin.

• Other Adventurous Projects

Submissions should be made by the participants themselves via Operating Authorities in sufficient time to reach the National Award Office at least <u>Three Months</u> prior to the date of departure. The Award cannot accept any responsibility concerning the suitability of venture for the participants concerned, all safety aspects, the adequacy of the training or emergency procedures. These responsibilities must rest with the Operating Authority.

Solo ventures would not normally constitute an Other Adventurous Project but any truly enterprising venture will be considered providing that the Operating Authority has approved and accepted the responsibility for the venture.

In giving approval for Other Adventurous Projects, the Award Office only confirms that the project is acceptable as a Gold qualifying venture in the Expeditions Section if it is successfully completed.

Proposals must state how all aspects of the venture will meet the requirements of the Award. Full explanations under the following headings will ensure the speedy consideration of an application:
1. The purpose of the venture.
2. The reasons why the venture will differ from the requirements and conditions of a standard Gold qualifying venture and should be considered as an Other Adventurous Project.
3. The duration of the qualifying part of the venture.
4. The names and ages of those involved and the role each will be taking in the planning of the venture.
5. The experience and skills of those involved which would justify their undertaking an Other Adventurous Project.
6. The nature of the environment in which the qualifying part of the venture will take place.
7. The planning, preparation and training, including any specific aspects related to the nature of the venture. Details of practice journeys.
8. The mode of travel during the venture.
9. The nature of the accommodation and catering arrangements.
10. Any special precautions or procedures in case of an accident or emergency.
11. How the proposed venture is to be supervised and assessed and who will receive the reports.

More information is available from Territorial and Regional Offices.

• Other Adventurous Projects

Supporting Roles and Responsibilities

The requirements and conditions set out in this Handbook are those necessary for the participants to gain their Award at the three levels. While many Operating Authorities are content to use these conditions and requirements alone, other Operating Authorities have additional requirements relating particularly to the training, experience and qualifications of the Instructors, Supervisors and Assessors involved in the Scheme. Since the Operating Authority are responsible for the safety and well-being of the participants and the approval of the Instructors, Supervisors and Assessors, adults must ensure that any additional requirements relating to the Operating Authority are fulfilled.

Instructors, Supervisors and Assessors have a most demanding role in the Expeditions Section. These responsibilities are increased by the nature of self-reliant unaccompanied ventures. Whilst no specific qualifications are insisted upon by the Award, Instructors, Supervisors and Assessors are strongly recommended that, where suitable national qualifications exist appropriate to the mode of travel and administered by the National Governing Bodies of the Outdoor Pursuits, these should be obtained.

Relevant qualifications are the Basic Expedition Training Award (BETA), administered by the Central Council of Physical Recreation, the Mountain Leader Award (Summer) administered by the Mountain Leader Training Board (MLTB). The British Canoe Union's (BCU) Instructor, Senior Instructor, Kayak/Open Canoe, Inland/Sea, and the Royal Yachting Association's (RYA) Dinghy Instructor, Senior Instructor (with tidal endorsement), RYA/DTp Yachtmaster Offshore Certificate.

INSTRUCTORS

Instructors have one of the most demanding roles within the Expeditions Section in terms of commitment of time and effort. The safety and well-being of the participants is dependent on the quality of the training, as is the quality and enjoyment of the total expeditioning experience.

Instructors must have the necessary skills and experience to deliver the common training syllabus based on safety and emergency procedures, First Aid, navigation and camp craft, and should also have skills related to the varying modes of travel. This frequently involves using more than one Instructor. No specific qualifications are stipulated by the Award, except in the case of preliminary First Aid training (see page 144). All Instructors should hold the appropriate National qualifications where they exist, or be of equivalent experience and approved by the Operating Authority. It is important that all Instructors should have extensive experience in the kind of environment in which the proposed venture is to take place so that they will have a realistic appreciation of the problems which the participants may encounter.

To ensure high standards of instruction, the training course should be planned beforehand and checked against the syllabus to ensure that there are no omissions. One Instructor or Leader within an Award Unit should have an overview of all the training and instruction and be mindful of all the conditions and requirements which the participants have to meet to ensure that the group is equipped in terms of recording and observation skills to fulfil the purpose of the venture, and that all members of the group are aware of the conditions under which the venture will take place.

It is important that Instructors always bear in mind that they are training young people to be self-reliant for unaccompanied ventures. Training should be progressive over the course of the training period. The Instructor must plan the sessions to enable the participants to become increasingly more self-reliant and dependent on their own resources. All participants must have the opportunity to develop their own leadership style. Training must be concerned with team building as well as developing individual talents and resources within the team to strengthen the group as a whole. This can be enhanced by regular reviewing sessions built into the training programme.

The practice journeys have a most important role in the training syllabus and there is great merit in some of these journeys being accompanied by the Instructor. This provides an opportunity to gain a real insight into the capabilities of the individuals thus enabling tuition to take place over a more extended period of time than in the more usual evening or lunch time sessions.

• Supporting Roles and Responsibilities - Instructors

SUPERVISORS

All ventures, including practice journeys, must be supervised by a suitably experienced adult who must accept responsibility for the safety and well-being of the group on behalf of the Operating Authority. The Supervisor, who is the agent of the Operating Authority, must be satisfied that the participants are fully trained and equipped to undertake the planned venture.

Supervision of the venture falls into two distinct categories:
- Practice and training ventures which may be accompanied or supervised by an Instructor and should be considered as part of the training process.
- Qualifying ventures which are assessed.

The Supervision of Qualifying Ventures
- Groups undertaking their qualifying venture must not be accompanied by an adult except in very special circumstances when, with written permission from the highest level within the Operating Authority, and not at Unit level, closer supervision may be permitted. Exceptions are made for some types of water ventures. In certain circumstances, for safety reasons, it may be important that contact with an adult should be easily available at night.
- With greater numbers of entrants in the older age range of 18 to 24 many participants are adults in their own right and are no longer 'in loco parentis'. The supervision of young adults would not need to be anywhere near as close as that for a group of 14 year olds embarking on their Bronze venture. There is, however, a responsibility to ensure that all are correctly advised and the responsibilities of care extends even to the 24 year olds.
- For ventures in normal, rural or open country the Supervisor should be present in the area of the venture. If they have not established a base in the immediate vicinity of the venture, then they must be sufficiently close to render help within a reasonable time if an emergency should arise.
- For ventures in Wild Country the Supervisor must be based in the vicinity of the area where the venture takes place. This requirement extends to Explorations on the sea, coast and remote areas of marshland.

• Supporting
Roles and
Respons-
ibilities
- Supervisors

190

- Ventures in estuaries or sheltered coastal waters should be supervised from a safety boat. The Supervisor and/or Assessor should be aboard yachts or keelboats in open sea areas.

- Supervisors should know the aims and objectives of the Expeditions Section and be familiar with the requirements and conditions which the participants have to fulfil.
- Supervisors should be sufficiently experienced and competent in the mode of travel to be able to provide safe and effective supervision.

The duties of the Supervisor, detailed below, are for Gold level ventures in Wild Country but will serve as a pattern for good and safe supervision of ventures at Bronze and Silver levels using all modes of travel.

Before the Venture

- Verify that the training has been completed and that the participants are properly equipped.
- Ensure that the *Record Books* have been signed.
- Check that the Notification Forms, route cards and other details have been completed and send them to the Assessor.
- Find a suitable base from which to supervise the venture.
- Ensure that the Initial Contact is made with the Assessor. Complete the arrangements for the First Meeting immediately prior to the venture.
- Participate in the First Meeting along with the Assessor and the group during the day or evening immediately prior to the venture.

During the Venture

- Visit the group once a day or as the needs of safety demand. Co-ordinate visits with the Assessor to ensure that the group is visited at the camp site each evening.
- Be responsible for communications and for keeping everyone informed of any changes in plans.

• Supporting Roles and Responsibilities - Supervisors

Role of the Supervisor

Outlined for a Gold level venture but serving as a pattern for all levels.

EXPEDITIONS
SUPERVISORS

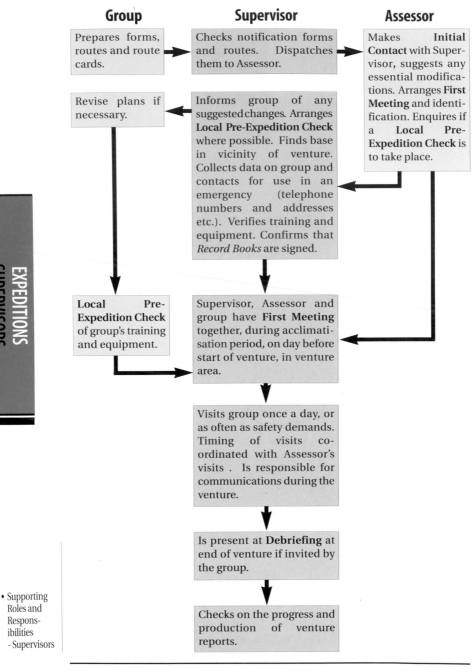

Group	Supervisor	Assessor
Prepares forms, routes and route cards.	Checks notification forms and routes. Dispatches them to Assessor.	Makes **Initial Contact** with Supervisor, suggests any essential modifications. Arranges **First Meeting** and identification. Enquires if a **Local Pre-Expedition Check** is to take place.
Revise plans if necessary.	Informs group of any suggested changes. Arranges **Local Pre-Expedition Check** where possible. Finds base in vicinity of venture. Collects data on group and contacts for use in an emergency (telephone numbers and addresses etc.). Verifies training and equipment. Confirms that *Record Books* are signed.	
Local Pre-Expedition Check of group's training and equipment.	Supervisor, Assessor and group have **First Meeting** together, during acclimatisation period, on day before start of venture, in venture area.	
	Visits group once a day, or as often as safety demands. Timing of visits coordinated with Assessor's visits. Is responsible for communications during the venture.	
	Is present at **Debriefing** at end of venture if invited by the group.	
	Checks on the progress and production of venture reports.	

• Supporting Roles and Responsibilities - Supervisors

After the Venture

- Be present at the oral Debriefing carried out by the Assessor, if invited by the group.
- Receive the reports of the venture if the participants decide to submit them to the Supervisor.

Supervisors should always carry with them all the relevant safety information which may be required. This will include the names, addresses and emergency contact numbers of the participants (usually their parents or guardian), the Assessor, a responsible person in the Operating Authority and Award Headquarters.

ASSESSORS

All ventures within the Expeditions Section must be assessed to ensure that each participant has fulfilled all the relevant conditions.

The Assessor must be an adult approved by the Operating Authority.

- At **Bronze** level the Assessor must not have been involved in any of the training or instruction of the group.
- At **Silver** level the Assessor should be independent of the Award Unit.
- At **Gold** level the Assessor must be independent of the Award Unit and not associated with it in any way.

For Gold assessments taking place in a designated Wild Country Area an Assessor from the appropriate Wild Country Panel or an Accredited Assessor from an Operating Authority should be used. If the Operating Authority does not use an Assessor from the Wild Country Panel or an Accredited Assessor, then the person must be of equivalent competence preferably holding an appropriate national qualification and must be approved by the Operating Authority. Every effort should be made by the Operating Authority to accredit the person at the earliest opportunity through the Assessor Accreditation Scheme.

The Award, in conjunction with Wild Country Panels and Operating Authorities, provides a national Accreditation Scheme for Wild Country Assessors in order to ensure a greater uniformity in the standard of assessment and to assist Local Pre-Expedition Checks and 'Open Golds'. *(For details contact Award Headquarters.)*

• Supporting Roles and Responsibilities
- Supervisors
- Assessors

Assessors have three main functions:

- To ensure that the conditions of the Expeditions Section of the Award are fulfilled.
- To advise on the safety of the venture. The ultimate responsibility rests with the Supervisor who is the agent of the Operating Authority.
- To safeguard the interests of the Award.

The role and responsibilities of the Assessor vary with the environment in which the venture takes place, the form of venture and the mode of travel. The responsibilities are detailed below for an Assessor in Wild Country at Gold level, but should serve as a statement of good and safe practice for all Assessors at both Bronze and Silver levels. The duties fall into three parts – before, during and after the venture.

Before the Venture

- Check the application forms or submissions to ensure that all the basic conditions and requirements are fulfilled.
- Scrutinise the plans, routes and foul weather alternatives and escape routes as soon as possible to enable the group to make any essential changes.
- Contact the Supervisor (The Initial Contact) and arrange a meeting (The First Meeting) with the participants and the Supervisor during the acclimatisation period prior to setting out on the venture (usually the day or evening before). Clarify whether a Local Pre-Expedition Check is being carried out. If the venture is an Exploration, check if a Mentor is involved and what contact, if any, will be made during the venture.
- Ensure that the training has been certified in the *Record Books* and that the required number of practice ventures have been completed.
- Check that the group is properly equipped and properly trained. This task is usually eased if a prior Local Pre-Expedition Check has been carried out.
- Arrange communications between the group, Supervisor and Assessor and confirm the visiting and checkpoint arrangements.
- Arrange or confirm the form and nature of the report and to whom it is being submitted.

• Supporting
Roles and
Respons-
ibilities
- Assessors

194

During the Venture

Visit at least one camp site to check camp craft, cooking and catering. Inspect a camp site after the group has left and observe the group en route.

- Meet with the group, normally once a day.
- Check the progress of observations, recording or investigatory work associated with the purpose of the venture.
- The Assessor, in full consultation with the Supervisor and the group, should not hesitate to require a group to modify their proposed routes for reasons of safety, weather conditions or a greater understanding of the limited capabilities of the group.

After the Venture

Meet the group at the end of the journey and carry out an oral Debriefing. This Debriefing enables the Assessor to share in the group's successful completion of the journey, and is an opportunity for the participants to express their feelings and reactions. The Debriefing should be concerned with overall impressions and achievements and should draw out the learning and personal development which has occurred to the individuals and to the group as a whole.

Either

- Receive an oral report relating to the purpose of the venture if prior arrangements have been made. Both pages of the *Record Books* may then be completed and signed. This must be distinct and separate from the oral debriefing.

or

- Confirm the arrangements which have been made concerning the submission of the reports. Complete and sign the page in the *Record Books* relating to the successful completion of the venture. If the participants have decided to submit their reports to the Assessor, then the Assessor and the participants should agree when this is to happen. On receipt of the reports, complete and sign the other part of the *Record Books* and return them to the participants.

• Supporting Roles and Responsibilities - Assessors

The Assessor's Role

The Assessor's role is much greater than just checking that the conditions and requirements have been fulfilled. Each year many ventures owe their success to the inspiration, encouragement and wise advice of the Assessor. Their detailed local knowledge of the area and weather conditions enables them to make a vital contribution ranging from guidance on the purpose of the venture to advising the Supervisor and the group on matters of safety and well-being. This judgement has been acquired by involvement with previous expeditions and a long association with the area. Guidance, while encouraging and enriching the experience, must never be intrusive or time consuming and should always be given at the appropriate moment. Assessors must always consult with the group and the Supervisor and be mindful that the venture belongs to the participants.

• Supporting
  Roles and
  Respons-
  ibilities
  - Assessors

The Significant Stages

Assessor receives notification forms and route tracing, usually via the Supervisor. →	Assessor checks and gives advice on essential modifications.
The Initial Contact. ←	The Assessor contacts the Supervisor, preferably by telephone. Arranges 'First Meeting' and finds out if there is to be a Local Pre-Expedition Check. Queries any problems concerning conditions or routes.
Local Pre-Expedition Check of training and equipment. ←	Carried out about a week before the venture at the group's home base, usually by a local Assessor.
The First Meeting. ←	Meeting between the Assessor, the group and the Supervisor on the day before the start of a venture in Wild Country. The most important of all the meetings - 'negotiate the contract'.
Meetings en-route and at camp sites. ←	As many as required to ensure that the conditions are fulfilled, usually about one a day.
Meeting at the end of the journey. The Debriefing. ←	Second only in importance to the 'First Meeting'. Involves the signing of the *Record Books* if the venture has been successful.
Assessor may receive written or other forms of report if the participants so decide. →	If the report is oral this may be received after the Debriefing at the end of the journey. Assessor signs and returns *Record Books* and reports.

EXPEDITIONS
ASSESSORS

• Supporting Roles and Responsibilities - Assessors

Expeditions Section Index

Skills

Skills

SECTION

CONTENTS

Aim of the Skills Section

To encourage the discovery and development of personal interests, and social and practical skills.

The Principles

This Section should stimulate young people to take up and persevere at satisfying and purposeful pursuits within a wide range of practical, cultural and social activities.

The choice can be either a continuing and progressive interest in an activity or the study of a topic of personal interest to the participant or a definite task to be completed.

In addition to developing skills, participation is intended to lead to contact with experienced people. This may be through membership of a club or group, or through the wealth of individual expertise available in the community.

Young people should have an opportunity to discover new talents and accept an on-going commitment.

Benefits to Young People

Although the specific benefits to young people depend on the choice of activity, the Skills Section should offer participants the opportunity to:

- **develop social and practical skills** by working alongside enthusiastic adults who volunteer to share skills and knowledge of a particular activity,
- **meet new people** by participating in different activities, linking in to local networks, building relationships with Adult Instructors and peers,
- **get organised** by understanding what is required and setting time and resources aside to follow the skill,
- **discover how to research information** by communication with the Adult Instructor, having access to the *Award Handbook* and other literature, making appropriate contacts in the community and identifying other sources of help and guidance,

- **try something new** particularly at Silver and Gold levels. At Bronze, it may be appropriate to follow an existing hobby or interest if this encourages young people to join the Scheme,
- **make real progress** by negotiating a programme involving an appropriate degree of challenge and reviewing achievements,
- **learn to enjoy working with adults** by building relationships, benefiting from their knowledge, appreciating their skills and sharing a mutual interest,
- **develop abilities** by acquiring knowledge, practising skills and achieving a degree of competence,
- **have fun** by sharing an activity with adults and peers,
- **discover new talents and raise self-esteem** by pursuing a new challenging activity.

Requirements

Individual progress and sustained interest over a period of time, leading to a deeper knowledge of the subject and the attainment of a reasonable degree of skill.

Type of Skill

The Skills Section offers young people a wide choice depending upon their personal preferences, abilities and the opportunities available. The Skill may be an existing interest or something entirely new to the participant.

There are over 200 Skills programmes to choose from. A complete list of Skills programmes available is given in the index on pages 264-266. Every effort has been made to provide cross references but if a particular activity is not listed it may be included under an alternative heading. For example Magic is listed under Conjuring, and Matchbox Collecting under Phillumeny.

A selection of sample programmes may be found in the following pages. All Skills programmes are contained in the *Skills Programmes* loose-leaf folder.

For convenience Skills programmes are listed under the following group headings:

- Collections, Studies and Surveys
- Crafts
- Life Skills
- Nature
- Recreative Skills
- Communications
- Graphic Arts
- Music
- Needlecrafts

A General Programme for each of these groups is detailed on the following pages and advice on how to use them is included under the heading, *How to Devise a New Skills Programme*.

Summary of Conditions

Participants should choose a Skill and follow it for a minimum period of:

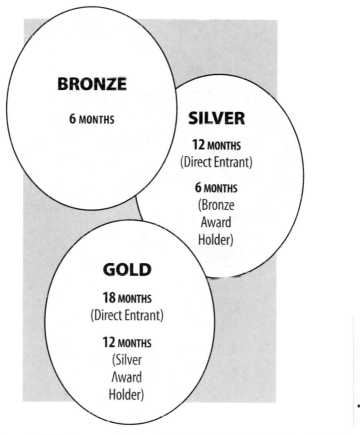

- Summary of Conditions

Conditions in Detail

It is recognised that there may be periods when participants are forced, through circumstances such as examinations, to defer active participation in their programme for an interval. For example, although the minimum period for completion at Bronze level is six months, it is not uncommon for a young person to spend twelve months completing their Skill.

Under certain circumstances, such as an unsatisfactory choice, lack of facilities, or movement of the Instructor or participant away from the area, the Skills may be changed **once** at any time during the period of an Award, but if two activities are undertaken, they are to be followed one after the other, not together.

Skills acquired in formal education, training and employment are not excluded, but participants must show adequate evidence of additional voluntary effort in their own leisure time.

The number of hours to be spent on the chosen Skill is not specified but regular effort during leisure time is required throughout the period.

The participant may follow the Skill independently or as a member of a group. Knowledge and experience may be acquired by attending a course or by individual enquiry.

PROGRAMMES

All programmes are for the guidance of participants and the adults helping in this Section. They are not prescriptive. There is no need to limit young people to one part of the programme. Starting at their own level of knowledge and experience, participants are free to select as broad or as restricted an aspect of their chosen Skill as they wish, but appropriate social, historical and cultural aspects are to be covered.

Safety requirements for any Skill are printed in bold type in the programme and must be followed.

To indicate the content appropriate to young people with varying degrees of knowledge and experience, most programmes are set out in three parts:

- *For beginners.*
- *For those with some knowledge.*
- *For the more advanced.*

The programme for beginners will not necessarily be appropriate at Bronze if the young person is already well acquainted with the chosen activity. Conversely, a participant at Gold tackling an unfamiliar subject might start with the beginners' programme.

Whilst participants are encouraged to make their own choice of activities, some advice may be needed, especially where young people are likely to benefit by taking up a new activity.

HOW TO DEVISE A NEW SKILLS PROGRAMME

If, after a thorough search of the index, participants cannot find their chosen activity, a programme should be devised in one of the following ways:

1. All activities in the Skills Section have been sub-divided into nine groups. A General Programme has been devised for each of these groups and they are detailed on the following pages.

   Using the appropriate General Programme as a guide, a proposed programme should be drawn up by the Instructor or a person knowledgeable in the activity, in consultation with the young person.

   The programme must:
   - focus on a specific activity, rather than comprise a series of 'tasters',
   - reflect the ability and experience of the young person,
   - be progressive and allow the young person to demonstrate achievement over a period of time,
   - contain appropriate safe working practices and legal requirements.

The programme should be approved by the Operating Authority before the activity is started and consultation with the Award's Territorial or Regional Office is advisable, particularly at the Gold level.

2. Topics from more than one programme may be combined to produce an individual programme. The combination of topics should focus on a particular theme and result in a comprehensive and progressive programme. This should be approved by the Operating Authority before the activity is started and consultation with the Award's Territorial or Regional Office is advisable, particularly at the Gold level.

3. If a number of Skills programmes may not be successfully combined or if none of the General Programmes appear to be appropriate to a participant's choice, then a new programme should be devised using the standard format: for beginners, for those with some knowledge and for the more advanced. This must be forwarded to Award Headquarters via the Operating Authority and the Award's Territorial or Regional Office for approval before commencement of the programme.

Note: It would be helpful if programmes produced as a result of 1 or 2 were forwarded to Award Headquarters so that the number of requests for a new activity may be monitored and the most popular included in future editions of Award literature.

INSTRUCTION AND ASSESSMENT

Instruction and assessment should be undertaken by Adult Helpers who are knowledgeable and experienced in the chosen activity or topic. They should be acceptable to the Operating Authority, relate easily and effectively to young people and have the necessary expertise and enthusiasm to guide and encourage participants in their efforts.

The Instructor and the Assessor may be the same person, but in some cases, particularly at Gold, independent assessment may be desirable.

• Conditions in Detail
- Programmes
- Instruction and Assessment

Each individual is to be assessed throughout the required period on:

• EFFORT • PERSEVERANCE • PROGRESS •

They should also have some understanding of the practical, cultural and social aspects of the chosen activity or topic. Group activities are to be assessed with regard to each individual's contribution to planning, execution and completion.

A young person qualifies in this Section if the Assessor, after consultation with the Instructor where applicable, is satisfied that:

- there has been a substantial commitment of genuine leisure time,
- the Skill has been consistently followed for the required time,
- genuine effort and individual progress have been made within the young person's capability.

• Conditions in Detail Instruction and Assessment

Record Books

The *Record Book* represents the experiences and achievements of a young person, and remarks should be personalised, positive and encouraging. It should always record success and achievement rather than failure.

In the event of a young person not satisfying the Assessor, he or she should be informed of the reason and no entry made in the *Record Book* until the conditions have been fulfilled.

Dates of starting and successful completion are to be entered in *Record Books*. Assessors should ensure that the date entered is the actual date on which the assessment was carried out and state clearly that any safety requirements have been met.

Bronze

SKILLS

Skill followed:

LEATHERWORK   (CRAFTS)

DATE STARTED: 24/8/92   COMPLETED: 17/9/93

Assessor's report

John has produced an excellent display of leatherwork for this section. He has designed and made various articles in leather so that he could take part in a local exhibition. All his work has been carefully made, and is of a high standard. His designs have been very imaginative as well as functional. John has incorporated many techniques including stitching, binding, weaving etc. A considerable amount of time & effort has been put into this project. Congratulations!

SIGNED C. Meheme   DATE 15/12/93

QUALIFICATION/EXPERIENCE Lecturer in F.E. (Craftwork specialisation)

33

Silver

SKILLS

Skill followed: (RECREATIVE SKILL)

MOTOR CARS- ENGINEERING & MAINTENANCE

DATE STARTED: 1/12/91   COMPLETED: 2/7/93

Assessor's report

Maya decided to follow this skill after successfully passing her driving test. She quickly became familiar with parts of the engine and the maintenance checks required. She has developed a good grasp of technical aspects which has lead to a broad understanding of modern car technology. She is able to communicate her knowledge clearly to others.

Maya's latest interest is in vintage cars.

SIGNED D. McDonald   DATE 2/7/93

QUALIFICATION/EXPERIENCE Associate Member Institute of Motor Industry

20

Gold

SKILLS PROGRAMMES

Collections, Studies and Surveys

Introduction

The chosen activity should give a balance between the attainment of knowledge and the application of practical skills. Activities may focus on a particular interest or embrace a broader range of historical, social and cultural topics relating to the chosen Skill. Programmes may be undertaken either by a group or on an individual basis.

For Assessment: evidence of individual progress, sustained interest and a commitment of genuine leisure time should be shown over the required period. This may take the form of a presentation, project or display. Group activities are to be assessed with regard to each individual's contribution to planning, execution and completion.

General Programme

Where a particular choice of Skill is not listed, a programme may be devised based on the following guidelines and bearing in mind the points made in the introduction. Any programme should encourage individual progress and sustained interest over a period of time, leading to a deeper knowledge of the subject and attainment of a reasonable degree of Skill. Before commencing the programme, participants should obtain approval from their Operating Authority.

Collections

1. Any collection should have a defined object and area of interest reflecting effort and imagination. It should not be a haphazard collection; the physical collection of objects on its own is not sufficient.
2. Research appropriate to the collection should be undertaken. This should include visits to libraries, museums, etc. and contact with specialist organisations and enthusiasts.
3. An understanding of the historical, social and cultural aspects of the collection should be developed.

Aeronautics
Aircraft Recognition
Anthropology
Archaeology
Architectural Appreciation
Astronautics
Astronomy
Ballet Appreciation
Bible Study
Church Architecture
Costume Study
Criminology
Entomology
Fine and Applied Arts and Design
Forces Insignia
Genealogy
Geology
Geometrical and Technical Drawing
Heraldry
Herpetology
Library and Information Skills
Local and Historical Survey
Map Making
Meteorology
Microscopy
Natural History
Numismatics (Coins)
Palaeontology
Period Furniture Appreciation
Philately (Stamps)
Phillumeny (Matchboxes)
Railways Affairs
Relief Modelling
Religions of the World
Ship Recognition
Theatre Appreciation
You and the Commonwealth
Zoology

• Collections,
  Studies and
  Surveys
  - General
    Programme

214

Studies and Surveys
1. The objects and area of interest of the study or survey should be clearly defined before commencing this activity and an understanding of the historical, social and cultural aspects should be developed.
2. The work should not be taken solely from existing books and wherever possible evidence of some original work should be given.
3. A summary and an interpretation should be made of the data/information collected.

Examples of Suitable Study Topics
1. The arts, music, dance or drama.
2. The life and times of a famous person, e.g. politician, sportsperson, media personality, dancer or musician.
3. An historical study, e.g. architecture, music, sports or politics.
4. An international or cultural study.
5. Transportation, e.g. its effects on the environment.

Examples of Suitable Surveys
1. Local villages or towns.
2. Local historical site(s).
3. Tourist attractions in an area.
4. Local language/dialects.
5. Local customs, songs, dances, etc.
6. Job opportunities for school leavers.

Collections, Studies and Surveys
Example Skills Programme

ASTRONOMY

Introduction
The study of Astronomy should give a balance between the attainment of knowledge and the application of practical skills and, throughout the programme, participants should have the opportunity to develop an understanding of related historical and scientific development. The activity may be followed either on an individual basis or as part of a group or club.

• Collections, Studies and Surveys
- General Programme
- Astronomy

For Assessment: evidence of individual progress, sustained interest and a commitment of genuine leisure time should be shown over the required period. This should take the form of a diary, log or note book. Group activities are to be assessed with regard to each individual's contribution to planning, execution and completion.

For beginners

Participants starting this activity should develop a good knowledge of:

1. The night sky as seen with the unaided eye from their home area.
2. The main constellations and the brighter stars.
3. Finding directions by the stars.
4. The seasonal changes in appearance of the night sky and the apparent motion of the Sun, Moon and planets.
5. a. The Earth-Moon and the Solar System.
   b. The Sun as a moving star and member of the Milky Way system or Galaxy.
   c. The Milky Way as one amongst countless other galaxies in the Universe.

For those with some knowledge

Participants should:

6. Compile a record of regular observations and suitable charts. This must include reference to at least one of the following:
   a. The phases of the Moon and its motion against the star background. The seasonal change in the apparent height of its path.
   b. The observed change in position of one of the five planets visible with the naked eye, to be made at regular intervals during the period.
   c. The apparent tracks of bright meteors, preferably observed during one of the regular meteor showers occurring during the year.
   d. The observed tracks of artificial satellites.
   e. Sunspot positions obtained by projection through binoculars or a small telescope. The observation of aurorae in appropriate locations.
7. Learn to make and use simple pieces of apparatus, e.g. a home-constructed clinometer, a simple two-lens telescope or other forms of sighting device.

• Collections, Studies and Surveys - Astronomy

8. Observe and record in a systematic manner any unusual object, e.g. a comet, which may be visible during the period.

For the more advanced
Participants should:
9. Make regular observations with binoculars or a simple telescope and produce a written record in diary form.
10. Produce a written paper on some aspect of astronomy which has appealed to them from their own observations. This should involve further reading, research and a development of their scientific and historical understanding of astronomy.

Collections, Studies and Surveys
Example Skills Programme

GENEALOGY (Family History)

Introduction
This activity should include as much practical work as possible, the aim of which is to study sources used by the family historian. Practical research into a family, not necessarily the participant's own, should form the basis of the programme at all levels. Participants are advised to plan their programme with the support and advice of either an appropriate historical society or with a local contact who has an interest in genealogy. This should include advice on the content of the practical research to be undertaken which should be methodical. Detailed records of all findings, positive and negative, and sources used should be kept in a notebook.

Participants from ethnic minority communities may wish to research their ancestral lineage, thereby providing a valuable insight into their cultural heritage. In this case contact should be made with an appropriate Genealogical Society. A research paper with useful contacts is available from Award Headquarters.

• Collections, Studies and Surveys
- Astronomy
- Genealogy

Programmes may be undertaken either by a group or on an individual basis.

For Assessment: evidence of individual progress, sustained interest and a commitment of genuine leisure time should be shown over the required period. At the end of the required period, participants should present their notebooks and other project work to the Assessor. The total project should be discussed, as should other ways in which the project may be developed in the future. Group activities are to be assessed with regard to each individual's contribution to planning, execution and completion.

For beginners
1. In preparation for practical research, participants should familiarise themselves with the following:
    a. The value of genealogical research.
    b. Family records, such as photographs, letters and diaries, tapes or accounts through interview.
    c. Accessing records of births, marriages and deaths.
    d. The census returns of 1841, 1851, 1861, 1871, 1881, 1891.
    e. Parish registers and gravestones as a valuable source.
    f. The use and limitations of the International Genealogical Index (IGI).
2. Practical Work - young people should:
    a. Carry out practical research, the extent of which should be negotiated with the Supervisor.
    b. Produce notebooks or another form of presentation of the research.
    c. If appropriate, produce charts which trace the family history.

For those with some knowledge
3. In preparation for practical research, participants should continue to keep notebooks and familiarise themselves with the following:
    a. County family history societies: Society of Genealogists; Federation of Family History Societies (FFHS) publications or other Genealogical Societies around the world.
    b. Parochial and Poor Law records, and published family histories.

• Collections,
Studies and
Surveys
- Genealogy

c. Non-conformist churches' records.
d. Wills and where they have been deposited.
e. Heraldry and the family historian.
f. The use of and possible voluntary contribution to the many modern indices available in record offices world-wide.

4. Practical Work - young people should continue to:
   a. Carry out practical research.
   b. Produce notebooks or other records of presentation of the research.

For the more advanced

5. In preparation for practical research, participants should continue to keep notebooks and familiarise themselves with the following:
   a. The extent and whereabouts of the principal genealogical records.
   b. The Public Record Office.
   c. The uses of computers in family history.
   d. Sources of information relating to specific professions, trades, callings and activities.
   e. The links between genealogy and social history.
   f. Methods of presenting genealogical records and findings of genealogical research.

6. Practical Work - young people should:
   a. Continue their practical research supplementing their findings with relevant collections of photographs, letters etc.
   b. Produce notebooks or other records of presentation of the research.
   c. Make a brief study of the evolution of surnames.

• Collections,
  Studies and
  Surveys
  - Genealogy

Communications

Introduction
These activities provide vehicles by which individuals express themselves, their beliefs and communicate with others. They call for an understanding of the various media as well as for an awareness of their potential and effects. Most of the activities require an acquisition of technical skills which provide the basis for communication and upon which ideas and creativity are expressed. An understanding of the historical, social and cultural aspects should also be developed. Programmes may be undertaken as a group or on an individual basis.

For Assessment: evidence of individual progress, sustained interest and a commitment of genuine leisure time should be shown over the required period. Group activities are to be assessed with regard to each individual's contribution to planning, execution and completion.

General Programme
Where a particular choice of Skill is not listed, a programme may be devised based on the following guidelines and bearing in mind the points made in the introduction. Any programme should encourage individual progress and sustained interest over a period of time, leading to a deeper knowledge of the subject and attainment of a reasonable degree of Skill. Before commencing the programme, participants should obtain approval from their Operating Authority.

A programme should include:
1. Visits to appropriate venues.
2. Membership of a specialist club or group, where appropriate.
3. An understanding of the importance of communication together with a knowledge of its historical, social and cultural background.
4. Communicating an idea or belief to others through a chosen medium.
5. Investigating systems/methods which make it possible for people with special needs to communicate effectively.

AMATEUR RADIO AND RADIO CONSTRUCTION

Introduction

This activity provides a vehicle by which individuals express themselves and communicate with others. The programme requires an acquisition of technical skills which provide the basis for communication and participants should be encouraged to develop an appreciation of the value of Amateur Radio in forming friendships with people in other countries and from different cultures. They should also develop an understanding of the historical aspects of Amateur Radio.

This programme, which may be undertaken either as a group or on an individual basis, calls for a high degree of personal involvement, especially as it involves verbal and written modes of communication.

Safety - Instructors should ensure that power for working models and experimental work is provided from batteries or low-voltage units. Those taking part should be fully aware of the dangers involved in the use of power supplies from AC mains and in high voltage circuits. They should also be conversant with the treatment for electric shock. Instruction should be given in the safe use of all tools appropriate to Amateur Radio work, e.g. screwdrivers, pliers, wire-cutters, soldering iron.

For Assessment: evidence of individual progress, sustained interest and a commitment of genuine leisure time should be shown over the required period which may take the form of working models, notebooks, diagrams, finished articles etc. Group activities are to be assessed with regard to each individual's contribution to planning, execution and completion.

SKILLS
PROGRAMMES

• Communications
  - Amateur Radio and Radio Construction

221

For beginners

Participants should:

1. Have an elementary knowledge of electricity, e.g. Ohm's Law, heating effect of a current, knowledge of simple units.
2. Have a very elementary knowledge of radio principles (radiation of radio waves, direct and reflected paths).
3. Identify the controls and operate a short wave radio.
4. Develop general knowledge of time zones and their relevance in determining the times of peak radio activity in different overseas countries.
5. Learn the International Phonetic Alphabet used in voice communication.
6. Prepare a simple log book giving details of 25 transmissions from broadcasting or amateur stations. (This should include date, time, frequency, quality of signal etc.)
7. Make correct use of simple tools used in radio construction (screwdrivers, pliers, wire cutters, soldering iron, etc.)
8. Construct a simple working circuit, e.g. crystal receiver, audio oscillator.
9. Use appropriate meters to measure voltage, current, resistance.

For those with some knowledge

Participants should:

10. Have a basic knowledge of direct and alternating current circuits, including resonant circuits and transformers.
11. Acquire simple knowledge of amplifying devices (transistors or valves) and their use in amplifiers and oscillators etc.
12. Have a more detailed knowledge of radio wave propagation, the role of the Ionosphere in producing fading and skip zones.
13. Understand the functions of the various stages of a radio receiver and the principle of the superheterodyne receiver.
14. Know the regulations governing amateur transmitters on such matters as who may use them, what types of message may and may not be sent, keeping records, avoiding interference to other radio users, etc.
15. Be able to send and receive Morse code signals at a speed of 5 words per minute.
16. Identify the controls of a radio transmitter and the methods for controlling and checking its frequency.

• Commun-
  ications
  - Amateur
  Radio &
  Radio
  Construction

17. Construct a more complex electronic device, e.g. a simple short-wave receiver, simple transmitter, power pack for deriving a low voltage regulated supply from the AC mains.
18. If possible, operate a low-power amateur transmitter and produce reports of contacts with at least ten amateurs in other countries. To do this the participant must pass the Novice Radio Amateurs Examination and obtain a transmitting licence. These Skill requirements can all be fulfilled by taking the Novice Radio Amateur training course run by the Radio Society of Great Britain (see Useful Addresses).

For the more advanced
Participants should:
19. Take a more advanced course in Amateur Radio and pass the Radio Amateur's examination run by the City and Guilds of London Institute. Courses leading to this qualification are held at many Adult Education Institutes and Further Education Colleges.
20. Operate as a licensed Radio Amateur for at least six months and keep records of contacts with twenty-five amateurs in other countries
21. Be able to send and receive Morse code signals at a speed of 12 words per minute.
22. Learn the common abbreviations and Q-code signals used in amateur radio practice.
23. Participate in at least two amateur contests or 'field days' or exercises in which local groups of radio amateurs provide communications for the emergency services.
24. Undertake, preferably in a group, the construction of a more sophisticated piece of electronic equipment, e.g. a transmitter for Single Sideband operation, a multi-band superheterodyne receiver, frequency counter.

Communications
Example Skills Programme

CIRCUS SKILLS

Introduction
This activity provides a vehicle by which individuals express themselves and communicate with others. The activities require an acquisition of technical and physical skills which provide the

basis for communication and upon which ideas and creativity are expressed. Circus Skills can incorporate physical activity, group discussion and individual or group participation. The programme calls for a high degree of personal commitment, as it involves physical, verbal and written methods of communication.

Participants should be of a fitness standard appropriate to enjoy and execute the skills learned, and the safety precautions in all aspects of performing Circus Skills must be adhered to. Instruction in the safe use of equipment must be given before commencement.

Participants are encouraged to join a workshop, club or course in order to learn Circus Skills. They should specialise in one chosen Circus Skill and have some knowledge of at least two others selected from the following five main disciplines:

- **Aerial:** Trapeze, Roman Rings, Aerial Ladder, Aerial Rope, Wire Walking and related skills.
- **Balance:** Trick-Cycling, Stilts, Ladder, Tight-Rope, Wire Walking, Perch, Roller Bolo, Slack Rope.
- **Manipulative:** Plate Spinning, Cigar Boxes, Club Swinging, Devil Sticks and Diabolo Sticks, Juggling (three ball and club).
- **Ground:** Aerobic, Handstands, Tumbling, Aerobatics.
- **Clowning.**

Participants should also learn about circus make-up and costumes, advertising and publicity and the cultural and historical background of the circus.

For Assessment: evidence of individual progress, sustained interest and a commitment of genuine leisure time should be shown over the required period. Group activities are to be assessed with regard to each individual's contribution to planning, execution and completion. Assessment should include a record of the young person's participation which can be in the form of a pictorial or written log, diary or video tape. A short presentation or performance of the Skill should be planned and, depending on the Circus Skill chosen, participants may co-ordinate some form of musical accompaniment.

• Commun-
  ications
  - Circus Skills

For beginners

Participants should:

1. Under experienced guidance, show evidence of continuous study, effort and achievement in one aspect of circus Skills, including partici- pation in a presentation.
2. Study one aspect of the circus and keep a scrapbook or log.
3. If possible, observe at least two events such as a circus or street performance and provide a critical comment on one of them.

For those with some knowledge

Participants should:

4. Under experienced guidance, show evidence of continuous study, effort and achievement in two aspects of Circus Skills, resulting in a final group presentation.
5. Read books and articles on a variety of aspects relating to the circus and produce a written or oral presentation on at least two books.
6. If possible, observe at least three events such as a circus or street performance and provide a critical comment on one of them.

For the more advanced

Participants should:

7. Under experienced guidance, make further study, effort and achievement on three chosen aspects of Circus Skills, result- ing in a final group presentation.
8. Show some knowledge of the historical development of the circus.
9. Carry out research on the international aspects of circus life, to include a study of performing arts in the ring.
10. If possible, observe at least four events such as a circus or street performance and produce a comparative analysis on at least two of them, with special reference to the aspect selected for special study.

Useful Organisations/Contacts: Association of Circus Proprietors of Great Britain, Circus Friends' Association.

• Commun- ications
- Circus Skills

Crafts

Introduction

These activities involve the development of a Skill through practical application. An understanding of the historical, social and cultural aspects should be developed, where appropriate. Programmes may be undertaken either by a group or on an individual basis. Due regard should always be given to safe working practices.

For Assessment: evidence of individual progress, sustained interest and a commitment of genuine leisure time should be shown over the required period. This may take the form of finished articles, sketchbooks, exhibitions, displays, etc. Group activities are to be assessed with regard to each individual's contribution to planning, execution and completion.

General Programme

Where a particular choice of Skill is not listed or where a number of topics cannot be successfully combined, a programme may be devised based on the following guidelines, bearing in mind the points made in the introduction. Any programme should encourage individual progress and sustained interest over a period of time, leading to a deeper knowledge of the subject and attainment of a reasonable degree of Skill. Before commencing the programme, participants should obtain approval from their Operating Authority.

Basketry
Boatbuilding
Bookbinding
Brass Rubbing
Cake Decoration
Candle Making
Canoe Building
Clay Modelling and Sculpture
Construction of Camp and
  Outdoor Equipment
Cookery
Corn Dollies
Cycle Maintenance
Egg Decorating
Electricity and Electronics
Enamelling
Fancy Ropework
Floral Art
French Polishing
Furniture Restoration
Glasswork
Jewellery
Kite Construction and Flying
Lampshade Making
Lapidary
Marquetry
Metalwork
Model Construction -
  Aircraft, Cars, Railways,
  Ships
Model Soldiers
Origami
Pewter Working
Pottery
Shoemaking
Taxidermy
Transport Restoration
Wine Making
Wood Carving
Woodwork
Young Engineers

A programme should include:

1. The range of materials available, their preparation, cost, characteristics and storing qualities.
2. The different applications, basic skills and variety of techniques involved in using the material.
3. **The care and safe use of tools and equipment. Precautions should be taken when working with substances requiring face masks and adequate ventilation.**
4. How to follow plans, diagrams, instructions, etc., progressing towards the production of a finished article.

5.   The development of ideas through design, planning and production stages for the more advanced.
6.   An opportunity to display finished items together with a presentation of the planning processes involved.
7.   The historical development of the craft, and regional and national variations.

KITE CONSTRUCTION AND FLYING

Introduction
This activity involves the development of a Skill through practical application. The participant should learn about the equipment used, its care and maintenance and the relevant historical, social and cultural aspects of Kite Construction and Kite Flying.

Due regard should be given to safe working practices. Participants should be instructed in the safe use of glues, the safety precautions required when using cutting tools and the hazards inherent in flying kites.

The programme may be undertaken either as a group or on an individual basis and, in order to develop their Skill, young people may like to join an appropriate group or course or take part in a competition or festival, such as an international kite flying festival.

For Assessment: evidence of individual progress, sustained interest and a commitment of genuine leisure time should be shown over the required period. This may take the form of finished articles, sketchbooks, exhibitions, displays etc. Group activities are to be assessed with regard to each individual's contribution to planning, execution and completion.

For beginners
Participants should:
1.   Acquire a general knowledge of the materials and equipment needed for making and flying kites.
2.   Understand the law in relation to kite flying.

SKILLS
PROGRAMMES

• Crafts
  - General Programme
  - Kite Construction and Flying

227

3. Have a general knowledge of the origins and history of kites.
4. Make a basic diamond kite out of paper or plastic and fly it.
5. Investigate different types of kites, including traditional kites from other countries, the materials and equipment used and basic kite construction.

For those with some knowledge
Participants should:
6. Make two kites:
   a. A single line kite.
   b. A steerable kite.
7. Display basic launching and stunt flying techniques.
8. Learn why kites fly.
9. Investigate the different uses of kites - past and present - and their historical development both in the United Kingdom and in other countries.
10. Research availability and prices of ready-to-fly kites and kite equipment from manufacturers and retailers in the United Kingdom.

For the more advanced
Participants should:
11. Design and make three kites:
    a. A fighting kite.
    b. A quad line steerable kite.
    c. Any other.
12. Make a wind turbine.
13. Display launching and stunt flying techniques and flying through a ground hook.
14. Display a stacker or train of kites.
15. Investigate a range of kite designs, flying lines, bridles, knots and reels.
16. Investigate one or more of the following:
    a. Aerial photography.
    b. Paradrops and skydivers.
    c. Regulations and classes for rokkaku fighting kites.
    d. International kite festivals and venues.
    e. Kite museums.
    f. Kite groups in the United Kingdom.

• Crafts
 - Kite
   Construction
   and Flying

TRANSPORT – RESTORATION

Introduction

These activities involve the development of a Skill through practical application. An understanding of the historical, social and cultural aspects should be developed, where appropriate. Programmes may be undertaken either by a group or on an individual basis. **Due regard should always be given to safe working practices.**

This programme can be adjusted to apply to the restoration of any form of transport, such as airplanes, cars, motorcycles, boats, trains, commercial vehicles, agricultural machinery. Before drawing up a specific programme of activity based on the following guidelines, the participant should consider joining an appropriate enthusiasts' club, society, group or class where expert advice and support will be available to them.

Any restorations carried out must be supervised by a person who is knowledgeable and experienced to ensure that the most sympathetic treatment and appropriate care is given to objects.

For Assessment: evidence of individual progress, sustained interest and a commitment of genuine leisure time should be shown over the required period. This may take the form of sketchbooks, studies, working drawings, photographic records or finished projects. Group activities are to be assessed with regard to each individual's contribution to planning, execution and completion.

For beginners

Participants should:

1. Learn about a variety of restoration techniques and the appropriate tools and materials. Be aware of their care and safe use. **Precautions should be taken when working with substances requiring face masks and adequate ventilation.**
2. Understand the mechanism by which rust/rot forms and where to look for it.

3. Have a knowledge of methods of eliminating rust and of surface preparation for painting.
4. Show competence in the use of resin-based filling materials.
5. Demonstrate a knowledge of painting techniques and when they are applicable.
6. Learn about the development of manufacturing materials and their effect on design. Investigate different sources such as museums, collections, illustrations, etc.

For those with some knowledge
Participants should:
7. Demonstrate a knowledge of lubrication and its effect on both engine and mechanical components, including running gear, where appropriate.
8. Know the basic principles of electric wiring, if appropriate.
9. Research the availability of replacement components.
10. Know the alternative methods of repairing holes in the bodywork and demonstrate at least one.
11. Know how to prepare for respray including the removal of certain components and the masking of others which cannot be removed.

For the more advanced
Participants should:
12. Develop a safe, working knowledge of welding and brazing techniques and an appreciation of when to use gas or electric welding.
13. Know how to respray using an air spray-gun.
14. Select a major component that requires repair or refurbishment, e.g. door skin or wing, engine, gearbox. Choose the appropriate materials and tools, carry out the restoration, reassemble and reinstall.
15. Undertake some repair to the interior of the vehicle, e.g. upholstery, headlining.
16. Keep a photographic or sketch record of the progress of a major restoration project.
17. Demonstrate a knowledge of the social relevance of a particular mode of transport by researching sources such as contemporary literature.

• Crafts
  - Transport
    Restoration

Graphic Arts

Introduction

Participants should understand the range of applications of graphics together with their role in communication, production and marketing. An awareness of the social role of graphic design in the community may be developed. These activities involve the development of a Skill through practical application and, wherever possible, ways of applying practical skills should be explored. Programmes may be undertaken either by a group or on an individual basis.

For Assessment: evidence of individual progress, sustained interest and a commitment of genuine leisure time should be shown over the required period. This should be in an appropriate format such as a sketchbook, folio of work, video recording or display. Group activities are to be assessed with regard to each individual's contribution to planning, execution and completion.

General Programme

Where a particular choice of Skill is not listed, a programme may be devised based on the following guidelines and bearing in mind the points made in the introduction. Any programme should encourage individual progress and sustained interest over a period of time, leading to a deeper knowledge of the subject and attainment of a reasonable degree of Skill. Examples of Graphic Arts that may be studied include computer graphics, animation and illustration. Before commencing the programme, participants should obtain approval from their Operating Authority.

A programme should lead to:
1. An awareness of the range of materials and techniques
2. An understanding of their advantages and disadvantages and where they may be most effectively used.
3. An appreciation of the constraints of working to a design brief involving the exploration and development of creative ideas from early stages through to a finished design.
4. An understanding of the use of colour, light and sound in graphic processes, as appropriate.

• Graphic Arts
 - General
  Programme

5. An awareness of the power of graphics to influence values and communicate through the mass media, and a subsequent understanding of the responsibility of the graphic designer to the community as a whole.
6. An awareness of how social and political change influences graphic arts.

Graphic Arts
Example Skills Programme

LETTERING AND CALLIGRAPHY

Introduction

This activity should include as much practical work as possible, preferably undertaken with others through a group or club. The programme involves practical work in lettering (drawn with pencil, pen or painted with a brush) and calligraphy (formal penmanship using the edged pen); the aim should be to develop a good all-round standard of practical work. Participants should also be aware of the historical development of lettering and calligraphy and its use for a variety of purposes today.

Study of the proportion and arrangement of letters. In all aspects of this programme, young people must be aware of the need for well designed work, the important factors being:

a. The proportion of individual letters.
b. The spacing between letters, words and lines.
c. The weight and density of the lettering and the balance of one area of writing with another.
d. The arrangement or layout of the writing in relation to the margins and blank spaces.
e. The use of colour in writing.
f The integration of illustration or decoration with the other elements.

For Assessment: work undertaken throughout the programme should be compiled into a portfolio of work for assessment. A selection of pieces should be mounted or presented in an appropriate way, e.g. exhibition, display. Group activities are to be assessed with regard to each individual's contribution to planning, execution and completion.

In each level young people should select and present for assessment from the following choices:

a. Practice sheets in brush and pen, or drawn lettering, and one fair copy of the alphabet showing related letters in their groups, or a complete alphabet after group study has been made.

b. A poem of not less than 14 lines written with an edged-pen in italic hand.

c. An inscription in painted Roman lettering including a date, or a poster for an exhibition (light letters on a dark ground or light and dark letters on a medium ground).

d. One example of prose of approximately 200 words written with an edged-pen for a double page opening of a manuscript book, including decorative capitals and a heading or an illustration.

e. A suitable example of a public notice in sans-serif block letters, e.g. 'Silence Please'.

f. Four varied examples from the following: a greetings card, a Christmas card, invitation to a party, recipe for a cake or other foods, menu for a steak house, fish restaurant or snack bar, notice for sale of work at a local school, advertisement for a fountain pen, monograms, design for wrapping paper or paper bags incorporating the name of a firm.

For beginners

Lettering

Participants starting this activity should:

1. Study and practise the skeleton alphabet in groups of letters. Paint the Roman alphabet with a brush in related groups of letters. Start with the capital letters, follow with the lower-case letters and numerals.

2. Study and practise a formal italic alphabet.

3. Draw and paint Sans Serif letters not less than 5 cm high, or draw and cut out Sans-Serif letters 5 cm, 7.5 cm, or 10 cm high, in white paper and arrange in words on black or coloured paper for practice in experimental spacing and layout.

Calligraphy

Participants should:

4. Start with the alphabet in skeleton form. The letters and their relative proportion to the circular 'O' should be studied and

• Graphic Arts
 - Lettering &
   Calligraphy

practised in groups, i.e. rectangular group of letters, round letters, wide letters, narrow and very narrow letters.

5. Ensure that writing with the edged-pen is practised, beginning with the lower-case letters, followed by simple capital letters and numerals and starting with a nib that is not less than Nib Six No. 1 (2.5mm) across its writing edge. A formal hand (the foundational hand) based on the circular 'O' should be used, also a formal italic hand made from a number of pen strokes.

6. Practise versal letters and flourished and swashed capitals, used for leading into the text or for adding to it.

7. Practise monograms, emblems for chapter headings and endings, and decorative borders related to the writing.

8. Illustrate writing in any medium, provided it is related in scale and weight.

For those with some knowledge
Participants should:

9. Continue the practise of lettering and calligraphy as suggested in the introduction. Finished examples of work should show evidence of an understanding of layout and design and the choice of good model alphabets.

10. Collect and mount in a sketchbook, or on sheets in a folder, examples of past and present day lettering and calligraphy, and give reasons for the choice. Examples should be included from newspapers, magazines, journals and book jackets, and participants should draw or take photographs of shop signs, street names, inn signs, etc.

For the more advanced
Participants should:

11. Continue to practise lettering and calligraphy and produce completed examples.

12. Make a study of lettering from the past and historical manuscript writing, by visiting churches for lettering on memorials, and museums for early manuscripts and historical documents. Rubbings can be made from slate or stone-incised inscriptions, on detail paper bought in a roll, the rubbing being done with a cobbler's heel ball.

PHOTOGRAPHY

Introduction

This activity should include as much practical work as possible, preferably undertaken with others through a group or club. Throughout the programme young people should develop a knowledge of the history and the different uses of photography. They should be encouraged to examine its impact in a variety of social and cultural contexts and develop an awareness of the effects of visual images on everyday life.

All taking part should understand the potential hazards of the chemicals used.

For Assessment: evidence of individual progress, sustained interest and a commitment of genuine leisure time should be shown over the required period. Some form of sketchbook or log book should be kept containing ideas and details of projects, and a portfolio of work should be compiled for assessment. Participants should be encouraged to work towards involvement in a display, exhibition, event or publication. Group activities are to be assessed with regard to each individual's contribution to planning, execution and completion.

For beginners

Participants starting this activity should:

1. Have a knowledge of the operation, care and maintenance of a 35mm SLR camera.
2. Be able to load and develop a black and white film in a 'daylight' tank.
3. Make contact prints from normal negatives on resin coated or fibre-based paper.
4. Take a series of twelve photographs on a theme of their choice and mount them in an appropriate way, e.g. in a portfolio or loose-leaf album. Enlargements, if necessary, may be processed professionally.

For those with some knowledge

Participants should:

5. Have a more in-depth knowledge of a 35 mm SLR camera

• Graphic Arts
- Photography

including the use of apertures, shutters, depth of field, lens focal lengths, etc. and develop an awareness of medium and large format cameras.

6. Prepare a series of twelve photographs based on a theme, e.g. landscapes, portraits, photo-journalism, advertising or fashion photography and mount them in an imaginative way, e.g. in a portfolio or in preparation for an exhibition.

7. Make a study either photographically or with mixed media, e.g. audio-visual, video, computers – illustrating a subject of special interest in the community or recording an event such as a newsworthy occasion.

8. Study the full process of photography. Make one enlargement of any subject. Participants should be responsible for taking the photograph, developing the film and printing the picture. The enlargement should be approximately 10"x 8" or 12"x 16". Exposure tables and calculators should be used to give correctly exposed negatives from outdoor subjects.

For the more advanced

Participants should:

9. Have knowledge of lighting and the use of filters for special effects by day and artificial lighting and flash.

10. Have knowledge of shading and retouching of enlargements made from any negative.

11. Know the basic rules of composition and lighting for portraiture.

12. Have knowledge of different types of developers and fixers in black and white photography and the action of the chemicals used.

13. Know about the different types of film emulsions and how they are used to produce different results.

14. Know the basic principles of colour processes and produce two samples.

15. Have an awareness of photography as a developing technology, e.g. the use of digital imaging technologies, sending images, manipulation.

• Graphic Arts
 - Photography

Life Skills

Introduction

These programmes provide opportunities for work on a group basis although this does not preclude participants from following them as individuals. They lend themselves to a structured course where individuals with specialist skills may be introduced to the group. They may also include a series of visits. The sessions can be spread over the whole of the required period with time for individual or group project work. An understanding of the historical, social and cultural aspects should be developed, where appropriate.

For Assessment: evidence of individual progress, sustained interest and a commitment of genuine leisure time should be shown over the required period. This may take the form of a diary, a record of the course work undertaken or a project which focuses on one aspect which may be of a personal interest to the participant. Group activities are to be assessed with regard to each individual's contribution to planning, execution and completion.

General Programme

Participants who wish to follow a more general Life Skills programme will find that many of the listed programmes are complementary; thus topics from more than one programme may be combined. For example, Money Matters and Consumer Affairs may be combined to produce an alternative programme. Any programme should encourage individual progress and sustained interest over a period of time, leading to a deeper knowledge of the subject and attainment of a reasonable degree of Skill. Before commencing the programme, participants should obtain approval from their Operating Authority.

The programme should provide opportunities, as appropriate, to:
1. Join a local club or society and participate in their activities.
2. Attend a suitable course which provides a progressive programme of training.
3. Harness local resources and invite contributions from local experts.
4. Acquire knowledge of a particular activity and understand the historical, social and cultural aspects.

5. Apply the knowledge by undertaking practical activities in real-life situations.
6. Demonstrate achievement by arranging a presentation, display or open debate.

HEALTH AND STYLE

Introduction
This programme provides an opportunity for working on a group basis although this does not preclude participants from following it as individuals. It lends itself to a structured course where individuals with specialist skills may be introduced to the group. It may also include a series of visits away from the group environment. The sessions may be spread over the whole of the required period with time for individual or group project work.

For Assessment: evidence of individual progress, sustained interest and a commitment of genuine leisure time should be shown over the required period. This may take the form of a diary, a record of the course work undertaken or a project which focuses on one aspect which may be of personal interest to the participant. Group activities are to be assessed with regard to each individual's contribution to planning, execution and completion.

For beginners
Participants should:
1. Attend sessions on at least four of the following:
   a. Skin care, to include cleansing, treatment of blemishes and the importance of skin protection with particular reference to the sun and harsh climates.
   b. Care of hair and/or beards and moustaches, to include advice on the choice of suitable styles.
   c. Care of the feet and the importance of correctly fitted footwear.
   d. Dental care.
   e. The part exercise and a balanced diet play in looking and feeling good.

2. Visit two of the specialists featured in the sessions under 1 and make a record of the visit, e.g. written project, scrapbook or photographs.
3. Attend a make-up or hair demonstration with a professional cosmetic consultant or hair stylist. This could include the opportunity to practise on a friend.
4. Have a discussion on the positive and negative influences of role models, such as TV personalities, musicians etc.

For those with some knowledge

Participants should:

5. Take part in sessions arranged to develop an understanding of issues relating to smoking, drug and alcohol abuse and sexually transmitted diseases/AIDS. It is advisable that a professional counsellor is invited to lead the sessions and that information is available on support organisations and educational resource material. Sessions could involve diverse methods such as discussions, debates, role play techniques, games/exercises, videos, etc.
6. Invite a specialist to talk about weight and diet problems, including bulimia, anorexia and the importance of balanced nutrition.
7. Visit a gym at a local health club or leisure centre and investigate the variety of toning and exercise equipment available. Together with an expert, participants should draw up an appropriate exercise and fitness plan for themselves. Alternatively, carry out a survey of young people's fitness levels by developing a fitness trial, under the guidance of a qualified Instructor.

For the more advanced

Participants should:

8. Either:
    a. Learn about the causes and effects of nutritional deficiencies and produce a project on their findings.
        or:

• Life Skills
  - Health and Style

    b.   Study the effects media images of health and beauty have on young people's tastes, fashions and trends.

9.   Investigate a selection of treatments, such as electrolysis, cosmetic surgery, orthodontics etc. Find out what is available through the National Health Service and the cost of private treatment.

10.   Arrange for a speaker to talk to the Unit on at least two complementary health treatments, e.g. homeopathy, reflexology, aromatherapy, osteopathy, hypnosis, acupuncture.

11.   Either:

    a.   Investigate the various services available at the local Health Centre, e.g. chiropody, dental treatments, well-women clinics. Produce a draft booklet or information poster which would be of help to a family moving into the area.

    or:

    b.   Become involved in or run a health education programme in a suitable venue such as a youth club. This could include health promotion work, involvement in health projects, such as Stop Smoking Clubs, health education courses and activities for younger children.

Life Skills
Example Skills Programme

YOUNG ENTERPRISE

Introduction

This programme is designed to give an opportunity for work with young people on a group basis, though this does not preclude participants from following it as individuals. It contains a variety of ideas for continued study. At all stages participants are expected to undertake projects in theory or practise on aspects which are of personal interest to them.

The programme can be tackled as a series of visits away from the group environment or by introducing skilled adults into the group or by combination of both. The sessions can be spread over the whole of the required period with time for individual or group project work, or by starting with a structured course and then specialising in certain aspects of the programme.

The Young Enterprise 'learning-by-doing' scheme provides for personal development within the framework of a team through the medium of a 'mini company'. In this way the participant handles real decision-making, plans, finance and personal relationships whilst accepting the consequences of their actions and attitudes.

The Young Enterprise scheme normally operates over an academic year of three terms averaging a total of eight months. To satisfy Silver and Gold level requirements, participants are expected to complete the additional period by continuing with Young Enterprise in the following year in the capacity of an assistant advisor. This involves using the expertise gained during the original experience to support young people taking part in Young Enterprise for the first time and helping the adult advisors drawn from industry and commerce. Thus participants make a social contribution whilst qualifying for the Skills Section.

For Assessment: evidence of individual progress, sustained interest and a commitment of genuine leisure time should be shown over the required period. This may take the form of a diary, a record of the course work undertaken or on the particular aspect of the project in which the participant has been involved. Group activities are to be assessed with regard to each individual's contribution to planning, execution and completion.

For beginners
Participants starting this activity should develop an awareness of:
1. The world of work.
2. Industrial organisation and management.
3. The importance of human relations in industry.
4. The importance of customer satisfaction.
5. The importance of product innovation.
6. The social significance of the creation of enterprise leading to sustained employment.
7. The importance of profit as a measure of business success.

For those with some knowledge
Participants should further their understanding of:
8. The working of businesses engaged in the manufacture of products or the provision of services.
9. The structure of business organisations.
10. Principle business functions.

• Life Skills
  - Young
    Enterprise

11. Departmental relationships and responsibilities.
12. The need for the efficient handling of human and physical resources and hence an understanding of the role of production processes, the importance of safety at work and of maintaining high standards of quality.
13. The application of marketing principles and practice.
14. The application of financial principles and procedures.

For the more advanced
As well as satisfying the requirements for the two previous parts of the programme, participants should develop an elementary knowledge of:
15. General management practice including chairmanship of meetings, report writing and evaluation.
16. Line and staff management with particular reference to sales and marketing, product research, design and development, production planning and control, management and financial accounting, company secretaryship, employee relations.
17. Internal and external relations.
18. Maintenance of records.
19. Company Law and practice, including formation and winding-up.
20. Corporate planning and control, including decision-making.

• Life Skills
  - Young
    Enterprise

Music

Introduction

There are a variety of individual programmes for music but where no programme is given for a particular activity, topics from more than one programme may be combined to produce an individual programme. An understanding of the historical, social and cultural aspects of music should be developed. Programmes may be undertaken either by a group or on an individual basis.

For Assessment: evidence of individual progress, sustained interest and a commitment of genuine leisure time should be shown over the required period. Group activities are to be assessed with regard to each individual's contribution to planning, execution and completion.

General Programme

Where a particular choice of Skill is not listed or where topics from more than one programme may not be successfully combined, participants may select one of the following options. Either choice should encourage participants to show individual progress, sustained interest and a genuine commitment to leisure time over a period of time, leading to a deeper knowledge of the subject and attainment of a reasonable degree of Skill.

1. Playing a musical instrument
   a. Receive instruction in the care and maintenance of the instrument.
   b. Develop competence in playing the chosen instrument.
   c. Develop the ability to read music at sight.
   d. Learn to play a particular style or a combination of styles of music.
   e. Play an instrument Individually or as part of a musical group, band or orchestra.
   f. If playing a percussion instrument, show ability to follow the part from a musical notation. Perform on any type of percussion instrument.

2. Singing
   a. Sing regularly either solo or as part of a group.

• Music
  - General
    Programme

b. Develop the ability to read music at sight and be able to sing, hum or whistle a short musical piece.

c. Take part in a performance or show, either solo or as a group member.

d. Develop competence in a particular style or a combination of styles of music.

JAZZ

Introduction

Those taking part should learn to read music and follow some acknowledged books of exercises and scales. They should also have some understanding of the history and development of Jazz, and of the social implications and consequences of this particular type of music. These might include such topics as the comparison and contrast of music from different countries or different periods, or an evaluation of the part played by music in times of rejoicing.

For Assessment: evidence of individual progress, sustained interest and a commitment of genuine leisure time should be shown over the required period. Group activities are to be assessed with regard to each individual's contribution to planning, execution and completion.

For beginners

Participants starting this activity should:

1. Be able to prepare and tune a chosen instrument to correct pitch and know about its elementary care.

2. Be able to play a scale and two tunes in each of three keys. The two tunes should be the same in each key. In the case of percussion instruments, they should be able to play two accompaniments in three different tempi.

3. Find out all they can about the part played by the chosen instrument in the development of jazz.

For those with some knowledge

Participants should:

4. Be able to sight read and play on the chosen instrument one tune selected by the Assessor in a fairly simple key. Vary as necessary for percussion.
5. Be able to play two prepared original choruses based on practised tunes and one improvisation on the tune read at sight.
6. If possible, follow the performance of a professional playing the chosen instrument, noting style, technique and rhythm.

For the more advanced

Participants should:

7. Be able to play at sight and improvise on three tunes chosen by the Assessor in three different keys. Vary for percussion.
8. Be able to improvise with other instruments, live or on record, on three further tunes, without preparation.
9. Prepare a study of the chosen instrument.

Music

Example Skills Programme

PAN PLAYING (Steel Bands)

Introduction

Those taking part should learn to read music and follow some acknowledged books of exercises and scales. They should have some understanding of the history and development of pan playing and of the social implications and consequences of this particular type of music. These might include such topics as the comparison and contrast of music from different countries or different periods, or an evaluation of the part played by music in times of rejoicing.

For Assessment: evidence of individual progress, sustained interest and a commitment of genuine leisure time should be shown over the required period. Group activities are to be assessed with regard to each individual's contribution to planning, execution and completion.

For beginners

Participants starting this activity should:

1. Draw a scale-chart of their pan (or set of pans) and write the

names of all notes on the appropriate segments.

2. Play the chromatic scales as well as the major and minor (harmonic) scales of C, F and G and their arpeggios.

3. Play the melody of five tunes of different rhythms and tempi, including at least one calypso, a current hit (non-calypso) and an excerpt from a classical composition.

4. Give a brief account of the history of the steel band movement in the Caribbean Islands.

For those with some knowledge

Participants should:

5. Draw scale-charts of all the pans in any one particular steel band writing the names of all notes on each pan or set of pans.

6. Play all major and minor scales and their arpeggios.

7. Sight read or improvise on a given melody. Play chord accompaniment for a given melody. Play a bass line for a given melody on either five or six bass.

8. Be able to describe the instruments in a local steel band and discuss their use in the steel orchestra as well as in other combinations.

For the more advanced

Participants should:

9. Prepare and rehearse for audition an arrangement of at least four minutes for a steel band of at least six pieces, e.g. two tenors, one double-second or double-tenor, one guitar, one cello, one tenor-bass or five bass. Drum kit and other percussion instruments may be added.

10. Know the general principles of keyboard harmony, the wholetone scales, the diminished scales and the modes.

11. Play at sight or improvise on three tunes in different keys chosen by the Assessor.

12. Make a detailed study of the latest developments in pan tuning and playing and the future of the pan or pans as musical instruments.

Nature

Introduction

Due regard should always be given to health hazards and safe working practices. An awareness of the social and cultural aspects should be developed where appropriate. Programmes may be undertaken either by a group or on an individual basis.

For Assessment: evidence of individual progress, sustained interest and a commitment of genuine leisure time should be shown over the required period. This may take the form of a written report, diary, display, talk or photographic record. Group activities are to be assessed with regard to each individual's contribution to planning, execution and completion.

General Programme

Where a particular choice of Skill is not listed, a programme may be devised based on the following guidelines and bearing in mind the points made in the introduction. Any programme should encourage individual progress and sustained interest over a period of time, leading to a deeper knowledge of the subject and attainment of a reasonable degree of Skill. Before commencing the programme, participants should obtain approval from their Operating Authority.

Participants should:
1. Join a local group or club concerned with nature, conservation, wildlife and the countryside and take part in their talks, meetings and activities.
2. **Understand the care and safe use of any tools or equipment where appropriate.**
3. Acquire knowledge of related health hazards, such as the use of pesticides or animal diseases.
4. Undertake research appropriate to the activity involving visits to nature reserves, Sites of Special Scientific Interest (SSSI's), museums and other places of interest.
5. Develop an understanding of the historical and social aspects where appropriate.

SKILLS PROGRAMMES

• Nature
  -General
    Programme

BIRD WATCHING

Introduction

This activity should include as much practical work as possible, preferably undertaken with others through a group or club. Participants should also show an understanding of the role birds play in the natural ecosystem, current bird conservation issues and organisations.

At all stages, those taking part should be aware of the patterns of study by group organisations.

Note: Collecting eggs, nests, feathers or other parts of birds is unnecessary for learning about birds. Collecting eggs is illegal and is still a threat to the future survival of some types of birds. Keeping wild birds as pets without a licence is also illegal.

For Assessment: each individual is to produce evidence of regular application to the interest over the required period. This may take the form of some kind of record such as a diary, log book or sketchbook. Group activities are to be assessed with regard to each individual's contribution to planning, execution and completion.

For beginners

Participants starting this activity should:

1. *Recognition* - be able to recognise and describe the essential field characters of 20 common species and know something about their habitats, habits, food and nests. Suggested supplementary activities are a garden bird feeding programme, a scrap-book of press cuttings and photographs etc. of birds, with comments on any features of special interest, or the construction of a bird-table and nest boxes.

2. *Fieldwork*
   a. Keep a diary or field notebook.
   b. Make at least one visit to a nature reserve or bird observatory recording the results in a diary.
   c. Regularly walk a route in an area near your home (e.g. garden, park, school grounds or wood) and make detailed observations of the birds and habitats that you see.

For those with some knowledge

Participants should:

3. *Structure* - be able to name and position the main features on a bird (e.g. crown, rump, supercilium primary feathers, secondary feathers).

4. *Recognition* be able to identify at least 50 species and know something of their habitats, foods, nests, conservation status and distribution in Britain.

5. *Adaptation* - be able to relate physical adaptations of the more important families of British birds to their different lifestyles.

6. *Fieldwork* - keep a diary or field notebook and embark on a detailed study of a single species, making notes on, for example, its song period, feeding behaviour, movements and habitat preferences.

7. *Migration* - study a book on migration and undertake fieldwork which should include the recording of arrival and departures dates of migrants and of any 'visible migration' and hard-weather movements that can be observed. A local reservoir or sewage farm might be suitable for this purpose.

8. *Protection* - have a basic knowledge of the laws which protect wild birds and the conservation of their habitats.

For the more advanced

Participants should:

9. *Structure* - have a detailed knowledge of the external features of birds and a basic knowledge of moult. An understanding of how the bird's wing functions. An elementary knowledge of the bird's internal anatomy (especially blood system, digestive system, air sacs and gonads).

10. *Recognition* - be thoroughly familiar with all the usual birds of the home area, including their songs and calls.

11. *Systematics* - have a knowledge of the systematic order of British birds and the relationship between each family group.

12. *Fieldwork* - Either:
    a. Take part in a national survey, e.g. Bird Breeding Survey, Wetland Bird Survey, ringing, nest record scheme. Useful

• Nature
- Birdwatching

contacts: British Trust for Ornithology, RSPB, Wildfowl and Wetlands Trust.

or:

b. Undertake a census by the mapping method of an area which might produce results of interest to conservation, e.g. gravel-pit, closed railway line, industrial wasteground.

or:

c. Make a more intense study of the species chosen from 6 above. Produce notes describing some aspect of the field-work.

13. *Migration* - know the main bird migration routes around the world, the current understanding of how and why migration occurs and the threats facing migrating birds.

14. If possible, take an active part in a local club, e.g. a YOC group or holiday, run by the junior section of The Royal Society for the Protection of Birds.

Nature
Example Skills Programme

CACTI GROWING

Introduction

This activity should include as much practical work as possible, preferably undertaken with others through a group or club. Participants should also develop an understanding of the historical development of cacti growing and its relevance in other parts of the world.

Note: Plants develop succulence in response to a dry period in their native habitat; the water stored in stem or leaf, or both, tides them over the dry resting period. In cultivation the resting period is equally important and the time of year varies for different plants. This rest period should, therefore, be taken into consideration when the six-monthly study periods are being assessed.

For Assessment: each individual is to produce evidence of regular application to the interest over the required period. This may take the form of some kind of record such as a diary, log book, sketchbook or photographic record. Group activities are to be assessed with regard to each individual's contribution to planning, execution and completion.

• Nature
 - Bird
   Watching
 - Cacti
   Growing

For beginners

Participants starting this activity should:

1. Start to make a collection of cacti and keep them in good growing condition.
2. Know the main parts of the world where cacti are found.
3. Know the meaning of genus and species.
4. Know the characteristics of succulents and cacti.
5. Be able to describe the true cacti and the name given to the families of cacti and succulents.
6. Be able to describe the yearly watering programme for cacti.
7. Visit a local horticultural show and discover how cacti are exhibited.

For those with some knowledge

Participants should:

8. Continue to add to their cacti collection and produce examples for examination and discussion with the Instructor.
9. Learn how to transplant and re-pot cacti.
10. Know how to recognise pests and diseases and outline the treatment and preventive measures.
11. Learn how to make up a suitable compost for cacti growing.
12. Find out about the most suitable food or fertiliser for cacti and how and when to apply it.
13. If possible, prepare two cacti for exhibition at a local horticultural show.

For the more advanced

Participants should:

14. Add to their existing collection.
15. Know the method of increasing stock - cutting, grafting, seed sowing.
16. Know the three main tribes of cacti (Pereskieae, Opuntieae, Cereeae), and some of the genera of each tribe.
17. Know some of the families of succulents and understand their individual properties.
18. Be able to identify cacti from photographs chosen by the Assessor.
19. If possible, prepare a group of cacti for exhibition.

• Nature
 - Cacti
   Growing

Needlecrafts

Introduction

The essence of these programmes is the practical application in learning the basic skills, stitches and appropriate choice of materials. It is also hoped that young people will be encouraged to be creative in making their own designs, patterns and colour schemes, especially at the more advanced stages. An understanding of the historical, social and cultural aspects of Needlecraft should also be developed where appropriate. Programmes may be undertaken either by a group or on an individual basis. **Due regard should always be given to safe working practices.**

Canvas Work (Needlepoint)
Crocheting
Dressing Dolls in National
  Costume
Dressmaking
Embroidery
Filography
Glove Making
Knitting
Leatherwork
Macramé
Patchwork
Pillow Lace Making
Quilting
Rug Making
Soft Furnishing
Soft Toy Making
Tatting
Weaving and Spinning

For Assessment: evidence of individual progress, sustained interest and a commitment to genuine leisure time should be shown over the required period. Group activities are to be assessed with regard to each individual's contribution to planning, execution and completion.

General Programme

Where a particular choice of Skill is not listed or where a number of topics cannot be successfully combined, a programme may be devised based on the following guidelines, bearing in mind the points made in the introduction. Any programme should encourage individual progress and sustained interest over a period of time, leading to a deeper knowledge of the subject and attainment of a reasonable degree of Skill. Before commencing the programme, participants should obtain approval from their Operating Authority.

A programme should include:

1. The range of materials available, their cost, preparation and characteristics.
2. The different applications, basic skills and variety of techniques involved in using the material.
3. **Instruction in the care and safe use of tools and equipment.**
4. How to follow plans, diagrams, instructions, patterns, etc. progressing towards the production of a finished article.

• Needlecrafts
  - General
    Programme

5. An opportunity to display samples and/or finished items.
6. The historical development of the craft and regional and national variations.

CANVAS WORK (NEEDLEPOINT)

Introduction

The essence of this programme is the practical application in learning the basic skills, stitches and appropriate choice of materials. An understanding of the historical, social and cultural aspects of canvas work should also be developed. This should include a focus on work which reflects the development of the craft regionally. Locally produced books of samplers and needlepoint patterns will help with this research and may inspire the participants to be creative in making their own designs, patterns and colour schemes, especially at the more advanced stages.

The programme may be undertaken either by a group or on an individual basis. **Due regard should always be given to safe working practices.**

For Assessment: evidence of individual progress, sustained interest and a commitment to genuine leisure time should be shown over the required period. Personal notebooks of stitches and designs, finished and ongoing work and evidence of visits to exhibitions, collections etc. should be included in the assessment. Group activities are to be assessed with regard to each individual's contribution to planning, execution and completion.

For beginners

Participants starting this activity should:
1. Learn basic needlepoint techniques, e.g. choosing canvas and needles appropriate to the project, preparing canvas, using a frame or hoop, centering work and starting/finishing stitches.
2. Learn to work the following stitches: tent, Scottish (diagonal), satin (Florentine) and rice (crossed corners). Keep a personal notebook illustrating these stitches.

SKILLS PROGRAMMES

• Needlecrafts
- General
Programme
Canvas Work
(Needlepoint)

3. Choose a canvas and appropriate yarn and make a simple sampler demonstrating the use of the four stitches above.
4. Learn how to follow a needlepoint pattern chart and work a simple article, e.g. small picture, pin cushion.
5. Develop their interest in canvas work by visiting at least one of the following venues: museums, exhibitions, collections.

For those with some knowledge
Participants should:
6. Research the variety of canvas and yarn suitable for needlepoint and add samples to their personal notebook.
7. Using a chart, work a more challenging pattern paying particular attention to starting and finishing yarn, even tension and extending the variety of stitches in the repertoire.
8. Learn how to transfer a design on to canvas and embroider a panel, chair or stool seat using a variety of stitches.
9. Take every opportunity to see both traditional and contemporary canvas work as seen in exhibitions, houses, museums and heritage centres.
10. Add details of these visits and new stitches learnt to a personal notebook.

For the more advanced
Participants should:
11. Continue to add to a notebook designs, stitches used and a record of visits to traditional and contemporary canvas work (see No. 9 above).
12. Either:
    Design a celebration sampler, e.g. birth, marriage, new home, and work in appropriate canvas and yarn.
    or:
    Work with others on a group needlepoint project, e.g. church kneelers, report of expedition, or panel depicting The Duke of Edinburgh's Award for display.
13. Learn how to stretch a finished canvas in preparation for framing.
14. Create several canvas work designs suitable for a variety of purposes, giving suggestions for colour and a selection of stitches.
15. Work one of the above designs and make up into the article of their choice.

• Needlecrafts
  - Canvas Work
   (Needlepoint)

PATCHWORK

Introduction

The essence of this programme is the practical application in learning the basic skills and appropriate choice of materials. An understanding of the historical, social and cultural aspects of patchwork should also be developed. This should include a focus on work which reflects the development of the craft in the participant's region. Young people should be encouraged to be creative in making their own designs, patterns and colour schemes, especially at the more advanced stages. Many heritage centres have libraries containing archives of quilting and its development in that region.

This programme may be undertaken either by a group or on an individual basis. Due regard should always be given to safe working practices.

For Assessment: evidence of individual progress, sustained interest and a commitment to genuine leisure time should be shown over the required period. A personal notebook of designs, both those worked as part of the programme and those admired on visits to heritage centres, collections, exhibitions etc. should be included in the assessment. Group activities are to be assessed with regard to each individual's contribution to planning, execution and completion.

For beginners

Participants starting this activity should:

1. Learn how to select appropriate fabrics and designs for patchwork.
2. Find out about the variety of templates available and how they can be made at home.
3. Make a small cushion using a hexagonal design, paying particular attention to the choice of fabric and colours.
4. Using a diamond patchwork design, make a small mat which should be lined and finished.
5. Develop their interest in patchwork by visiting at least one of the following venues: museums, exhibitions, collections, heritage centres, etc.

• Needlecrafts
  - Patchwork

6. Keep a notebook showing fabrics and designs used and details of visits in No. 5 above.

For those with some knowledge
Participants should:

7. Using diamond, hexagonal and log cabin patchwork, experiment with the variety of effects and patterns to create three small samples.
8. Use a favourite pattern from the finished samples and design and make an article of their choice suitable for a birthday present.
9. Continue to add details of designs to the notebook.

For the more advanced
Participants should:

10. Make a study of patchwork quilts, e.g. American quilts or the development of quilts in their region.
11. Add all research to their notebook.
12. Create several patchwork designs suitable for a variety of purposes, giving suggestions for fabric and colour.
13. Plan a quilt in patchwork in the design of their choice. Work a section measuring 60cm x 105cm. The full quilt may be finished subsequently or, if suitable, the section may be lined and made into a cot cover.

• Needlecrafts
  - Patchwork

Recreative Skills

Introduction

Those choosing these activities should be encouraged to join a club which is properly constituted and affiliated, directly or indirectly to the national body governing the activity. Programmes may be undertaken either by a group or on an individual basis.

Where appropriate, the participant should learn about the equipment used and its care and maintenance, the rules and scoring for the games concerned, the historical and social aspects of the activity and the organisation and work of the governing body at national and local levels.

Some of these programmes contain certain safety and legal requirements, indicated in bold type, which must be followed and due regard should always be given to safe working practices. Some activities may require additional insurance cover.

For Assessment: evidence of individual progress, sustained interest and a commitment to genuine leisure time should be shown over the required period. Group activities are to be assessed with regard to each individual's contribution to planning, execution and completion.

General Programme

Where a particular choice of Skill is not listed, a programme may be devised bearing in mind the points made in the introduction. Any programme should encourage individual progress and sustained interest over a period of time, leading to a deeper knowledge of the subject and attainment of a reasonable degree of Skill. Before commencing the programme, participants should obtain approval from their Operating Authority. A programme could include such activities as Table and Indoor games.

A programme should include:
1. **Instruction in the care and safe use of tools and equipment.**
2. Provision for progression in the activity as the standard of participation improves.

• Recreative
  Skills
  - General
    Programme

3. The keeping of a record of participation in the activity.
4. Membership of a specialist club or group, where appropriate.
5. Finding out about the origins and development of the activity.

FISHING

Introduction

Wherever possible, those choosing this activity should join a club which is properly constituted and affiliated directly or indirectly to the National Federation of Angling. The participant should become knowledgeable about equipment used and its care and maintenance and about the rules and regulations concerning fishing and its historical development. Throughout participation in this programme participants should be aware of the conservation aspects of angling.

For Assessment: each individual is to produce evidence of regular application to the activity over the required period which may take the form of club membership, attendance record, results achieved, diary or log and should not be solely on the standards of Skill attained.

For beginners

Participants starting this activity should:
1. Undertake as much practical work as possible and keep a diary and general notebook.
2. Gain knowledge of fishing found locally - game, coarse, sea.
3. Gain practical experience of the methods of fishing in these local waters, e.g. fly fishing, spinning, long trotting, pole fishing, worming.
4. Have an elementary knowledge of one of the different types of fishing to be found in the British Isles, e.g:
   a. Game - trout, sea trout, salmon.
   b. Coarse - perch, roach, tench, pike, bream.
   c. Sea - bass, mackerel, shark.
5. Find out about the variety of tackle available - i.e. rods, reels and lines.

6. Learn about basic methods of rod construction, e.g. glass and carbon fibre, cane.
7. Learn how to care for and maintain fishing tackle.
8. Have knowledge of close seasons.
9. Learn elementary knots.

For those with some knowledge
Participants should:
10. Gain as much practical experience as possible in fishing, tackle making and maintenance.
11. Read about types of fishing found in the British Isles, where to look for each type and what species a certain type of water is likely to yield.
12. Have experience of one of the following - game, coarse or sea fishing.
13. Gain further practical experience of a variety of fishing, e.g. fly fishing, spinning, pole fishing, long trotting.
14. Develop a knowledge of baits:
    a. Choice of baits.
    b. Legal and illegal baits.
    c. How weather conditions affect the choice of bait.
15. Understand what type of tackle to use for different fishing conditions and the appropriate rods, reels and lines.
16. Learn about materials used in rod-making and the differences between rods for fly fishing and spinning.
17. Learn about fish breeding, hatchery work, maintenance of stock, and make visits to appropriate venues where possible.

For the more advanced
Participants should:
18. Have a knowledge of fishing in other countries, e.g. distribution, species, methods of catching.
19. Gain a more detailed knowledge of British fishing.
20. Do more practical and theoretical work in the following fields:
    a. Game fishing.
    b. Sea fishing.
    c. Coarse fishing.

• Recreative Skills - Fishing

21. Have knowledge of more sophisticated and modern rod design and construction. Build a rod out of modern materials. Have some idea of what factors affect the design of a rod, e.g. type, weight, action, material.
22. Have knowledge of fish culture, pollution and its prevention and the work undertaken by the National Rivers Authority.
23. Have knowledge of reel and line design and the appropriate choice for different types of fishing.

Recreative Skills
Example Skills Programme

MARKSMANSHIP

Introduction

Marksmanship is the ability to deliver successive shots into a chosen area of a target on demand. It requires a unique blend of technical knowledge and physical control to achieve this outside the normal demands of speed, strength and agility seen in more dynamic sports. For the purposes of the Award, emphasis should be placed on regular practice with the rifle or pistol, during which time the other technical knowledge can be built up. **Safety is of paramount importance. Target shooting has an excellent safety record and all practice and learning must be based on a foundation of safe conduct and responsibility in using the rifle or pistol.**

Attendance at a National Smallbore Rifle Association affiliated club is generally required although air gun shooting may be carried out on a safe purpose-built range under the supervision of a competent person.

The disciplines that may be followed are:
- Air Rifle at 10 metres or 6 yards.
- Air Pistol at 10 metres or 6 yards.
- .22 Rifle (prone position) at 15, 20 or 25 yards.

For Assessment: each individual is to produce evidence of regular application to the activity over the required period which may take the form of club membership, attendance record, results achieved, diary or log. Assessment should not be solely on the standards of Skill attained.

For Beginners

Participants starting this activity should:

1. Develop a knowledge of the sport of Target Shooting which must include:
   a. **Safety rules.**
   b. **The law relating to themselves and the type of gun they are using.**
   c. Range etiquette.
   d. The names of the parts of the gun they are using.
   e. Basic competition procedures and the different types of competition.
   f. The type of target that is used for their particular discipline.
   g. How to load and operate the chosen gun in a safe manner.
   h. How to fire a shot with the gun supported.
2. Display an ability to shoot, under supervision, with the gun supported but without the need for verbal instruction. **They must observe and operate within the safety rules in force at the time without need for correction.**
3. Gain experience in the shooting discipline of their choice. The gun may be rested in a suitable manner on some form of support so that the aim is steadied but the gun is not clamped or restrained mechanically in any way. Actual practical experience should be gained in:
   a. Gun mounting.
   b. The hold.
   c. Aiming and correct sight picture.
   d. Breathing.
   e. Trigger control.
   f. Follow through.
   This practical experience should be gained during proven regular attendance at a shooting range at least once per fortnight.

For those with some knowledge

Participants should:

4. Have a more general knowledge of the sport of target shooting which must include the above items and also:
   a. The basic equipment used in their discipline and how it is used.
   b. How the equipment is adjusted and the effects of the adjustments (including the sling in the prone position).

• Recreative Skills - Marksmanship

c. How to adjust sights and the use of the spotting scope.

d. How to keep a shooting diary and what items to include.

e. How to fire a shot with the gun unsupported in the manner associated with their discipline.

5. Be able to place 10 consecutive shots in the black aiming mark of the relevant air rifle or pistol target, or within the 7 ring on the prone rifle target.

6. Experience the elements of shooting technique outlined above but using the rifle or pistol unsupported. They must also experience shooting in a pistol competition.

For the more advanced

Participants should:

7. Possess the previously outlined information and in addition:

a. Compile a brief resume of one Olympic shooting discipline which should include its rules and history.

b. Know how to clean and maintain a gun properly and the effects of this on accuracy.

c. Know the basic elements of shooting technique related to their discipline.

d. Know the organisational structure of the discipline locally, regionally, nationally and internationally.

e. Know the different types of scoring, and be practised in the type used in their discipline including the use of a scoring gauge.

8. Either:

a. Demonstrate the ability to make a minimum score in a shoulder-to-shoulder competition (not within the same club). The minimum scores are shown in the table below. The current NSRA targets must be used for each discipline.

	6 yards	10 metres	
Air Rifle	86	84	
Air Pistol	83	80	

	15 yards	20 yards	25 yards
Prone .22 Rifle	87	87	87

• Recreative
  Skills
  - Marksman-
    ship

or:

b. Demonstrate the ability to supervise a shooting activity at the beginners' level (this is restricted to participants over the age of 17). Part of this requirement is obtaining the NSRA Range Officers' Certificate.

The scores outlined are a guide for the examining officer and may be increased if he or she feels that they are insufficiently challenging for the participant. In the air rifle and air pistol disciplines the examining officer may make allowance for the use of recoiling guns. However the use of recoilless guns should be encouraged where circumstances permit.

9. Organise a shooting activity under guidance and supervision. They must also participate in a shoulder-to-shoulder competition but not within the same club.

• Recreative
Skills
- Marksman-
ship

Skills Programmes – Index

The programmes listed below are available in the Skills Programmes loose-leaf folder. A selection of Skills Programmes is contained in this Handbook and, for these, the relevant page number is shown. In exceptional circumstances a limited number of single programmes are available from The Award Scheme Ltd by sending a stamped, self-addressed envelope.

SKILLS
INDEX

SKILLS INDEX

• Skills Programmes - Index

PR

Physical Recreation

SECTION

The Duke of Edinburgh's Award Handbook

Physical Recreation

Aim of the Physical Recreation Section

To encourage participation in Physical Recreation and improvement of performance.

The Principles

This Section offers a wide range of programmes in the belief that:
- Involvement in some form of enjoyable physical activity is essential for physical well-being.
- A lasting sense of achievement and satisfaction is derived from meeting a physical challenge.
- The activities listed are enjoyable in themselves and can lead to the establishment of a lasting active lifestyle.
- Young people should have the opportunity to make a choice, then negotiate a personal programme of participation and achieve an objective.

Benefits to Young People

Participation in the Physical Recreation Section should provide opportunities to:

- **enjoy keeping fit** by choosing an activity which is in itself enjoyable, and which leads to the establishment of a lasting, active lifestyle,
- **improve fitness** by taking part in an activity on a regular basis to improve physical health and well-being,
- **discover new abilities** by following an activity which presents a challenge,
- **raise self-esteem** through improvement of performance and reaching the minimum requirements,
- **extend personal goals** by involvement in different experiences and meeting new people,
- **respond to a challenge** by extending physical fitness and performance to the limit of ability,
- **derive a sense of achievement** from meeting a physical challenge.

PHYSICAL RECREATION
INTRODUCTION

Requirements

Assessed participation in organised Physical Recreation and achievement of individual progress.

Types of Physical Recreation

The Physical Recreation Section offers young people a wide choice depending upon their personal preferences, abilities and the opportunities available. The young person may already be involved in the activity or it could be something entirely new.

The scope of the Section means that all young people should be able to take part from those who are natural athletes or games players to those who are not so keen on active sport and those who have special needs.

There are other possibilities not included in the list below. For example, many activities have versions specifically adapted for wheelchairs, e.g. wheelchair basketball, and the list is therefore intended to be inclusive rather than exclusive. **However, before undertaking any other activities, proposals must first be submitted to the National Award Office for approval via the Operating Authority and the appropriate Territorial or Regional Office.**

Activities are divided into the following three categories:

● Activities with Set Standards. These are usually National Governing Body Awards but, in the case of Physical Achievement and Swimming, standards have been set by The Duke of Edinburgh's Award.

▲ Activities with Participation Programmes.

△ Activities which are covered by the general Team Games participation programme.

Types of Physical Recreation

- ▲ Aerobics *(see Fitness Activities)*
- ● Archery
- ● Athletics
- ● Badminton
- △ Baseball
- ● Basketball
- △ Boccia
- ▲ Bowling - Tenpin
- ▲ Bowls - Carpet, Crown Green, Flat Green
- ▲ Boxing
- △ Camogie
- △ Canoe Polo
- ● Canoeing
- ● Carriage Driving
- ▲ Caving & Potholing
- △ Cricket - Outdoor, Indoor
- ▲ Croquet
- ● Cross Country Running
- △ Curling
- ● Cycling
- ● Dance - Acrobatic, Ballet, Ballroom, Classical Greek, Disco, Highland, Latin American, Modern, Old Time, Stage, Tap
- ▲ Dance - English Traditional (Country and Morris, Step and Sword), Indian Classical (Kathak), Irish Traditional (Ceili and Irish Step), Scottish Country, Scottish Highland, Welsh Folk
- ● Diving
- ● Fencing
- ▲ Fitness Activities - Circuit Training; Exercise Machines / Multi-gym; Exercise to Music including Aerobics, Aquarobics, Step Aerobics; Running; Skipping
- ▲ Fives - Eton, Rugby
- △ Football and Gaelic Association Football
- ● Golf
- ● Gymnastics - Rhythmic, Sports Acrobatics, Gymnastics for Women & Girls, BAGA Awards
- ▲ Gymnastics - Educational
- ● Hang Gliding
- △ Hockey - Field, Ice, Indoor, Street / Roller
- △ Hurling
- ● Judo
- ▲ Keep Fit
- △ Korfball
- △ Lacrosse

- ● Martial Arts
- ▲ Medau Rhythmic Movement
- ● Modern Biathlon, Pentathlon and Triathlon
- △ Netball
- △ Octopushing
- ● Orienteering
- ● Parachuting
- ● Paragliding
- ▲ Petanque
- ● Physical Achievement
- △ Polo
- ▲ Real Tennis
- ● Riding
- ▲ Rock Climbing
- △ Rounders
- ● Rowing and Sculling
- △ Rugby League Football
- △ Rugby Union Football
- ▲ Running *(see Fitness Activities)*
- ● Sailing and Windsurfing
- ● Sand and Land Yachting
- ● Skating - Ice, Roller
- ● Skiing - Alpine
- ▲ Skiing - Nordic (Cross Country)
- ▲ Skipping *(see Fitness Activities)*
- ▲ Squash
- △ Stoolball
- ● Sub Aqua
- ● Surfing
- ● Swimming
- ● Table Tennis
- ▲ Tennis
- ● Trampolining
- △ Volleyball
- △ Water Polo
- ● Water Skiing
- ● Weightlifting
- ● Weight Training (free weights)
- ● Windsurfing *(see Sailing)*
- ▲ Wrestling
- ▲ Yoga (Hatha)

Note: This list is not exhaustive, but any proposed additions must first be submitted to the National Award Office for approval via the Operating Authority and the appropriate Territorial or Regional Office.

● standard
▲ participation
△ team sport

• Types of Physical Recreation

Summary of Conditions

Participants should select one activity and:

- Show improvement over a period of time.
- Obtain the stipulated number of points.

The minimum number of points required is:

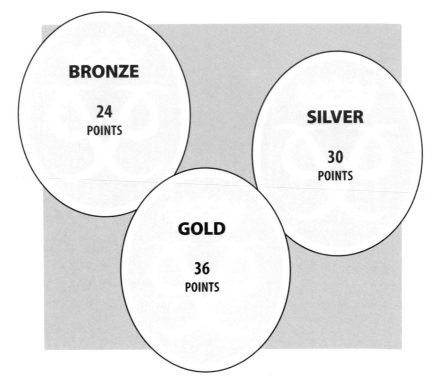

Activities are divided into three groups:

- ● Activities which have relevant National Governing Body Awards or, in the case of Physical Achievement and Swimming, set standards of The Duke of Edinburgh's Award.
- ▲ Activities which have participation programmes listed.
- △ Activities which are covered by the general Team Games participation programme.

Points are awarded for participation and improvement and, in addition, for certain designated sports, by obtaining standards.

Conditions in Detail

IMPROVEMENT

To qualify, participants must show improvement of overall performance in the chosen activity, show effort during the period of participation and make progress based upon their initial knowledge and ability.

This should be assessed as a continuing process throughout the period of participation, with regard to improvement in the following areas:

Application   Attendance and willingness to involve themselves during each practical session, appropriately attired and equipped.

Technique   Understanding of the techniques applicable to the activity.

Skill   Development of individual and/or co-operative skills appropriate to the activity.

Tactics   Appreciation of individual or group co-operative tactics necessary to the activity at their level of participation.

Fitness   Improvement of physical fitness specific to the activity.

Rules   Knowledge of rules appropriate to the level of activity at which the participation is involved.

Safety   Knowledge of safety regulations and appreciation of dangers inherent in the activity.

THE POINTS SYSTEM

The minimum number of points required to qualify for each Award is as follows:

BRONZE	24 points
SILVER	30 points
GOLD	36 points

• Conditions in Detail

Points are to be awarded differently depending on whether the activity is one with set standards or a participation programme:

A. Activities with Set Standards including those set by The Duke of Edinburgh's Award

Participation, improvement and achievement of set standards
Participants should choose an activity and:

1. First, using the Governing Body syllabus, participate and demonstrate improvement over a period of time. Participants must obtain at least 12 points over a minimum period of six weeks before attempting a standard. Points should be awarded on the basis of two points for each hourly session (one for each half hour), outside curriculum or work time. Not more than two points per week or four points per alternate weekend can be counted.

2. Then, when ready and **after** a period of more than six weeks, attempt a Governing Body standard. Points should be awarded for standards on the basis of the tables given on pages 284-290 of this book: 6, 12, 18 or 24 points may be awarded, depending on the level achieved.

3. If further points are needed to reach the required minimum number, continue with participation sessions and improvement.

Notes on Standards
1. Only points scored for one National Governing Body standard achieved in the activity may qualify.

2. Points gained for standards achieved and participation must be in the same activity. However, Operating Authorities have the discretion to waive this rule if, for exceptional reasons, such as moving away from the area, the participant no longer has access to the required facilities, although points gathered for standards in one activity cannot be added to those gained for standards in another in order to reach the required total.

3. Standards gained before starting work for an Award may not be counted. Participants should either gain the next higher proficiency award (but not an Instructors' Certificate) or take up a new activity.

4. In some cases separate standards or tables are shown for males and females; for all other activities one table gives standards for both sexes.
5. Standards **should** be attempted but, where an individual is unable to achieve the lowest standard shown, they may qualify by participation and personal improvement alone. In such cases, they **must** use the relevant Governing Body syllabus for measurable or certified standards as a working programme.
6. Further details of the standards in each activity should be obtained from the appropriate National Governing Body. The standards listed on pages 284-290 of the *Award Handbook* are those from the British Governing Bodies. Where these do not exist, the standards of the English Governing Bodies have been published. In these cases, the appropriate standards of the Governing Bodies of Scotland, Wales and Northern Ireland may be used instead.
7. Most activities in this group have relevant standards set by the appropriate National Governing Body of Sport, but for Physical Achievement and Swimming, The Duke of Edinburgh's Award has set its own standards and these are listed on pages 292 295.

B. Activities with Participation Programmes, including Team Games

Participation and improvement

Participants should:

1. Choose an activity and participate in it for a minimum of:

> **BRONZE** 12 weeks
>
> **SILVER** 15 weeks
>
> **GOLD** 18 weeks

2. Show improvement over the period of participation.
3. Gain the appropriate number of points.
   Points should be awarded on the basis of two points for each hourly session (one for each half hour), outside curriculum or work time. Not more than two points per week or four points per alternate weekend can be counted.

• Conditions in Detail

Notes on Participation Programmes

1. Guidelines for participation-only programmes and team sports are listed on pages 300-339.
2. Safety requirements in bold type must be observed in all cases.
3. The programmes are for guidance and not to be taken as rigid syllabi. Participants should start the programme at their own level of ability and experience and should cover as much of it as they can in the time it takes to qualify.
4. In exceptional circumstances, for example where availability of local facilities seriously limits usage such as in rural areas, the qualifying points may, at the discretion of Operating Authorities, be built up by undertaking a second activity, but a minimum of 12 points for participation must be gained in each activity. Activities cannot be undertaken concurrently.

INSTRUCTION AND ASSESSMENT

1. **Warm Up and Cool Down Sessions**

   Warm up and cool down periods are essential for all physical activity sessions. These should included static stretch exercises for all the main muscle groups and some cardio vascular work. The cooling down period should involve similar exercises gradually reducing the level of activity and allowing the muscles to return to their normal resting length.

2. **Safety and Good Practice**

   The publication, *Safe Practice in Physical Education*, published by the British Association of Advisers and Lecturers in Physical Education is recommended to all Instructors since it covers all aspects of safety both in general terms and specific to every activity. Copies may be available through the Local Authority or the Operating Authority.

3. Adults can assist in the Physical Recreation Section by being an Instructor, i.e. the person who coaches or supervises sessions or an Assessor, i.e. the person who carries out the final assessment. They must be knowledgeable and experienced in the activity, acceptable to the Operating Authority and, where appropriate, to the National Governing Body of Sport. It is essential that adults relate easily and effectively to young people.

4. Instructors and Assessors are normally suitably qualified Award Leaders, PE teachers, Club Officials, Club Instructors or National Governing Body Assessors. For most activities with set standards, Instructors and Assessors must be

• Conditions in Detail
- Instruction and Assessment

recognised by the appropriate National Governing Body of Sport, whose advice should be sought in such matters. For participation-only programmes, advice is given in some of the individual programmes detailed on pages 300-329.

5. At Bronze level, the Instructor and the Assessor may be the same person. At Silver level, the Instructor should normally be independent of the Assessor. At Gold level, the Assessor must be independent of the Instructor.

6. For all levels, assessment should be made at both the initial and final stages to confirm that there has been improvement. This is particularly important for participation-only programmes.

7. For the final assessment, the Assessor must be satisfied that, after consultation with the Instructor, the young person has:
   • shown effort during the period of participation,
   • made progress based upon their initial knowledge and ability,
   • shown improvement in the areas outlined above.

Note: It is advisable that an individual's choice of activity in the Physical Recreation Section be approved in advance by the Operating Authority to avoid disappointment by the Section being completed incorrectly.

Record Books

The *Record Book* represents the experiences and achievements of a young person and therefore remarks should be personalised, positive and encouraging. It should always record success and achievement rather than failure.

At all levels the activity, dates and points for participation are to be entered in *Record Books* by Instructors.

In the event of a young person not satisfying the Assessor, he or she should be informed of the reason and no entry made in the *Record Book* until the conditions have been fulfilled.

For activities with participation-only programmes, an Assessor's report is required and for activities with set standards, the Assessor should check that the standards attained are entered correctly.

PHYSICAL RECREATION

ACTIVITIES WITH PARTICIPATION PROGRAMMES ▲
POINTS REQUIRED: 24

ACTIVITY ROCK CLIMBING

DATES STARTED 04/05/94   COMPLETED 01/10/94

	SESSIONS		POINTS
NUMBER OF HOURLY SESSIONS ATTENDED	16	AT 2 POINTS EACH	2
OR NUMBER OF HALF-HOURLY SESSIONS		AT 1 POINT EACH	
		TOTAL	32

SIGNATURE OF
COACH OR INSTRUCTOR Anita M. Baker

Assessor's report: Kim has worked extremely hard to achieve a good standard in her climbing and shows tenacity. She is knowledgeable about the skills, procedures and equipment necessary to climb safely, including belay systems and climbing calls.
She has √climbed both on indoor walls and outside crags at Windgather and Aaden Rocher.
A sound member of the climbing team.

IMPROVEMENT: It is certified that this participant has shown improvement in application, technique, skill, tactics, fitness, knowledge of rules, appreciation of hazards and knowledge of safety precautions, as appropriate to the activity chosen

SIGNED Catrina Watson   DATE 6/10/94

QUALIFICATION/POSITION SPSA (BMC) Training Course

21

Bronze

PHYSICAL RECREATION

ACTIVITIES WITH RECOGNISED STANDARDS ●
POINTS REQUIRED: 30

ACTIVITY **BADMINTON**

DATES STARTED: **9/10/93**   COMPLETED **13/3/94**

	SESSIONS		POINTS
NUMBER OF HOURLY SESSIONS ATTENDED	9	AT 2 POINTS EACH	18
OR NUMBER OF HALF-HOURLY SESSIONS	2	AT 1 POINT EACH	2
		SUB TOTAL (A)	20

STANDARDS ATTAINED (check Award Handbook for points)

ACTIVITY	EVENT(S)	STANDARD(S)	
BADMINTON	BADMINTON ASSOC. OF ENGLAND - CARLTON AWARD	BRONZE	12

	SUB TOTAL FOR STANDARDS (B)	12
David demonstrated enormous improvement particularly in tactics	PLUS SUB TOTAL (A)	20
	TOTAL POINTS (A+B)	32

IMPROVEMENT: It is certified that this participant has shown improvement in application, technique, skill, tactics, fitness, knowledge of rules, appreciation of hazards and knowledge of safety precautions, as appropriate to the activity chosen.

SIGNED _L. Van Patten_   DATE **13/3/94**
INSTRUCTOR

SIGNED _Alison Lee_   DATE **13/3/94**
ASSESSOR

QUALIFICATION/POSITION _Badminton Assoc. of England Coach_

36

Silver

PHYSICAL RECREATION

ACTIVITIES WITH PARTICIPATION PROGRAMMES ▲
POINTS REQUIRED: 36

ACTIVITY Ice Hockey

DATES STARTED: 1.1.94   COMPLETED: 23/6/94

	SESSIONS		POINTS
NUMBER OF HOURLY SESSIONS ATTENDED	20	AT 2 POINTS EACH	2
OR NUMBER OF HALF-HOURLY SESSIONS		AT 1 POINT EACH	
		TOTAL	40

SIGNATURE OF COACH OR INSTRUCTOR _Julian Dogo_

Assessor's report: Fiona has attended sessions regularly and has obtained the basic skills of skating forwards and backwards whilst controlling the puck. She has obtained the first level required in addition though, as well as to make up controlling the puck and in mastering drills both for offensive and defensive play. She chose to continue her involvement in the game.

IMPROVEMENT: It is certified that this participant has shown improvement in application, technique, skill, tactics, fitness, knowledge of rules, appreciation of hazards and knowledge of safety precautions, as appropriate to the activity chosen.

SIGNED S. Ross

QUALIFICATION Ice Hockey Coach.   DATE 26/6/94

23

Gold

ACTIVITIES WITH NATIONAL GOVERNING BODY STANDARDS

ARCHERY

Full details available from The Grand National Archery Society

ATHLETICS

Obtain either:

AAA Five Star Award	Three	Four	Five	Outstanding Performance
or:				
Scottish AAA Thistle Award	Blue	Bronze	Silver	Gold
POINTS:	**6**	**12**	**18**	**24**

BADMINTON

Obtain a Badminton Association of England Carlton Award

	Intermediate	Bronze	Silver	Gold
POINTS:	**6**	**12**	**18**	**24**

BASKETBALL

Obtain an English Basketball Association Star Award

	Two Star	Three Star	Four Star	All Star
POINTS:	**6**	**12**	**18**	**24**

CANOEING

Tests of Personal Performance. Obtain the appropriate <u>level</u>:

Open Canoe	-	1	2	3/4
Kayak (closed cockpit)	-	1	2	3/4/5
Kayak (open cockpit)	-	1	2	3
Surf	-	1	2	3/4/5

Competition - Standards

500m	Blue	Bronze	Silver	Gold
Marathon 13.5 miles	-	Bronze	Silver	Gold
Marathon 26.0 miles	-	Bronze	Silver	Gold

Competition - Racing

Sprint Racing ⎫	-	Complete	150% or	120% of
Wild Water Racing ⎪	-	an event	promotion	winner's time
Slalom Racing ⎬	-		by one division	
Marathon Racing ⎭	-			

Specific Events

Devizes/				
Westminster ⎫	for	-	-	for full
Trans Pennine ⎬	each stage	-	-	completion
NABC 100	completed	-	-	of course
mile test ⎭				
POINTS:	**6**	**12**	**18**	**24**

Full details available from the British Canoe Union

CARRIAGE DRIVING

Obtain a standard from the British Driving Society

	Pre-lim Grooms	Level I	Level II	Level III
POINTS:	6	12	18	24

CROSS COUNTRY RUNNING

Obtain either:

AAA Five Star Award	Three	Four	Five	Outstanding Performance
POINTS:	6	12	18	24

or:

Scottish AAA Thistle Award

	Blue	Bronze	Silver	Gold
POINTS:	6	12	18	24

CYCLING

Undertake either:

Time Trial - 1000 metres Standing Start

	1.43	1.32	1.26	1.20
	(2.00)	(1.42)	(1.36)	(1.30)
POINTS:	6	12	18	24

or:

Time Trial - 4000 metres Standing Start or (3000 metres Standing Start)

	6.34	6.00	5.40	5.20
	(5.26)	(5.02)	(4.50)	(4.30)
POINTS:	6	12	18	24

or:

Reliability Trial - 80 kilometres, 50 miles, normally ridden in a small group on a road but the conditions are not competitive amongst the members of the group and each individual is timed over the set distance. The course may be a circuit covered one or more times, especially if the start can also be the finish, but the circuit should not be too small, i.e. not covered more than two or three times

	3.54	3.36	3.18	3.00
	(4.42)	(4.18)	(3.54)	(3.30)
POINTS:	6	12	18	24

or:

Road Time Trials - 10 miles and 25 miles

Details available from Road Time Trials Council

Notes: Time Trials to be ridden under competitive conditions on a hard-surfaced cycle track. The Tests are to be judged by British Cycling Federation officials of Divisional or National status or, in the case of Reliability Trials, officials of the Cyclists' Touring Club. Road Time Trials are to be assessed by the Road Time Trials Council.

For guidance and a copy of the draft programme for mountain biking please contact the Operating Authority or Territorial/Regional Office.

Where standards for females are different from males, they are shown in brackets.

PHYSICAL RECREATION STANDARDS

- Carriage Driving
- Cross Country Running
- Cycling

DANCE

Obtain a proficiency Award from one of the following:
International Dance Teachers' Association, Imperial Society of Teachers of Dancing, Royal Academy of Dancing, The British Association of Teachers of Dancing, The British Ballet Organisation, The National Association of Teachers of Dancing.

Ballet, Tap, Stage, Modern, Acrobatic, Classical Greek

	III	IV	V or Pre-elementary	Elementary Higher Award
POINTS:	6	12	18	24

Highland, Ballroom, Disco, Latin American, Old Time

	Bronze or III	Silver or IV	Gold or V	Higher Award
POINTS:	6	12	18	24

DIVING

Obtain a proficiency Award of the Amateur Swimming Association

	-	4 Star	1 metre diver	Bronze
POINTS:	6	12	18	24

FENCING

Obtain a proficiency Award of the Amateur Fencing Association

	Yellow Grade 1	Green Grade 2	Blue Grade 3	Orange Grade 6
POINTS:	6	12	18	24

GOLF

Obtain either a:
Certified CONGU handicap (for males)

	40*	27	22	16
POINTS:	6	12	18	24

or:
Certified LGU/ILGU handicap (for females)

	(54*)	(35)	(29)	(18)
POINTS:	6	12	18	24

or:
Merit Award from the Golf Foundation

	Blue Prelim	Green Par	Bronze Birdie	Silver Eagle
POINTS:	6	12	18	24

*Where standards for females are different from males, they are shown in brackets. (*unofficial handicap)*

GYMNASTICS

Obtain a proficiency Award of the British Amateur Gymnastics Association

	III	IV	V	Higher Award
Rhythmic Gymnastics	1	2	3	-
Sports Acrobatics	3	2	1	-
Gymnastics for Women and Girls	-	-	Single Gold	Double Gold
BAGA Awards	2	1	-	-
POINTS:	6	12	18	24

HANG GLIDING

Obtain a Pilot Rating Certificate of the British Hang Gliding and Paragliding Association

	Elementary Pilot Certificate	Club Pilot Certificate	Cross Country Pilot Certificate	Advanced Pilot Certificate
POINTS:	6	12	18	24

JUDO

Obtain a certified grade of the British Judo Association

Those holding a junior grade

	5th Mon Yellow 2 Tags	8th Mon Orange 2 Tags	10th Mon Green 1 Tag	13th Mon Blue 1 Tag

Those holding a senior grade

	8th Kyu Bottom Orange	7th Kyu Top Orange	5th Kyu Top Green	4th Kyu Bottom Blue
POINTS:	6	12	18	24

MARTIAL ARTS

Obtain a grading from one of the following Governing Bodies:-
British Aikido Board, British Council of Chinese Martial Arts, British Ju Jitsu Association Governing Body, British Kendo Association, British Taekwondo Council, United Kingdom Tang Soo Do Federation, British Karate Federation, English Karate Governing Body, Scottish Karate Board, Welsh Karate Federation
Note: Due to the nature of Martial Arts as traditional combat systems it is essential that Operating Authorities closely monitor the involvement of Award participants. Those young people wishing to undertake Martial Arts for the Physical Recreation Section must seek approval from their Operating Authority prior to commencing the activity.

	Lowest awardable grade	Second lowest awardable grade	Third lowest awardable grade	Fourth lowest awardable grade
POINTS:	6	12	18	24

MODERN BIATHLON, PENTATHLON AND TRIATHLON

Obtain the required number of points as laid down in the *Modern Pentathlon Association Rulebook* in the required disciplines

Biathlon	1500	1800	2100	
Pentathlon	1300	1700	2300	2900
Triathlon	3500	4200	4600	5000
POINTS:	6	12	18	24

ORIENTEERING

Obtain an Award of the British Orienteering Federation

	Orange	Red/Light Green	Green/Bronze	Brown/Blue/Silver/Gold
POINTS:	6	12	18	24

PARACHUTING

Obtain a qualification of the British Parachute Association (minimum age 16)

	'A' Licence	'B' Licence	'C' Licence
	-			
POINTS:	6	12	18	24

PARAGLIDING

Obtain a rating from the British Hang Gliding and Paragliding Association

	Student Pilot	Club Pilot	Pilot	Advanced Pilot
POINTS:	6	12	18	24

RIDING

Obtain an Efficiency Standard of the

Riding Club	Grade 1	Grade 2	Grade 3	Grade 4
Pony Club	D Standard	C Standard	B Standard	A Standard
British Horse Society	Progressive Test 5	Progressive Test 10	Progressive Test 12	-
POINTS:	6	12	18	24

ROWING AND SCULLING

Obtain a proficiency Award from the Amateur Rowing Association

	Watermanship or 50km	Sculling	250km	500km
POINTS:	6	12	18	24

SAILING AND WINDSURFING

Obtain a proficiency Award from the Royal Yachting Association

Cruising	-	Competent Crew	Day Skipper	Coastal Skipper
Young Sailors Scheme	Start Sailing 2	Start Sailing 3	Red or White Badge	Blue Badge
Dinghy (Adult)	Level 1	Level 2	Level 3 or 4	Level 5
Keelboat	Level 1	Level 2	Level 3 or 4	-
Windsurfing	Level 1	Level 2	Level 3 or Comp 1	Level 4 or Comp 2
POINTS:	6	12	18	24

SAND AND LAND YACHTING

Pass a sailing test of The British Federation of Sand and Land Yacht Clubs

	-	-	Sailing Pilot	-
POINTS:	6	12	18	24

SKATING

Ice - Pass a test judged by officials of the National Ice Skating Association of UK

	Basic 1-4	Basic 5-8	Advanced Figure 1-4 or Dance 1-3	Advanced Figure 5-8 or Dance 4-6
POINTS:	6	12	18	24

Roller - Pass a judged test by officials of the British Federation of Roller Skating

	Basic Skills Grades 1-4	Basic Skills Grades 5-8	Preliminary Figure/Free/ Dance Medal Test	Bronze Figure/Free/ Dance Medal Test
POINTS:	6	12	18	24

Ice or Roller 1/2 mile - mins and secs

	2.21 (2.28)	2.09 (2.16)	1.57 (2.04)	1.45 (1.52)
POINTS:	6	12	18	24

Where standards for females are different from males, they are shown in brackets.

SKIING

Alpine - Obtain a British Alpine Ski Award. (Details from the English Ski Council, Scottish National Ski Council or Ski Council of Wales.)

	Two Star	Three Star	Four Star	Five Star
POINTS:	6	12	18	24

For details of Freestyle (ballet) and Grass Skiing contact the English Ski Council

SUB-AQUA

Obtain an Award from the British Sub-Aqua Club

	Snorkel Diver	Open Water Snorkel Diver	Novice Diver	Sports Diver
POINTS:	6	12	18	24

SURFING

Obtain an Award from the British Surfing Association

	-	Single Fin	Twin Fin	Three Fin
POINTS:	6	12	18	24

SWIMMING

Obtain either a standard or score points. Details on page 297.

TABLE TENNIS

Obtain a Skills Award from the English Table Tennis Association

	Rookie Award	Improvers' Award	Players' Award	Matchplayer Award
POINTS:	6	12	18	24

TRAMPOLINING

Obtain a proficiency award of the British Trampoline Federation

	Preliminary Award	Elementary Bronze	Elementary Silver	Elementary Gold
POINTS:	6	12	18	24

WATER SKIING

Obtain a national grade of the British Water Ski Federation

	Bronze	Silver	Gold	-
POINTS:	6	12	18	24

WEIGHTLIFTING

Obtain a certified grade of the British Amateur Weight Lifters' Association based on two competition lifts

	-	Yellow	Orange	Green
POINTS:	6	12	18	24

WEIGHT TRAINING (FREE WEIGHTS)

Obtain a certified grade of the British Amateur Weightlifters Association based on all round Weight Training Awards

	-	1 Star grade	2 Star grade	3 Star grade
POINTS:	6	12	18	24

ACTIVITIES WITH SET STANDARDS
OF THE DUKE OF EDINBURGH'S AWARD

PHYSICAL ACHIEVEMENT
Introduction

All the events may be undertaken either outdoors or indoors (e.g. gymnasium or club hall). The only equipment needed is a size five football or netball, a chair or similar item, gym mat, markers, tape measure and a watch.

Undertake all seven events and select six to count. At least one point must be scored in each of the six events counted. The maximum score in any event is five points. A reasonable rest is to be allowed between each event. The tests may be spread over two sessions.

Description of Events

Test should be undertaken in the following order:

SPEED TEST
Run ten times between two lines marked on the ground or floor 9 metres apart. The score is determined by the time in which this exercise is completed.

Speed Test

BALL SPEED BOUNCE
Using a netball or size five football, stand behind a line 2 metres from wall. Hold ball with two hands against chest. Ball must be thrown with two hands so as to rebound from the wall into both hands behind the restraining line. Count the number of times the ball is successfully caught in 30 seconds. (It is recommended that a brick wall or similar solid surface is used for this event to ensure a satisfactory rebound.)

Ball Speed Bounce

• Physical
Achievement
- Speed Test
- Ball Speed
Bounce

TRUNK CURL TEST

(To be performed on a towel, mat or suitable equivalent). Lie on the back with legs bent. A 90 degree angle should be maintained between the upper and lower legs. Place hands on cheeks. Ankles should not be held. Sit up, curling trunk and head until both elbows touch upper legs and then return to the starting position. Although the feet may leave the floor, the right angle between the upper and lower legs must be maintained. The score is the number of curls completed in one minute.

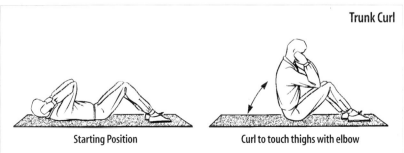

Trunk Curl

Starting Position   Curl to touch thighs with elbow

BAILEY BRIDGE

Start in the front support position (body in straight line supported by hands and toes only) with shoulders near to and facing a chair, stool or box on which a small object should rest (e.g. bean bag, duster, 5 cm. cube of wood). The seat of the chair should be approximately 45cm. from the floor. Take the object from the chair seat with one hand, place it on the floor, pick up the object with the other hand and replace it on the chair. Continue cycle. Count the number of times the object is successfully placed on the chair in thirty seconds.

Bailey Bridge

Starting Position

45cm

Lift article off
chair and place
on floor

Return with
other hand

• Physical
Achievement
- Trunk Curl
Test
- Bailey Bridge

PUSH-UP

Hand/foot version: Lie face down on the floor, hands under shoulders, palms flat on the floor. Straighten arms, without locking, to lift body, leaving only palms and toes on floor. Bend elbows until nose touches the floor or return to starting position. Repeat push-up. Scoring ceases if the body sags. The score is the number of push-ups completed in one minute.

Starting Position

Push-Up (hand/foot version)

Push Up

Lower until nose touches floor

or:

Hand/knee moderated version: Lie face down on the floor, hands under shoulders, palms flat on the floor with lower legs bent upwards from the knees. Straighten arms, without locking, to lift body, leaving only the palms and knees on floor, so that knees, hips and shoulders are in a straight line. This straight line should be maintained and the hands should not be allowed to move back towards the knees. Bend elbows until nose touches the floor or return to starting position. Repeat push-up. The score is the number of push-ups completed in one minute.

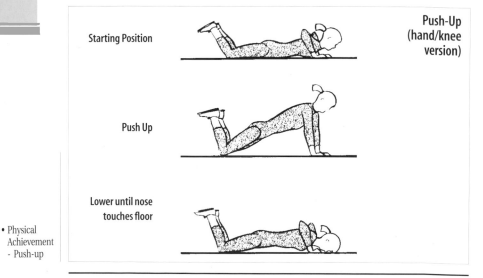

Starting Position

Push-Up (hand/knee version)

Push Up

Lower until nose touches floor

• Physical Achievement - Push-up

SINGLE LEG SQUAT THRUST

Starting Position: Set up two lines 50cm apart. Crouch with both hands placed flat on the floor and with the toes touching the front line. Take one leg back so that the foot is on the floor behind the rear line.

The test: Change legs so that each foot is alternately thrust over the rear line, with the hips remaining high. The score is the number of single leg squat thrusts, i.e. when each foot crosses the line, completed in the thirty seconds.

Single Leg Squat Thrust

Starting Position

Change Legs

50cm

RUN

Twenty laps of a rectangular circuit 12 metres by 8 metres, each corner marked by a small object. The score is determined by the time in which this exercise is completed.

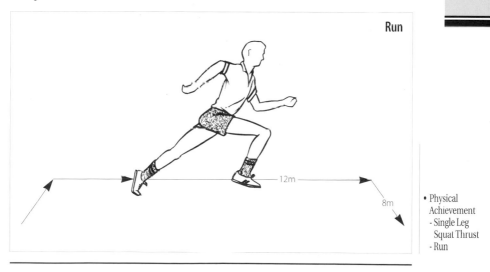

Run

12m

8m

• Physical
  Achievement
  - Single Leg
    Squat Thrust
  - Run

Physical Achievement - Scoring

Scoring - Males

TEST:		1	2	3	4	5
Speed Test	Time (secs)	28	26	25	24	23
Ball Speed Bounce	No. of catches in 30 secs	30	35	40	45	50
Trunk Curl Test	No. in 1 minute	20	28	34	40	45
Bailey Bridge	No. in 30 secs	12	17	19	21	22
Push-Up hand/foot version	No. in 1 minute	15	23	27	34	50
Or Push-Up hand/knee moderated version	No. in 1 minute	25	37	44	58	68
Single Leg Squat Thrust	No. in 30 secs	40	60	70	76	82
Run	Time (mins &secs)	4.20	4.00	3.40	3.20	3.10

Scoring - Females

TEST:		1	2	3	4	5
Speed Test	Time (secs)	32	28	27	26	25
Ball Speed Bounce	No. of catches in 30 secs	20	26	32	36	38
Trunk Curl Test	No. in 1 minute	10	20	28	32	36
Bailey Bridge	No. in 30 secs	12	16	18	20	22
Push-Up hand/foot version	No. in 1 minute	8	14	18	24	30
Or Push-Up hand/knee moderated version	No. in 1 minute	14	24	28	40	45
Single Leg Squat Thrust	No. in 30 secs	35	50	65	72	80
Run	Time (mins & secs)	4.50	4.30	4.10	3.50	3.40

• Physical
  Achievement
  - Scoring

SWIMMING

Non-Swimmers
Learn to swim at least 20 yards (18.3 metres) - 12 points.
For the test, jump or dive in and swim unaided without stopping.

Swimmers
Either:
1. Obtain one of the following Governing Body qualifications or:
2. Pass a Duke of Edinburgh's Award Composite Speed Test

a) Governing Body qualifications
Amateur Swimming Association - Proficiency in Personal Survival

	Level 2	-	-	-
POINTS:	6	12	18	24

Swimming Challenge Awards

	-	Bronze	Silver	Gold
POINTS:	6	12	18	24

Swimming Teachers' Association Survival Award

	-	Bronze	Silver	Gold
POINTS:	6	12	18	24

Amateur Swimming Association - Synchronised Swimming Award

	Pre-lim Synchro	Grade 1	Grade II	Grade III
POINTS:	6	12	18	24

b) Composite Speed tests
Swim 25 yards or 25 metres without turns. This should be undertaken three times, each time using a different stroke. All three are to be taken during a single session, but not continuously. At least one point should be scored for each stroke - the maximum score for any one stroke is 10 points.

STROKE	POINTS:	1	2	3	4	5	6	7	8	9	10
25yds Backstroke (without a dive)	Secs.	27	26	25	24	23	22	21	20	19	18
25yds Breaststroke	Secs.	29	28	27	26	25	24	23	22	21	20
25yds Butterfly	Secs.	26	25	24	23	22	21	20	19	18	17
25yds Freestyle	Secs.	24	23	22	21	20	19	18	17	16	15
25m Backstroke (without a dive)	Secs.	30	29	28	27	26	25	24	23	22	21
25m Breaststroke	Secs.	32	31	30	29	28	27	26	25	24	23
25m Butterfly	Secs.	29	28	27	26	25	24	23	22	21	20
25m Freestyle	Secs.	27	26	25	24	23	22	21	20	19	18

PHYSICAL RECREATION STANDARDS

• Swimming

BOWLING (TENPIN)

General Requirements

1. The aim is to achieve a consistent scoring average. Throughout the period of participation, young people should keep a certified personal score card and a note of any problems which result in low scoring. For assessment, the Instructor should issue a certificate confirming that instruction has taken place on a regular basis.

2. Instruction and assessment should be carried out by any BTBA qualified Instructor, or school teacher in possession of a BTBA Teachers Certificate. For details of local Instructors, please contact the British Tenpin Bowling Association.

Programme

Participants should:

1. Have a full knowledge of scoring and pin positioning by numbers.
2. Know how to choose a bowling ball to fit the hand.
3. Be able to demonstrate the four step approach to right and left hand bowlers.
4. Have knowledge of correct stance, follow-through and the importance of hand, wrist and thumb positioning.
5. Know about the various types of bowling shoes.
6. Be able to demonstrate the straight ball, hook ball and the reasons for the use of spot and arrow markings on the lane.
7. Show good manners, courtesy to other bowlers and sportsmanship within the Bowling Centre.
8. Have knowledge of lane dimensions and materials and of pin and ball composition with their respective weights.
9. Bowl regularly with a recognised League affiliated to the BTBA and consistently improve their scoring average.
10. Observe competitive Bowling such as an area BTBA Championships.

British Tenpin Bowling Association

• Bowling
 - Tenpin

BOWLS

Carpet Bowling

Participants should:
1. Know the basic rules as published in the *Scottish Carpet Bowling Association Handbook.*
2. Have knowledge of the various woods and how to choose them, and of the requirements for correct equipment.
3. Deliver bowl competently.
4. Take part in friendly singles matches.
5. Be able to place the woods consistently.
6. Compete in a team singles match.
7. Demonstrate drawing, guarding, chap-and-lie and striking.
8. Compete in friendly doubles matches.
9. Play in a major competition, showing skill in all basic plays.
10. Understand how to complete score sheets, and tournament draws of varied kinds.

Scottish Carpet Bowling Association

Crown Green Bowls

Participants should:
1. Know the Laws of the Game as published in the *British Crown Green Handbook.*
2. Have an awareness of the aims and functions of the British Crown Green Bowling Association and its County Associations.
3. Understand the handicap system in Crown Green Bowls.
4. Have a working knowledge of score cards and tournament sheets.
5. Be able to deliver a bowl both finger and thumb bias competently.
6. Obtain a high enough standard of play to gain a position in a club team.
7. Play in an open competition.

British Crown Green Bowling Association Handbook

Flat Green Bowls

Participants should:

1. Know the basic laws as published in the *English or Scottish Bowling Association Yearbook*. Obtain the *EBA Guidance for New Bowlers*.
2. Know the requirements regarding correct dress, i.e. whites or greys, correct footwear, waterproofs.
3. Know the types and sizes of bowls and how to choose the correct size and weight to suit the player.
4. Learn how to place the mat correctly and demonstrate how to deliver the jack to a required length including the correct way to deliver a bowl for forehand and backhand.
5. Play in friendly single games.
6. Know the rules regarding singles, pairs, triples and fours games, including ends required to be played for each game.
7. Know and be able to demonstrate, according to the level of skill attained, shots which can be played in a game: the draw, resting out a bowl, trailing the jack, follow through shots, fire or drive, block or stopper, touching bowl on the green, touching bowl in the ditch, resting a bowl, resting a bowl adjacent to the jack.
8. Play in club events.
9. Learn the correct method of measuring and be able to use different types of measuring equipment: spring measure, string measure, callipers, feeler gauges and wedges.
10. Understand how to complete score cards, how club match results are calculated and how to mark singles matches.
11. Know the duties of each player in pairs, triples and fours.
12. Play in different types of game.
13. Learn the tactics of play by taking part in club games.
14. Play in individual competitions.

English Bowling Association

• Bowls
 - Flat Green
   Bowls

BOXING

General Requirements

1. Instructors must be approved by the Amateur Boxing Association.
2. Participants must secure the approval of the Operating Authority in writing before undertaking this activity.
3. Parental permission must be gained in writing before commencing this activity if the participant is under 18 years.

Programme

Instructors should follow the course of instruction in a club approved by the Amateur Boxing Association.

CAVING AND POTHOLING

General Requirements

1. Caving or potholing is the exploration of natural and sometimes mined underground systems and a primary motive should be the desire to learn about such places. A vital element in caving is the satisfaction and pleasure obtained from personal discovery and not the mere overcoming of a natural obstacle or competing against other cavers.
2. The exploration of a cave is a group activity – but the group should be small, both for mobility underground and so that each person is an integral member. As far as possible each member of the party should be self-reliant at the level of difficulty attempted.
3. Participants must realise that caves are a unique and fragile environment and any damage will have a lasting effect. Conservation must be learned at the outset.
4. **All caving and potholing expeditions must be led by an experienced adult caver who has completed the Local Cave Leader Assessment Scheme or who holds the Cave Instructor Certificate, or an experienced person approved by the Operating Authority.**

*Note: The Caving Code and the Conservation Code is contained in the leaflets **So You Want to Go Caving** and **Protect our Caves**. These, and advice on leadership are obtainable from The National Caving Association.*

Programme

Participants should:

1. Be aware of and understand the need for ensuring that visits to caves cause no damage. Ensure the highest standards of behaviour and know the Conservation Code.

2. Appreciate the importance of suitable clothing and personal equipment, such as boots, helmet, lighting, belt, and know what to look for when selecting it.

3. Know about underground hazards such as deep water, rock falls, hypothermia, getting lost, and appreciate the difficulty of rescue after even a minor accident.

4. Know about weather and flooding, particularly when to avoid caves with active streamways and in times of rain or unsettled weather.

5. Know what to do in the event of an accident or underground emergency. Have knowledge of basic First Aid.

6. Know what to include in group emergency equipment: First Aid kit, spare lighting, food, whistle, survival bags.

7. Have knowledge of and be able to call out the Cave Rescue.

8. Have a basic understanding of cave formation and features.

9. Be conversant with equipment for pitches and other obstacles: handlines, traverse lines, lifelines, ladders, cowstails, harnesses. Be able to demonstrate how to tie appropriate knots, tie onto the rope and belay using the Italian Hitch method. (The extent to which this area is covered will depend on the caves available. Single Rope Techniques may be learnt but only if taught and supervised by an adult with the Cave Instructor Certificate.)

10. Learn about and discuss the care and maintenance of equipment.

11. Demonstrate commitment and improve skills by descending a variety of caves and by following an associated activity, e.g. cave photography, cave surveying, keeping a log, or learning more about the equipment used.

12. Organise and lead at least one expedition of appropriate difficulty.

National Caving Association

• Caving and
Potholing

CROQUET

General Requirements

1. Association Croquet is a game where skill in making individual shots and knowledge of tactics are equally important. Variations of the game are played in many back gardens up and down the country, but the official game is played to the rules of The Croquet Association, the game's governing body.
2. At club level, the game is played on a lawn 35 yards long by 28 yards wide, and many croquet clubs provide coaching for beginners throughout the season. Addresses of individual croquet clubs, publications to help the beginner and advanced player, and copies of the official rules can be obtained from The Croquet Association.

Programme

Participants should:

1. Know the basic laws of the game, as published by The Croquet Association in the booklet *Basic Laws*.
2. Join a croquet club, if possible, and obtain some coaching.
3. Understand the basic stroke sequence: roquet, croquet, continuation shot.
4. Practise single ball shots: taking position, hoop running, roquet, rush.
5. Practise two ball shots: take-off, stop shot, drive, roll, split shot.
6. Practise hoop approaches: rush, croquet shot, run hoop, roquet.
7. Practise playing 4-ball breaks.
8. Understand common faults: crush, double hit, push.
9. Obtain a Croquet Association Handicap. Play handicap games with other clubs.
10. Know and understand theory and tactics:
    a. 4-ball break.
    b. 3-ball break.
    c. The standard opening.
    d. How to use bisques to set up a break.
11. Play games at a croquet club with experienced players.
12. Enter a Croquet Association Tournament as either an individual or a member of a team.

Practice targets

1. Roquets: (6 feet): 7 out of 10, (12 feet): 4 out of 10.

• Croquet

2. Hoop running and taking position: place a ball on the yard line in front of hoop 1. Using 20 shots, take it through the first 6 hoops in order and then hit the peg.

3. 4-ball break: make a 4-ball break through 6 hoops using 3 bisques.

The Merit Awards awarded by The Croquet Association may be used as a good indication of performance.

The Croquet Association

DANCE

If the appropriate form of Dance is not included in the standards section, reference should be made to the following section on Dance as a participation activity. Programmes for the following forms of Dance are included below:

- English Traditional Dance (Country and Morris, Step & Sword).
- Indian Classical Dance (Kathak).
- Irish Traditional Dance (Ceili and Irish Step).
- Scottish Country Dancing.
- Scottish Highland Dancing.
- Welsh Folk Dancing.

Other forms of Dance, such as Manx, Traditional Chinese or Polish Dance, may be undertaken as a participation activity but a programme should first be drawn up and submitted to the participant's Operating Authority (and at Gold to Award Headquarters) for approval, before commencement of the programme. For further advice on possible contacts or information contact the Award Headquarters.

English Traditional Dancing

General Requirements

The English Folk Dance and Song Society (EFDSS) publishes annually a directory of Country Dance Clubs and Morris, Sword and Step Dance Teams throughout Britain. Participants are advised to join one of these in their locality for instruction and guidance. The EFDSS can recommend suitable Assessors.

English Country Dancing

General Requirements

Participants should be able to dance in any position in the set and demonstrate understanding of the music, rhythm and phrasing as well as knowledge of a variety of steps and figures.

Programme

Participants should:

1. Be able to perform a varied programme choosing 3 dances from List A and play, whistle or sing 3 accompanying tunes.
2. Be able to perform a varied programme choosing 3 dances from A, 2 dances from B and play, whistle or sing 4 accompanying tunes.
3. Be able to perform a varied programme:
   a. Choose 3 dances from each of Lists A, B and C and play, whistle or sing 6 of the accompanying tunes.
   b. Call any dance from List A.
   c. perform a dance which the participant has composed to show:
      - Knowledge and understanding of the partnership between appropriate figures and musical phrasing.
      - Originality and innovation.
      - An understanding of the necessary components in creating a dance in the traditional style.

List A:
   Up the Sides and Down the Middle, Nottingham Swing, The Rifleman, Ninepins, Drops of Brandy, Circle Waltz, Galopede, Yorkshire Square Eight, Hullichan Roundabout.

List B:
   Black Jack, Dorset Four Hand Reel, Bonny Breast Knot (Sussex Version), Bonny Breast Knot (Somerset and Devon), Morpeth Rant, Hunt the Squirrel, Speed the Plough, Double Lead Through Triumph (Dorset), Cottagers.

List C:
   Fandango, Shrewsbury Lasses, Bishop, Trip to Highgate, The Militia, Green Sleeves and Yellow Lace, Newcastle.

Notes: For Dances in Lists A & B see Community Dance Manuals (published by EFDSS), for those in List C contact EFDSS Librarian.

• Dance
  - English
    Country
    Dancing

Morris, Sword and Step

General Requirements

As with all team dancing, the participants should be constantly aware of the other members of the team and work together as a whole. Each person should be able to dance in any position in the team.

Programme

Participants should:

1. Be able to perform 2 dances from one or more of the following traditions:
   a. Cotswold Morris.
   b. Border Morris.
   c. North West Morris.
   d. Longsword/Rapper.
   e. Step/Clog.
2. Be able to perform 4 dances from at least 2 of the categories listed above.
3. Be able to perform:
   either: 3 Cotswold Morris dances
   or: 3 Border Morris dances
   or: 3 North West Morris dances
   and either: 1 Longsword/Rapper dance
   or: a solo traditional dance e.g. Morris Jig, Broom Dance, Step/Clog Dance.
4. Give a brief description of the historical/social background to each of the dance traditions performed.

Indian Classical Dance (Kathak)

Introduction

Kathak is one of the most well-known classical dance styles of the Indian sub-continent. It originated and was developed in the Northern Region as a story-telling, recitative, mimetic art form. The main features of this dance form are expressive and graceful movements of the body, emphasis on footwork and different types of pirouettes. It is usually accompanied by traditional Indian music, percussive and melodic, which complements the dance.

General Requirements

1. Good body posture.
2. Good sense of rhythm.
3. Good power of concentration and alertness.
4. Time and commitment to practise outside class hours.

Programme

Participants should:

1. First:
   a. Dance Tatkar in three speeds.
   b. Memorise the syllabus of Tatkar and recite in the three speeds.
   c. Perform the basic Hasta – s and co-ordinate with Tatkar.
   d. Learn the 5 step-spin and 8 step-spin in first two speeds (Bhramari).
   e. Perform three Tihae with Padhant.
   f. Dance three Tukra with Padhant that involve the above Bhramari(s).
2. Then:
   a. Dance the 5 step and 8 step Bhramari in the third speed.
   b. Learn two Tukra that use the above Bhramari.
   c. Become familiar with the concept of Taala, recognise it on Tabla and dance with the Tabla. Undertake rhythm exercises on Taala.
   d. Learn one Tez-Amad.
   e. Dance a footwork that involves three varieties of syllables.
3. And then:
   a. Dance five Tukra and five Tihai in Teental with the accompaniment of Tabla and also do the Padhant of each
   b. Dance and recite a Kavitta with emphasis on facial expression.
   c. Dance a Lari or Laya-bant with emphasis on facial expression.
   d. Learn a Vandana.

Institute of Indian Art and Culture

PHYSICAL RECREATION

PARTICIPATION PROGRAMMES

• Dance
 - Indian Classical
   Dance (Kathak)

Irish Traditional Dancing

General Requirements

1. Irish Dancing should be performed gracefully. The carriage of the body should be natural, upright and with the arms hanging in a relaxed manner by the sides. In Ceili Dancing, when performing hand movements, dancers should hold their hands at shoulder level. Knowledge of both the music and the time signature for each dance is required, e.g. Light Jig, Single Jig and Treble Jig – 6/8, Slip-Jig – 9/8, Reel – 2/4 or 4/4, Hornpipe – 4/4.

2. Participants may follow either or both of the set programmes. Each programme is progressive and commences with basic requirements. The first programme is for Irish Ceili Dancing and includes a selection of the popular figure dances normally danced at Ceilis. The second programme is for Irish Step or Solo Dancing for individual participants and covers both the basic and advanced solo dances.

Programme for Traditional Irish Ceili Dancing

The dances in this section are figure dances in group formation, as distinct from Irish step or solo dances. They are simple and easy to perform and require a knowledge of only the most elementary steps. These dances lend themselves well to recreational and social use.

Participants should be able to perform:

1. a. Promenade step (in both double jig and reel rhythm).
    b. Side step (seven and two threes).
    c. Jig step (both rise and grind and sink and grind).
2. a. Advance and retire.
    b. Swing round.
    c. Right and left wheel.
3. a. The Walls of Limerick.
    b. The Siege of Ennis.
    c. The Bridge of Athlone.
4. a. The Siege of Carrick.
    b. Rinnce Mor.
    c. The Harvestime Jig.
5. a. The Full Chain.
    b. Four sevens.
    c. The Square.

• Dance
 - Irish
 Traditional
 Dancing

6. a. The Antrim Reel.
   b. The Four Hand Reel.
   c. The Fairy Reel or Glencar Reel.
7. a. The Double Quarter Chain.
   b. Slip sides.
   c. The High Cauled Cap.
   d. The Eight Hand Jig.
8. a. Lannigan's Ball.
   b. The Eight Hand Reel.
   c. The Three Tunes.
   d. The Sixteen Hand Reel.

Programme for Traditional Irish Step Dancing

The following programme is progressive and should be followed by individual participants. There is a greater emphasis on the footwork in step dancing and care should be taken to ensure that the feet are crossed. The right foot should be placed in front of the left at the start of each dance with the toes pointing outwards.

Participants should:
1. Be able to perform:
   a. Promenade Step (in both Double Jig and Reel rhythm).
   b. Side Step (seven and two threes).
   c. Jig Step (both rise and grind and sink and grind) and explain the rhythm for the Jig 6/8 and the Reel 2/4 or 4/4.
2. Be able to perform:
   a. The basic Solo Reel.
   b. The light Double Jig.
3. Be able to:
   a. Identify the rhythm of the Single Jig and the Slip Jig.
   b. Perform the basic Single Jig.
   c. Perform the basic Slip Jig.
4. Be able to perform:
   a. The Double Reel.
   b. Basic Treble Jig.
5. Be able to:
   a. Identify the rhythm of the Hornpipe.
   b. Perform St. Patrick's Day (Traditional).
   c. Perform the basic Hornpipe.
6. Be able to perform:
   a. The Blackbird (Traditional).
   b. Advanced Double Reel.

• Dance
  - Irish
    Traditional
    Dancing

7. Be able to perform:
   a. The Job of Journeywork (Traditional).
   b. The Advanced Slip-Jig.
8. Be able to perform:
   a. The Garden of Daisies (Traditional).
   b. Advanced Treble Jig.
   c. Advanced Hornpipe.

Scottish Country Dancing

General Requirements

In Scottish Country Dancing a knowledge of the basic steps and formation is more valuable than the memorisation of isolated dances.

Note: This programme has been compiled to make it possible to work through it using only the following books: 'Sixteen Popular Country Dances', '24 Favourite Country Dances', 'The Book of Graded Scottish Country Dances'. The alternative dances, however, are chosen from other books.

Programme

Participants should:

1. Be able to perform the following steps rhythmically in reel and jig time:
   a. Skip change of step.
   b. Slip step.
   c. Pas de Basque.
   d. The 'stepping-up' step.
2. Know the following formations:
   a. Four hands across.
   b. Right and left.
   c. Down the middle and up.
   d. Allemande.
   e. Cast off.
   f. Poussette.
   g. Four hands round.
3. Be able to perform the following dances, one from each pair to be selected:
   a. The Highland Fair – *Graded Book* or Cumberland Reel – *Book 1.*
   b. The White Cockade – *24 Favourite Country Dances* or The Isle of Skye – *Book 10.*

c. Lady Catherine Bruce's Reel – *Graded Book* or The Bob of Fettercairn – *Book 6*.

d. Corn Rigs – *24 Favourites* or The River Cree – *16 Popular Country Dances*.

4. Know the following:
   a. Strathspey travelling step.
   b. Strathspey setting step.

5. Know the following formations:
   a. Reel of three.
   b. Six hands round.
   c. Set and turn corners.
   d. Set and turn corners, followed by reel of three.
   e. Adaptation of all known formations except Poussette to Strathspey rhythm.

6. Perform the following dances (one from each pair):
   a. Dumbarton Drums – *24 Favourites*.
   b. Jenny's Bawbee – *24 Favourites* or Monymusk – *16 Popular Dances*.
   c. Speed the Plough – *24 Favourites* or The Fairy Dance – *Book 3*.
   d. Mrs Macleod – *24 Favourites* or I'll Mak'ye Fain to Follow Me – *Book 6*.

7. Know:
   a. One reel time setting step, e.g. Pas de Basque and coupé.
   b. One Strathspey setting step, e.g. Glasgow Highlander's step.

8. Know the following formations:
   a. Set to and turn corners, followed by reel of three.
   b. Turn corner and partner.
   c. Double triangles.
   d. Set to corner, turn right to face partner, etc.

9. Perform the following dances (one from each pair):
   a. Madge Wildfire's Strathspey – *16 Popular Dances* or The Earl of Home – *Book 12*.
   b. Duke of Perth – *24 Favourites* or Dalkeith's Strathspey – *Book 9*.

PHYSICAL RECREATION

PARTICIPATION PROGRAMMES

• Dance
  - Scottish
    Country
    Dancing

313

c. Lord Rosslyn's Fancy – *16 Popular Dances* or My Mither's Comin' in – *Book 15*.
d. Lady Susan Stewart's Reel – *24 Favourites* or General Stuart's Reel – *Book 10*.
e. The Eightsome Reel – *24 Favourites* or The Buchan Eightsome – *Book 21*.

Royal Society of Scottish Country Dancing

Scottish Highland Dancing

General Requirements

1. Participants should start the programme at their own level of aptitude and experience and should cover as much of it as they can in the time it takes to qualify.

2. Information on this activity and advice concerning assessment, which should be conducted by an Assessor approved by the Board, can be obtained from the Scottish Official Board of Highland Dancing. Only steps approved by the Board may be used. If participants wish to include alternative National Dances, contact the SOBHD for advice.

Programme

Participants should:

1. Be able to dance:
    a. The Highland Fling (4 Steps) 1st step Shedding; 2nd Toe-and-Heel; 6th Crossover; 8th last Shedding.
    b. Sword Dance (2 slow and 1 quick) 1st step Addressing the Sword; 4th Pointing; 8th Crossing and Pointing.
    c. Sean Triubhas (3 slow and 1 quick) 1st step Brushing; 2nd Side Travel; 4th Backward Travel; 11th Toe Heel and Rock.

2. Be able to dance these dances using the following steps:
    a. The Highland Fling (4 steps) 1st step Shedding; 4th Rocking; 7th Shake and Turn; 8th Last Shedding.
    b. Sword Dance (2 slow and 1 quick) 1st step Addressing the Sword; 2nd Open Pas-de-Bas; 7th Open Pas-de-Bas Quick Step.
    c. Sean Triubhas (4 slow and 2 quick) 1st step Brushing; 3rd Diagonal Travel; 4th alter Backward Travel; 5th Travelling Balance; 10th Shedding the Backstep; 12th Pointing and Backstep.

d. Strathspey and Reel of Tulloch (2 Strathspeys) setting steps – 3rd step Toe-and-Heel; 6th Crossover. Tulloch (4 parts) setting steps – 1st step Pas-de-Bas; 6th Balance and Round the Leg; 4th Brushing; Last step Highcutting.

3. Be able to dance the following 4 dances using the steps indicated:

   a. Highland Fling (4 steps) 1st step Shedding; 2nd Backstepping; 6th Crossover; 8th Last Shedding.

   b. Sword Dance (3 slow and 1 quick) 1st step Addressing the Sword; 5th Diagonal Points; 3rd Toe-and-Heel; 8th Crossing and Pointing (Alternate Method for Bar 1).

   c. Sean Triubhas (4 slow and 2 quick) 1st step Brushing; 2nd Side Travel; 5th Travelling Balance; 8th Side Heel and Toe; 11th Toe Heel and Rock; 13th Heel-and-Toe and Shedding.

   d. Strathspey and Reel of Tulloch (2 Strathspeys) setting steps – 3rd step Toe-and-Heel; 5th Alt Second Backstepping; (2 Highland Reel). Setting steps 10th step Shuffle; Last Highcutting.

4. Be able to dance the following 4 dances using the steps indicated:

   a. Highland Fling (6 steps) 1st step Shedding; 2nd Backstepping; 4th Rocking; 5th Second Backstep; 6th Alt Crossover; 8th Alt Last Shedding.

   b. Sword Dance (2 slow and 2 quick) 1st step Addressing the Sword; 5th Diagonal Points; 7th Open Pas-de-Basque Quick Step; 8th Crossing and Pointing.

   c. Sean Triubhas (4 slow and 2 quick) 1st step Brushing; 2nd Side Travel; 7th High Cut in Front and Balance; 6th Alt Lead and Shedding.

   d. Strathspey and Highland Reel (2 Strathspey) Setting steps 3rd step Toe-and-Heel; 5th Alt Second Backstepping; (2 Highland Reel) Setting Steps 10th step Shuffle; Last Highcutting).

Scottish Official Board of Highland Dancing

Welsh Folk Dancing

For information and queries regarding assessment refer to the Welsh Folk Dance Society.

Participants should:

1. Understand and be able to perform basic movements and steps including:
    a. Forward and Back, Siding, Stors (hands across).
    b. Circles, arming, setting, Promenade, Gypsy, Heys (various).
    c. Figure of Eight, Step Hop, Reel step, Balance and Swing.
2. Follow brief instructions to dance social dances including:
    a. Simple longways (Cofi o'r Dre).
    b. Double circle (Ffarwel i'r Marian).
    c. Simple circle (Cylch y Cymry).
    d. Sicilian Circle (Robin Ddiog).
    e. Square Dance (Clawdd Offa).
3. Be able to dance two longways duple minor dances chosen from:
    a. The Welsh Jig.   b. St. David's Day.
    c. Croen y Ddafad Felen. d. Sweet Richard.
    e. The Welsh March.
4. Be familiar with:
    a. Different dance rhythms including: Jig, Reel, Waltz, March.
    b. The way folk dance is handed down through the generations.
5. Perform three dances suitable for display such as:
    a. Arglwydd Caernarfon.
    b. The Llanover Reel.
    c. Tŷ Coch Caerdydd.
    d. Powell's Fancy.
    e. Meillionen.
    f. Dawns Gwyl Ifan.
6. Either:
    a. Perform a solo dance in the Welsh tradition, e.g. Dawns Morfa Rhuddlan, Yr Hudoles, Dawns y Glocsen.
       or:
    b. Teach a younger group two dances from section 2.

Welsh Folk Dance Society

• Dance
  - Welsh Folk
  Dancing

FITNESS ACTIVITIES

Introduction
Any **one** of the following activities can be followed as a participation programme:
- **Circuit Training.**
- **Exercise Machines/Multi-gym.**
- **Exercise to Music including Aerobics, Aquarobics and Step Aerobics.**
- **Running.**
- **Skipping.**

The aims of this programme are:
1. To encourage participation in a personal health and fitness programme.
2. To enable participants to show an improvement in general fitness.
3. To develop, in each participant, a knowledge of how to maintain and monitor fitness for a healthy and enjoyable lifestyle.

General Requirements
1. The qualification of the Instructor for each activity is given under each separate heading but it is important that such a person is experienced in working with young people.
2. **All equipment used should be in good condition and the working area must provide space for each participant to exercise safely.**
3. Instructors must be made aware that the activity is being undertaken as part of The Duke of Edinburgh's Award.
4. The ratio of Instructors/class members must be sufficiently low to allow supervision of the individual.
5. Participants should:
   a. Wear suitable clothing and footwear
   b. Have an understanding of warming up prior to exercise and cooling down after exercise.
   c. Understand why exercise is an important component of health.
   d. Be taught to recognise the onset of fatigue and withdraw from any session as soon as the symptoms are recognised.
   e. Not adopt any exercise position which results in pain or discomfort.

• Fitness Activities

Circuit Training and Exercise Machines/Multigym

General Requirements

Instructors should be qualified PE teachers or approved for these activities by the Operating Authority. Where free weights, exercise machines or similar resistance exercise equipment is used, the Instructor must have taken an appropriate course to qualify for such use.

Programme

Select at least five 'Stations' ensuring that at least three cater specifically for muscular strength, muscular endurance and cardiovascular training.

Participants should be provided with 'exercise cards' which state clearly the load/distance/ repetitions/time as appropriate for each individual with provision for adjustment.

Exercise to Music
including Aerobics, Aquarobics and Step Aerobics

General Requirements

1. In each of these three activities the key principles of aerobic activity are:
    -   Warm up, stretching and pulse raising.
    -   Aerobic build-up.
    -   Muscular strength and endurance.
    -   Cool down.

2. Progression is made as a participant's fitness and understanding of the activity increases either by the intensity and/or speed and/or duration of the exercises, with variations of those exercises and/or the range of movement involved. The frequency of participation also has a marked effect on progression.

1. Aerobics

Instructors should either:

a. Be a qualified PE teacher with appropriate experience of aerobic exercise.

or:

b. Hold an RSA Exercise to Music qualification.

or:

c. Hold an equivalent qualification approved by the Operating Authority.

2. Aquarobics

Instructors should either:

a. Be a qualified PE teacher with appropriate experience of aerobic exercise and have attended a course related to aquarobics.

or:

b. Hold an RSA Certificate in Exercise to Music and have attended a course related to aquarobics.

or:

c. Hold an equivalent qualification approved by the Operating Authority.

3. Step Aerobics

Instructors should either:

a. Be a qualified PE teacher with appropriate experience of aerobic exercise and have attended an additional course related to step aerobics.

or:

b. Hold an RSA Certificate in Exercise to Music and have attended a course related to step aerobics.

or:

c. Hold an equivalent qualification approved by the Operating Authority.

Note: Participants in this activity should be made aware of the safety practices in step assembly, the height at which to work and movement off and onto the step.

• Fitness Activities
- Exercise to Music including Aerobics, Aquarobics, Step Aerobics

Running

General Requirements

Instructors should be knowledgeable and experienced in the activity and acceptable to the Operating Authority.

Note: If running on roads, light coloured or reflective clothing should be worn, especially in poor visibility.

Participants should:

1. Demonstrate knowledge of prevention and basic treatment of injuries which may occur such as blisters, sprained ankles, shin soreness etc.
2. Appreciate the nutritional and fluid intake requirements for longer distance running.
3. Wear clothing which will maintain an appropriate body temperature.

Programme

Participants should:

1. Develop from walk to run/ walk to run a set distance.
2. Increase the distance over a period of weeks (e.g week 1 = 2 miles, week 12 = 6 miles).
3. Decrease the time for a set distance.
4. Increase the distance for a set time.
5. Increase the number of running sessions per week (e.g. week 1 = 1 session, week 12 = 3 sessions).

Skipping

General Requirements

Instructors should be knowledgeable and experienced in the activity and acceptable to the Operating Authority.

Programme

Over the period of participation, participants should develop speed and duration, and increase the frequency of training sessions, in each of the following exercises:

1. Slow spring steps with rebound (plain skips).
2. Running steps (on the spot and travelling).
3. Step-hop (with knee raising).
4. Pas-de-Bas and at least two other dance steps.
5. All the above with changes of tempo, with backward and forward turning rope and with methods of turning to face another direction.
6. Perform four different sequences of steps taken from items 1 to 5 above.

FIVES

Eton Fives

General Requirements

Participants should know something about the origins of Eton Fives and the method of play and participate in competitive matches.

Programme

Participants should have a knowledge of:

1. Mastering service throw.
2. Mastering returns of service (the Cut).
3. Returning the Cut.
4. Use of both hands.
5. Volleying.
6. Shots off the Pepper Pot.
7. Straight drives
8. Angled shots.
9. Positional play.
10. Tactics.
11. Advanced techniques.
12. Scoring.
13. Rules of the game.
14. Equipment.

Eton Fives Association

Rugby Fives

General Requirements

Participants should know about the origins of Fives and be aware that Rugby Fives is only one of three officially recognised forms of the game.

Programme

Participants should:

1. Know the rules of the game of Rugby Fives and be able to keep the score in both singles and doubles.
2. Be able to serve and receive service with a reasonable degree of competence against an opponent of a similar standard.
3. Be able to play the ball with either hand with a reasonable degree of control over the direction and strength of the stroke.
4. Strive to enlarge his repertoire of strokes, as well as being able to drive the ball hard and low. Be able to play lobs and drop shots and to make use of the angles. (Although a majority of shots will be played after the ball has bounced, the ability to volley should also be developed).
5. Develop the ability to predict, as quickly as possible, how the path of the ball, struck by an opponent, will be affected by contact with the walls of the court in order to move to a suitable position from which next to play it.
6. Show an appreciation of the importance of good positioning and of the need to move during a rally, not only so as to be in a good position to play shots but also so as to enable opponent(s) to do likewise.
7. Be aware of what constitutes good court manners and know when a let should be asked for and/or offered.
8. Develop an understanding of tactics so as to play appropriate shots during the course of a rally.
9. Show an ability to work in conjunction with a partner in doubles so that the two of them function as effectively as possible as a unit.
10. Always strive to improve the standard of play.
11. Participate in competitive events within the club.
12. Participate in inter-club events.

Rugby Fives Association

GYMNASTICS – EDUCATIONAL

Note: For other forms of Gymnastics, see the section on Governing Body standards.

General Requirements

1. The aim is to increase the participant's understanding of movement (as applied to gymnastics) and ability to make use of this knowledge.
2. The participant should therefore be able to:
   a. Show technical competence. This demands precision in the use of whichever bodily, dynamic or spatial factors are chiefly involved.
   b. Answer with inventiveness and accuracy tasks which can be interpreted in a wide variety of ways.
   c. Work with a partner – while they work, participants should prove that they can observe accurately and show adaptability and sensitivity to one another's actions.
   d. Perform sequences – a sequence should consist of three or more main actions neatly linked with one another either directly or by definite actions.

Programme

Participants should be able to perform:

1. **In floor work – create a sequence:**
   a. Containing contrasts of quick and slow movements.
   b. Using bending and stretching movements.
   c. Using twisting and turns with travelling.
   d. Using rolling and balancing the weight on the hands.
2. **On simple apparatus:**
   a. On window ladders or wall bars, either:
      - make a rhythmic pattern of movement including climbing, hanging leg gestures and balance
      or:
      - make as continuous a sequence of twisting movement as possible and include some upside-down positions.
   b. Arrange a combination of apparatus (box and bars, horse and forms, etc.) and show the following on it:
      - a sequence which shows contrasts of speed
      - a sequence showing a variety of ways of vaulting on, off and over the apparatus
      - a sequence based on a movement idea of their own choice.

• Gymnastics
 - Educational

3. **In floor work:**
   a. Create a sequence using bending and stretching with movement on the spot, travelling and jumping and showing clear use of high and low levels. Make a sequence with twisting movements (including fixing various parts of the body while moving the rest).
   b. Working with a partner, show a sequence in exact unison involving large far reaching, slower movements contrasting with smaller more compact, quicker movements. Working with a partner, show a sequence involving the bearing of one another's weight in a variety of ways and showing economy and continuity.

4. **On simple apparatus:**
   (As for item 2, but co-operating with a partner.)

5. **On main apparatus:**
   a. Design their own symmetrical apparatus arrangements for working in unison with a partner on any of the tasks in 2b.
   b. On suitable apparatus, make a sequence to show the different uses of the arms in moving on, off or over apparatus, e.g. different grips with the hands, bearing the weight on both arms or one arm.

Note: Action should reveal a high level of technical skill as well as the features of the second level sequences.

Criteria:
- Skilful and accurate rather than spectacular movement.
- Accuracy of repetition in both practised and improvised sequences.
- A balance of work, so that no part of the body and no one type of movement is shown to the exclusion of the rest.

6. **Control of Balance:**
   a. Show balancing on a variety of large or small parts of the body:
      - on the broad side of a form
      - on apparatus which is waist high or higher
      - on the floor.
   b. Show balancing as in a. showing a variety of methods of launching the body away from the point of support, catching and recovering the body's equilibrium in a new place:

• Gymnastics
- Educational

- on the floor
- on the broadside of a form and mat
- on higher apparatus with mats.
  c. Show balancing while sliding and/or spinning:
    - down inclined forms
    - on the floor given additional impetus by a partner.

7. **Control of rhythm:**
   a. Make a sequence showing clear fluctuation of speed and strength containing the following actions in the order given: run, jump into roll, balance on hands, run leap, roll, spin:

   - using your own natural rhythm
   - changing the rhythm so that the quick and/or strong stresses come at different points in the sequence.
   b. With a partner compose a sequence using the five basic jumps and bearing one another's weight:
    - without apparatus
    - using double bars.

8. **Control of Pattern:**
   a. Make a floor sequence using the four basic body shapes and at least four of the basic body actions.
   b. Combine with a partner to make a sequence showing patterns on apparatus, e.g. a window ladder.
   c. Working in a group of three show:
    - supporting and balance
    - supporting flight to make patterns using the four basic body shapes first on the floor and then make another sequence on suitable apparatus.

9. **Apparatus Arrangement:**
   a. Devise and demonstrate the use of an apparatus arrangement which offers full opportunity for flight with:
    - swinging
    - twisting
    - jumping

• Gymnastics
 - Educational

KEEP FIT

General Requirements
1. The aims of the programme are to:
    a. Obtain some understanding of the basic principles underlying The Keep Fit Association's work.
    b. Be aware of the physical, mental and social objectives of the work carried out in a keep fit class.
    c. Practically experience keep fit movement and improve in performance.
2. People requiring any help with regard to training and assessment should write enclosing a stamped, addressed envelope to The Keep Fit Association.

Programme
Under the tuition of a qualified Keep Fit Association Teacher, participants should:
1. Understand the preliminary warming up and conditioning of the body as a preparation of exercise.
2. Move in a well co-ordinated way while performing movements based on the activities of transference of body weight, travelling, gesturing, turning, jumping and holding stillness.
3. Use the variety of accent and rhythm obtained by stressing the weight, time, space and flow elements of movement.
4. Highlight the physical objectives inherent in each particular movement phase.
5. Move with confidence in all areas of the space surrounding the body.
6. Work with sensitivity to others while moving freely in the general space of the working area and/or when working with a group towards a specific movement objective.
7. Understand the safety aspects of movement and exercise.

The Keep Fit Association

MEDAU RHYTHMIC MOVEMENT

General Requirements
1. The aims of the programme are:
    a. To achieve economy of effort, good body alignment and posture, suppleness, harmony and freedom in natural whole body movement.

b. To encourage participation in Medau Rhythmic Movement as a recreative activity.
2. Assessment should be carried out in consultation with a qualified Medau trainer.

Programme
Participants should:
1. Regularly attend a Medau Rhythmic Movement class and wear suitable clothing.
2. Show an understanding of the basic principles of Medau Rhythmic Movement and be able to demonstrate:
    a. Movements using resilience and swing.
    b. Travelling movements of walking, running, skipping and jumping.
    c. Work with balls, hoops, clubs and other hand apparatus as an aid to movement training.
    d. Floorwork exercise.
3. Develop a sense of rhythm and aural perception.
4. Have some understanding of the various applications of small apparatus to movement training.
5. Understand movement in relation to health and posture.
6. Develop sensibility and adaptability to working with partners and in groups.
7. Show progress in rhythmical sense and gain a deeper understanding of the functions of rhythm and music in Medau Movement.
8. Have some knowledge of Medau Breathing Movement.

The Medau Society

PÉTANQUE

General Requirements
Instruction and assessment should be carried out by a qualified British Pétanque Association Coach. Details may be obtained from the BPA.

Programme
Participants should:
1. Know something about the origins of the game of Pétanque.
2. Understand the rules associated with the game.
3. Understand how a game is organised.
4. Understand and demonstrate the different tactics required by both the pointer and the shooter in a game of Pétanque.

• Medau Rhythmic Movement
• Pétanque

5. Demonstrate a good understanding of the scoring system required in the game of Pétanque.
6. Understand what is meant by the terms:
   a. Cochonnet.
   b. Pointeur.
   c. Tireur.
   d. La ravanche.
   e. La belle.
   f. La donnée.
   g. Un biberon.
   h. Le couloir.
   i. Un gratton.
   j. Une mêlée.
7. Demonstrate the correct method of throwing a boule, showing an ability to apply backspin, left sidespin and right sidespin.
8. Demonstrate the correct method of shooting in Pétanque.
9. Understand and demonstrate the following:
   a. Un carreau.
   b. Une raspaillette.
   c. La portée (or la plombée).
   d. La demi-portée.
   e. La roulette.
   f. La roulette dirigee.
   g. Bonne maman.
   h. La devant-de-boule.
   i. Une casquette.
10. Understand the rules associated with throwing out the jack.
11. Compete in at least ten Pétanque games, keeping a record of their score and showing improvement.

British Petanque Association

REAL TENNIS

General Requirements

The aim is to develop knowledge and basic skills in order to participate effectively in the sport.

Programme

Participants should:
1. Have knowledge of court characteristics, equipment and historical development.
2. Know basic rules, etiquette and scoring.
3. Have an understanding of basic tactics and positional play in singles and doubles.
4. Understand the principles underlying the grip, footwork and stroke production.
5. Be able to deliver different types of service.
6. Be able to return service and rally by developing the following strokes:
   a. The basic floor shot (forehand and backhand).
   b. The volley (forehand and backhand).

    c.   Playing off the back wall.

    d.   Playing off the side walls and tambour.

    e.   The lob.

    f.   The force.

7. Have an awareness of safety and fitness considerations.

8. Participate in friendly and competitive games.

9. Participate in club tournaments and/or inter-club matches.

10. Understand handicaps and the handicap system (singles and doubles).

11. Develop a knowledge of international events and players.

Tennis and Rackets Association

ROCK CLIMBING

General Requirements

1. Instruction in the practical aspects of this Rock Climbing programme should be directly supervised by people holding an SPSA or a higher Award such as BMG, Aspirant BMG, MIC or MIA. Instructors should operate only in the environments for which they are qualified.

2. Throughout the programme the emphasis should be on the enjoyment of moving over rock and the ways in which this can be done controlling the essential adventure within a framework of safety.

3. Those items marked with an asterisk (*) can only be effectively demonstrated on outdoor cliffs but otherwise everything can be practised and demonstrated either on artificial climbing walls or on cliffs.

Programme

1. **The crag environment**

    Participants should:

    a.   Appreciate the needs of other crag users particularly regarding safety, noise, litter and have an awareness and understanding of the issues and problems affecting access to climbing areas.

    b.   Consider these needs whilst at the crag and leave the crag in the same or better condition than that on arrival.

    c.   Understand the ways and means of reducing the erosion of the crag environment.*

    d.   Have an awareness of access restrictions.*

2. **Equipment**
   Participants should know how to:
   a. Secure and adjust a climbing harness correctly.
   b. Fit a helmet and take responsibility for wearing it as necessary.
   c. Choose suitable ropes and understand the usage of full, half and twin ropes.
   d. Choose appropriate clothing, including footwear and equipment for the crag and the climb being undertaken.

3. **Ropework**
   Participants should have familiarity with the knots used in climbing (overhand, figure of eight, bowline, clove hitch) and be able to:
   a. Tie rope directly into climbing harness.
   b. Tie to karabiner using clove hitch and/or a figure of eight knot.
   c. Tie to multiple anchors – equalising the load.
   d. Coil a rope.

4. **Rope work whilst climbing**
   Participants should be able to:
   a. Choose secure anchors.
   b. Place a sling and karabiner on a spike and on a thread belay.
   c. Place a variety of artificial chockstones and camming devices for use as belays.*
   d. Choose appropriate position and stance for top roping* and bottom roping.
   e. Choose appropriate position and stance for belaying a leader.
   f. Attach rope to friction/belay device – sticht, tuber, ATC, figure of eight descendeur or similar and correctly take in rope through the device.
   g. Pay out and take in rope for a leader climbing a pitch placing running belays.
   h. Perform lower-offs from the bottom.

• Rock Climbing

5. **Climbing**
   Participants should:
   a. Use a workable system of communications between climbers, particularly 'safe' and 'climb when ready'.
   b. Understand and demonstrate the use of various types of belays.
   c. Climb carefully and efficiently at an appropriate standard demonstrating the techniques of climbing a variety of rock features such as slabs, arêtes, chimneys, cracks, etc.
   d. Undertake single-pitch climbs.
   e. Perform an abseil using a safety rope.
   f. Be lowered by another climber.
   g. Practise climbing down.
   h. Undertake multi-pitch climbs.*
   i. Use a variety of rock climbing venues.

6. **Interpreting guide books**
   Participants should have:
   a. An understanding of the grading system.
   b. An appreciation of the effects of conditions on graded climbs.
   c. A knowledge of crag features and be able to recognise them.

7. **Emergency Procedures**
   Participants should consider the emergency procedures while engaged in climbing, i.e.:
   a. What emergency equipment to carry.
   b. Where to get help.
   c. Nearest telephone.
   d. Where to find shelter.*

SKIING – NORDIC (CROSS-COUNTRY)

General Requirements
1. The aim is to encourage young people to explore the environment, whilst increasing their competence and skiing in a safe and responsible way.
2. **All skiing ventures must be led or accompanied by an experienced and appropriately qualified person.**

• Rock Climbing
• Skiing
  - Nordic (Cross-Country)

Programme

Participants should progress through the following programme and:

1. Learn to carefully plan all skiing ventures properly before they take place. This must involve the following:
   a. Checking of equipment, which must be adequate for the terrain.
   b. Knowledge of the terrain.
   c. Knowledge of the prevailing weather conditions.
   d. A sufficient level of technical competence and physical fitness for the terrain.
2. Have knowledge of safety precautions, the casualty code, map reading and the use of a compass in sub-zero conditions and when travelling on snow as laid out in the Expeditions Section of the *Award Handbook.*
3. Have an understanding of the possible hazards of open country and adverse weather conditions and know the precautions and equipment required for safe cross-country skiing.
4. Be able to execute the following on moderate terrain:
   a. A simple kick (step) turn to the left and to the right.
   b. Climbing a slope on skis using a direct ascent and then the herringbone.
   c. Traversing downhill across a slope long enough to show complete control.
   d. Travelling downhill and doing a snowplough turn to the left and to the right.
   e. Running easily and smoothly along a level terrain on skis.
5. Undertake cross-country skiing ventures which are in progressively more difficult terrain, i.e. machine-cut trails, following an experienced leader cutting the tracks, making new tracks across undisturbed snow.
6. Undertake suitable physical training such as dry cross-country skiing, circuit training, walking, running, hill running, mountain biking, roller-skiing or rollerblading.
7. Be able to make a cross-country tour on skis across undulating ground. Suggested distance of eight kilometres (five miles).
8. Be able to:
   a. Perform a kick (step) turn to both the right and the left on the side of a steep slope.
   b. Perform a christie or swing stop turn to either the right or the left.

• Skiing
  - Nordic
  (Cross-
  Country)

9. Be able to:
   a. Explain how bumps can be used to help when running on the flat or climbing, and demonstrate this technique.
   b. Travel downhill over an uneven surface.
   c. Perform a skating turn on the flat.
   d. Demonstrate the method of resting the arms when running on the flat or when climbing.
10. Be able to:
   a. Traverse up a slope incorporating kick (step) turns without breaking the rhythm of the climb.
   b. Descend in a confident manner over variable terrain.
   c. Perform skating turns through wooded country.
11. Continue to make cross-country tours on skis across undulating ground of not in excess of 1500 metres, gradually increasing distances, e.g. from eight to fifteen kilometres.

Note: For other forms of skiing, see the section on Governing Body standards on page 289.

SQUASH

Programme

Participants should:
1. Be able to play straight forehand and backhand drives.
2. Be able to play high lob service.
3. Know the basic scoring and rules.
4. Be able to play side-wall shots (forehand and backhand).
5. Be able to play strokes off the backwall including boost from corners.
6. Know correct positioning of player on court.
7. Be able to play drop shots.
8. Master short angle shots.
9. Be able to play basic lobs and volleys.
10. Understand the basic tactics of the game.
11. Be accomplished at the cross court drive.
12. Be able to play a variety of services.
13. Participation in competitive games.
14. Be able to play cross court and backhand lobs.
15. Understand rules including faults.
16. Improve length and control of all strokes.
17. Understand the more advanced tactics.
18. Participate in club or inter-club games.

Squash Rackets Association

• Skiing
  - Nordic
    (Cross-
    Country)
• Squash

TEAM SPORTS

Team Sports include:
- Baseball • Boccia • Camogie • Canoe Polo • Cricket • Curling • Football • Gaelic Association Football • Hockey • Hurling • Ice Hockey • Indoor Cricket • Indoor Hockey • Korfball • Lacrosse • Netball • Octopushing • Polo • Roller Hockey • Rounders • Rugby League Football • Rugby Union Football • Stoolball • Street Hockey • Volleyball • Water Polo.

General Requirements

1. It is not possible to produce detailed programmes separately for each team game, but the following programme can be adapted to meet the particular requirements of most team games.

2. Young people who are still undergoing full-time education may not count participation in school teams if the matches and training sessions are during curriculum time. It is only acceptable where it can clearly be shown that a young person is putting genuine voluntary effort into training sessions, in leisure time, and that the team is playing matches outside

normal school hours.

3. Those taking part in any team games should join a club or team which is properly constituted and affiliated directly or indirectly to the National Body governing the game. Where Governing Bodies have their own Awards, participants are encouraged to undertake their programmes as part of their participation sessions; the additional Awards may help to provide greater motivation and encourage good techniques and practice.

Programme

Participants should:

1. Have a sound knowledge of the laws of the game.
2. Attain a reasonable proficiency in the basic skills of the game in order to participate and compete in a serious game.
3. Show a knowledge of the care and maintenance of equipment.
4. Compete in appropriate club competitions.
5. Show skills and an improvement in standard of play.
6. Develop an appreciation of tactics and positioning play.
7. Be selected and play in a team which has proper fixtures.

TENNIS

Participants should develop the following:

1. Simple racket control.
2. Racket/ball co-ordination.
3. Self-feed controlled hit to target – forehand/backhand.
4. Partner-fed controlled hit to target over barrier – forehand/ backhand.
5. An understanding of simple game rules.
6. Forehand/backhand.
7. Forehand/backhand volley.
8. Underarm serve.
9. The ability to play out a point.
10. Forehand rally (x10).
11. Forehand/backhand volley with depth.
12. Overarm serve.
13. Point play.
14. The ability to rally with depth (x10).
15. Approach shot to net then volley.
16. Serve, approach to net to volley return.

17. The rally with movement.
18. Forehand-only rally with depth using full court.
19. Interception volleys with reach.
20. Overhead smash.
21. Lob.
22. Drop shot.
23. The ability to serve to target areas.
24. Return of serve.
25. Sequence of 5 shots using the basic strokes.
26. An understanding basic tactics for doubles and singles.
27. The vision for shot selection within the match situation.
28. Variations of spin (topspin/slice).
29. Reactions to match situation and detailed knowledge of 'reading' the game.
30. Match analysis.

Participants should play friendly singles and doubles games and, as they become more competent, club and inter-club matches, leading to open, area or County championships.

Lawn Tennis Association

WRESTLING (FREESTYLE)

General Requirements

1. The aim is to provide the participant with a consistent and systematic programme for learning freestyle wrestling techniques safely whilst having fun. The programme provides the participant with the skills necessary to take part in actual freestyle wrestling competition.

2. The primary goals for Supervisor and participant alike are:
   a. Instil a proper attitude towards training.
   b. Emphasise the aerobic – anaerobic aspects of wrestling.
   c. Improve skill levels.
   d. Improve knowledge and execution of techniques.
   e. Understand the international rules.
   f. Develop an aggressive, positive and offensive attitude towards participation.

3. Wrestling, at all levels, must always be conducted under the supervision of a qualified Coach/Instructor.

4. **Throughout the programme, safety must be uppermost in the minds of both participant and Supervisor. Wrestling must take place on a suitable mat.**

Programme

Throughout the programme, the participant must adopt the Total Wrestling concept promoted by the International Federation. This concept demands full aggressive activity by the wrestler. Wrestlers must be mentally and physically prepared to wrestle in the centre of the mat throughout the entire match and be willing to take risks in order to score points. Defensive wrestling must be aggressive counter-wrestling, not merely moves avoiding combative situations.

Participants should:

1. Have an understanding of the possible hazards involved in a contact sport such as wrestling.
2. Know the precautions, equipment required and hygiene rules of wrestling.
3. Understand the need for wrestlers to be matched according to weight.
4. Demonstrate a correct and thorough warm-up before and cool-down immediately following wrestling practice.
5. Be able to demonstrate the seven basic skills which provide the wrestler with mobility and power:
   a. Stance – ability to keep the head, neck, back, hips, elbows and legs in a prescribed position to each other.
   b. Motion – ability to move the body from one position on the mat to another in a lateral or circular direction and remain in good position.
   c. Changing levels – ability to move the hips up and down in relation to the opponent whilst remaining in good position.
   d. Penetration -ability to move the hips directly into, under and through the opponent whilst remaining in a good position.
   e. Lifting – ability to move the opponent's body mass in an upward direction up and/or off the mat.
   f. Backstep – ability to move the hips into and under the opponent whilst twisting backwards into their body.
   g. Backarch – ability to control the body and remain in balance whilst driving the hips into and under the opponent whilst moving from the feet into a high arching back bridge.

• Wrestling (Freestyle)

6. Demonstrate one variation of each technique below against a co-operative partner and show increased skill in executing techniques against increasing resistance:
   a. Sit out.
   b. Double leg takedown.
   c. Single leg takedown.
   d. Fireman's carry takedown.
   e. Duck under to control.
   f. Head snap to control.
   g. Ankle pick up to control.
   h. Crossface to pin.
   i. Arm bar to pin.
   j. Half Nelson to pin.
   k. Waist hold and far ankle breakdown.
   l. Cross ankle turn over.
   m. Gut wrench.
   n. Arm roll.
   o. Shoulder throw.
   p. Hip throw.
   q. Cradle.
   r. Turk ride.
   s. Olympic lift.
   (For each technique, the wrestler should be able to demonstrate an effective counter-attack. The wrestler should also be fully aware of the competition points scoring for each technique.)
7. Take part in competition against opponent within training sessions and show improvement in technique. Emphasis should not be on actual match result but successful technique used in a competition situation.
8. Demonstrate knowledge of the international wrestling rules by taking part as a referee in a wrestling competition within training session.
9. Undertake appropriate conditioning of specific relevance to wrestling. Emphasis should be placed on flexibility, strength and aerobic/anaerobic training. Particular emphasis should be given to strengthening the neck (always under supervision).
10. Take part in inter-club competitions.

British Amateur Wrestling Association

• Wrestling
  (Freestyle)

YOGA (HATHA)

General Requirements

Yoga is the uniting or joining of a healthy body and disciplined mind. In the postures or asanas, the quality of body use is as important as a degree of accomplishment. Asanas are not intended to be gymnastic exercises, they are

positions for the body in which one remains steady, calm, quiet and comfortable – physically and mentally – a balanced and harmonious state.

Programme

Participants should:

1. Know and understand the rules and advice of practice – precautions, clothing, limbering, etc.
2. Develop movement and co-ordination in basic asanas, i.e. all movements of the spine, forward, backward and side bending postures, rotation or twisting postures, plus inverted and balancing poses.
3. Acquire knowledge of basic breathing techniques.
4. Learn to relax during and after postures.
5. Develop and improve ability and quality of the postures – classical asanas.
6. Expand further the breathing control – to synchronise breathing and movement.
7. Develop the knowledge and practise of several techniques of relaxation and concentration.
8. Continue as in items 1-7 with greater quality of movement and greater depth of understanding and meaning in the asanas.
9. Develop through practice a deeper awareness of oneself and others.
10. Study and practise pranayama (control of breath).

British Wheel of Yoga

• Yoga

PHYSICAL RECREATION SECTION INDEX

PARTICIPATION PROGRAMMES

PHYSICAL RECREATION

• Physical
Recreation
Index

340

Residential
Project
SECTION

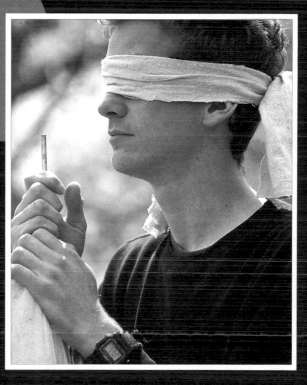

Residential
Project

Aim of the Residential Project
(an additional requirement for the Gold Award)

To broaden young people's experience through involvement with others in a residential setting.

The Principles

The intention is to introduce young people to some form of purposeful enterprise **in the company of others who are not already known to them.**

Benefits to Young People

The Residential Project should give young people the opportunity to:

- experience an unfamiliar environment,
- build new relationships and show concern for others,
- work as part of a team towards shared goals,
- accept responsibility for and to each other,
- develop communication skills,
- show initiative,
- enjoy living and working with others.

Requirement

To undertake a shared activity, either through voluntary service or training, in a residential setting away from home and in an unfamiliar environment. Participants may require briefing or training prior to or during the Residential period so that they are able to contribute fully to the activity and derive full benefit from the experience.

Conditions

Where and What?
Residential settings may typically be in centres, youth hostels, sailing ships or camps. Staying with a family or 'Home Stays' are not acceptable.

Provided it conforms to the general conditions, the type of residential experience is to be the young person's own choice, freely made and without any financial gain.

The Project must provide opportunities for broadening interests and experience – it is the ideal incentive to try a new activity. Under some circumstances, however, it may be related to existing interests or activities being followed in other Sections of the Award. (The qualifying venture of the Expeditions Section cannot be regarded as a Residential Project.)

With Whom?

In order to fulfil the objectives of the Residential Project, it is probably most beneficial for participants to join projects **individually.** Otherwise only a small minority of those taking part should be the young person's usual companions at home, or in school, work or youth group.

If young people are to make new friends and build new relationships this aspect is essential.

For How Long?

The Project should take place over at least five consecutive days with at least four nights spent away.

In exceptional circumstances, such as limited leave availability, and after consultation with, and at the discretion of, Operating Authorities, this commitment can be spread over a series of weekends provided that they involve at least four nights away; that they fall within a 12-month period; that the same activity is pursued and that progressive training is provided.

When?

For some, completing this Section at the start of their Gold Award can provide the motivation to continue; for others, leaving this element until later, when they are more mature and ready for a more ambitious project, can afford them maximum benefit.

Suitable Opportunities

Young people must choose for themselves the type of Residential Project they wish to undertake. Some will select projects where the majority of participants are of their own age group whilst others may choose to be part of a small team working with young children or elderly people.

Different types of Residential may achieve different outcomes; thus, before making a choice, the main purpose must be clear. For example, a self-catering activity weekend run in a small hostel or camping barn, which involves young people in the planning and decision-making is likely to be more successful in promoting relationships with others and teamwork than a holiday play scheme based on a large residential centre which provides catering and Instructors. This option, on the other hand, may offer more opportunities for taking responsibility and showing concern for others.

Physical activities can develop personal skills such as problem solving and a sense of achievement, whilst a drama course can improve communication skills and confidence. With adequate planning, however, with sufficient time being allocated for reviewing and reflection, most of the benefits and outcomes can be achieved during most types of Residential Project.

Again, the essential ingredient of the Residential is that it intensifies the opportunities to establish new relationships, to adopt new roles and responsibilities, and to share the sense of excitement and achievement in fulfilling a worthwhile goal. All this as well as being most enjoyable.

• Suitable
Opportunities

Suitable opportunities generally fall into one of the following categories:

Conservation or Environmental Work

- Archeological projects.
- Conservation projects such as: Acorn Camps, BTCV Work Camps, Cathedral Camps, Earthwatch Europe, National Trust.
- Inner city regeneration projects.
- Preservation work on canals, inland waterways, steam railways.

Service to Others

- Holiday camps for disadvantaged children or disabled people.
- Projects organised by Churches and voluntary organisations.
- Residential Community Projects such as building playgrounds or redecorating village halls.
- Voluntary work with elderly people.
- Voluntary work with relief organisations.

Activity-Based

- Creative courses such as art, drama or photographic courses.
- Outdoor adventure courses such as: Brathay and Endeavour Explorations, Ocean Youth Club, Outward Bound, Raleigh International, Sail Training Association, YHA Great Escapes.
- Voluntary Youth Organisations' Activity Camps.

Personal Training

- Issue-based or awareness-raising courses.
- Coaching and instructional courses.
- Spiritual and personal development training courses.
- Youth Leadership training courses.

A range of Residential opportunities is published regularly in *Award Journal*.

• Suitable
Opportunities

Preparation

1. A discussion with the Award Leader prior to making the final choice will enable participants to think through the value of a particular opportunity for personal development.
2. It is essential that the Project complies with the safety criteria of the Operating Authority and the requirements and conditions of the Award. Participants should seek guidance and approval from their Operating Authority prior to committing themselves.
3. Once the choice of Residential Project has been made, individual participants should contact the relevant organisation or course organiser in order to obtain further details.
4. Before enrolling, each participant should identify a suitable Assessor approved by the Operating Authority and who is present throughout the period of residence.

The Assessor should be briefed about the requirements and aims of the Residential Project and given a copy of the relevant *Notes for Adult Helpers*.

Assessment

On arrival at the Residential venue, the participant should remind the Course Leader and other Course Tutors or Instructors that the project will form part of a Gold Award; a meeting should be arranged with the Assessor during, and at the end of, the Project to review progress and discuss issues related to the experience and assessment.

Young people should be assessed on their personal standards, relationships with others, responsibility, initiative and general progress during the Residential period.

Confirmation of Project

Before a booking is confirmed for a Residential Project, Leaders and participants should be sure that it adheres to the following criteria:

- Attendance at the event is the free choice of the participant rather than being a compulsory course.
- The participant will be joining the event alone; alternatively, only a small minority of participants on the project should be known to the young person at home, school or at work.
- The Residential offers opportunities to broaden experience and involve the participant in purposeful enterprise in the company of others.
- Its duration is not less than 5 consecutive full days (4 nights).
- The participant will be in attendance for the full period required by the event, living and working with the same team of people.
- The Residential provides opportunities to develop maturity and to accept responsibility.
- There are opportunities for the participant to be adequately assessed throughout the full period, rather than merely qualify by attendance.
- The Assessor will be present throughout the period of residence and directly involved with the participant.
- The Assessor is aware of the criteria for assessment and the procedures for signing the *Record Book*.

Record Books

The *Record Book* represents a young person's experiences and achievements and remarks should therefore be personalised, positive and encouraging. It should always record success and achievement and, whenever possible, should be completed before the participant leaves the Project.

In the event of the Assessor not being satisfied that the participant has fulfilled the assessment criteria by the end of the Project, the young person should be informed of the reason and no entry should be made in the *Record Book*. The Assessor should encourage the participant to undertake another Project.

RESIDENTIAL PROJECT

ACTIVITY PHOTOGRAPHIC WORKSHOP

PURPOSE To learn about & explore aspects of Photography

PLACE Media Centre, Bristol

DATE OF ATTENDANCE FROM 1/8/94 TO 6/8/94

Assessor's report: *(including personal standards, relationships with others, responsibility, initiative and general progress).*

For Megan, meeting and working with others with a common enthusiasm for photography proved to be a very enjoyable and rewarding part of the residential. Although a good team member she was keen to express her own personal style - she showed considerable artistic flair and interpreted her ideas in an imaginative way, producing prints of outstanding quality for the final exhibition

SIGNED A Chandler DATE 7/8/94

QUALIFICATION Course Tutor & Lecturer in Photography

26

Gold

RESIDENTIAL PROJECT

ACTIVITY CHILDREN'S CAMP FOR THOSE WITH DIABETES

PURPOSE SERVICE TO OTHERS

PLACE BARLBOROUGH, DERBYSHIRE

DATE OF ATTENDANCE FROM 14/8/93 - 18/8/93 TO 25/8/93 - 28/8/93

Assessor's report: *(including personal standards, relationships with others, responsibility, initiative and general progress).*

Kevin proved himself to be an excellent leader, showing a high level of initiative and responsibility with the children. Always cheerful and caring, he showed affection and was particularly sensitive to their needs. He was a willing and hard working member of the team and communicated well with the other leaders who respected his commitment. He was a pleasure to be with.

SIGNED S Khan DATE 28/8/93

QUALIFICATION B.DA. Holiday Warden.

26

• Record Books

351

Useful
Addresses
and Index

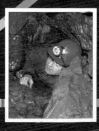

Useful Addresses

• **Age Concern:** Astral House, 1268 London Road, London SW16 4ER. Tel: 0181 679 8000

• **Air Training Corps:** RAF Cranwell, Sleaford, Lincolnshire NG34 8HB. Tel: 01400 261201

• **Amateur Athletic Association of England:** 225a Bristol Road, Edgbaston, Birmingham B5 7UB. Tel: 0121 440 5000

• **Amateur Boxing Association of England:** Crystal Palace National Sports Centre, London SE19 2BB. Tel: 0181 778 0251

• **Amateur Rowing Association:** The Priory, 6 Lower Mall, London W6 9DJ. Tel: 0181 741 5314

• **Amateur Swimming Association:** Harold Fern House, Derby Square, Loughborough, Leicestershire LE11 5AL. Tel: 01509 618700

• **Army Cadet Force Association:** Duke of York's Headquarters, E Block, Kings Road, London SW3 4RR. Tel: 0171 730 9733

• **Badminton Association of England:** National Badminton Centre, Bradwell Road, Loughton Lodge, Milton Keynes MK8 9LA. Tel: 01908 568822

• **Boys' Brigade:** Felden Lodge, Felden, Hemel Hempstead, Hertfordshire HP3 0BL. Tel: 01442 231681

• **Brathay Exploration Group:** Brathay Hall, Ambleside, Cumbria LA22 0HP. Tel: 01539 433942

• **British Aikido Board:** 6 Halkingcroft, Langley, Slough, Berkshire SL3 7AT. Tel: 01753 819086

• **British Amateur Gymnastics Association:** Ford Hall, Lilleshall National Sports Centre, Nr.Newport, Shropshire TF10 9NB. Tel: 01952 820330

• **British Amateur Weightlifters Association:** Grosvenor House, 131 Hurst Street, Oxford OX4 4HE. Tel: 01865 200339

• **British Amateur Wrestling Association:** The Wrestling Academy, 41 Great Clowes Street, Salford M7 1RQ. Tel: 0161 832 9209

• **British Association of Teachers of Dancing:** 23 Marywood Square, Glasgow G41 2BP. Tel: 0141 423 4029

• **British Ballet Organisation:** Woolborough House, 39 Lonsdale Road, Barnes, London SW13 9JP. Tel: 0181 748 1241

• **British Canoe Union:** John Dudderidge House, Adbolton Lane, West Bridgford, Nottingham NG2 5AS. Tel: 01159 821100

• **British Cave Rescue Council:** Pearl Hill Farm, Dent, Sedbergh, Cumbria LA10 5TG. Tel: 01539 625412

• **British Council for Chinese Martial Arts:** c/o 110 Frensham Drive, Nuneaton, Warwickshire CV10 9QL. Tel: 01203 394642

• **British Crown Green Bowling Association:** 14 Leighton Avenue, Maghull Liverpool L31 0AH. Tel: 0151 526 8367

• **British Cycling Federation:** The National Cycling Centre, Stuart Street, Manchester M11 4DQ. Tel: 0161 230 2301

• **British Driving Society:** 27 Dugard Place, Barford, Nr. Warwick CV35 8DX. Tel: 01926 624420

• **British Federation of Roller Skating:** Lilleshall National Sports Centre, Nr. Newport, Shropshire TF10 9AT. Tel: 01952 825253

• **British Federation of Sand and Land Yacht Clubs:** 23 Piper Drive, Long Whatton, Loughborough, Leicestershire LE12 5DJ. Tel: 01509 842292

• **British Fencing Association:** 1 Baron's Gate, 33-35 Rothschild Road, London W4 5HT. Tel: 0181 742 3032

• **British Hang Gliding and Paragliding Association:** The Old School Room, Loughborough Road, Leicester LE4 5PJ. Tel: 01162 611322

• **British Horse Society:** British Equestrian Centre, Stoneleigh Park, Kenilworth, Warwickshire CV8 2LR. Tel: 01203 696697

• **British JuJitsu Association:** 29 Ringstead Crescent, Sheffield S10 5SH. Tel: 01142 666733

• **British Judo Association:** 7a Rutland Street, Leicester LE1 1RB. Tel: 01162 559669

• **British Karate Federation:** 5a Tram Road Side, Treharris, Mid Glamorgan CF46 5ET. Tel: 01443 411944

• **British Kendo Association:** Chapel House, 19 Chapel Place, Ramsgate, Kent CT11 9RY. Tel: 01843 585596

• **British Mountaineering Council:** 177-179 Burton Road, West Didsbury, Manchester M20 2BB. Tel: 0161 445 4747

- **British Orienteering Federation:** Riversdale, Dale Road North, Darley Dale, Matlock Derbyshire, DE4 2HX. Tel: 01629 734042

- **British Parachute Association:** 5 Wharf Way, Glen Parva, Leicester LE2 9TF. Tel: 01162 785271

- **British Petanque Association:** 12 Ensign Business Centre, Westwood Park, Coventry CV8 8JA. Tel: 01203 421408

- **British Red Cross Society:** 9 Grosvenor Crescent, London SW1X 7EJ. Tel: 0171 235 5454

- **British Schools Exploring Society:** 1 Kensington Gore, London SW7 2AR. Tel: 0171 591 3141

- **British Ski & Snowboarding Federation:** 258 Main Street, East Calder, Livingston, West Lothian EH53 0EE. Tel: 01506 884343

- **British Sports Association for the Disabled:** Solecast House, 13-27 Brunswick Place, London N1 6DX. Tel: 0171 490 4919

- **British Sub-Aqua Club:** Telford's Quay, Ellesmere Port, South Wirral L65 4FY. Tel: 0151 357 1951

- **British Surfing Association:** T2 Champion's Yard, Penzance, Cornwall TR18 2SS. Tel: 01736 360250

- **British Taekwondo Council:** 163a Church Road, Redfield, Bristol BS5 9LA. Tel: 0117 955 1046

- **British Ten Pin Bowling Association:** 114 Balfour Road, Ilford, Essex IG1 4JD. Tel: 0181 478 1745

- **British Trampoline Federation:** 146 College Road, Harrow, Middlesex HA1 1BH. Tel: 0181 863 7278

- **British Trust for Conservation Volunteers:** 36 St Mary's Street, Wallingford, Oxfordshire OX10 0EU. Tel: 01491 839766

- **British Trust for Ornithology:** National Centre for Ornithology, The Nunnery, Thetford, Norfolk IP24 2PU. Tel: 01842 750050

- **British Water Ski Federation:** 390 City Road, London EC1V 1QA. Tel: 0171 833 2855

- **British Waterways:** Willow Grange, Church Road, Watford, Hertfordshire WD1 3QA. Tel: 01923 226422

- **British Wheel of Yoga:** 1 Hamilton Place, Boston Road, Sleaford, Lincolnshire NG34 7ES. Tel: 01529 306851

- **Campaigners:** Campaigners House, Colney House, St.Albans, Hertfordshire AL4 0NQ. Tel: 01727 824065

- **Camping and Caravanning Club:** Greenfield House, Westwood Way, Coventry CV32 8JH. Tel: 01203 694995

- **Central Council for Physical Recreation:** Francis House, Francis Street, London SW1P 1DE. Tel: 0171 828 3163

- **Children's Society:** Edward Rudolf House, Margery Street, London WC1 0JL. Tel: 0171 837 4299

- **Church in Wales:** Children's Officer, Woodlands Place, Penarth, South Glamorgan CF6 2EX. Tel: 01222 705278

- **Church Lads' and Church Girls' Brigade:** 2 Barnsley Road, Wath-upon-Darne, Rotherham, South Yorkshire S63 6PY. Tel: 01709 870335

- **Church of England:** General Synod Board of Education (Children) Church House, Dean's Yard, Westminster, London SW1P 3NZ. Tel: 0171 222 9011

- **Church of Ireland:** Canon Houston McKelvey, 19 Upper Lisburn Road, Belfast BT10 0GW. Tel: 01232 619008

- **Church of Scotland:** Board of Parish Education, St. Colm's Centre, 18 Inverleith Terrace, Edinburgh EH3 5NS. Tel: 0131 332 0343

- **Council for Environmental Education:** University of Reading, London Road, Reading, Berkshire RG1 5AQ. Tel: 01734 756061

- **Council for the Protection of Rural England:** Warwick House, 25 Buckingham Palace Road, London SW1W 0PP. Tel: 0171 976 6433

- **Countryside Commission:** John Dower House, Crescent Place, Cheltenham, Gloucestershire GL50 3RA. Tel: 01242 521381

- **Croquet Association:** Hurlingham Club, Ranelagh Gardens, London SW6 3PR. Tel: 0171 736 3148

- **Cyclists Touring Club:** Cotterell House, 69 Meadrow, Godalming, Surrey GU7 3HS. Tel: 01483 417217

- **English Association for Snooker & Billiards:** 27 Oakfield Road, Clifton, Bristol BS8 2AT. Tel: 0117 923 9600

- **English Basketball Association:** 48 Bradford Road, Stanningley, Pudsey, West Yorkshire LS28 6DF. Tel: 0113 2 361166

- **English Bowling Association:** Lyndhurst Road, Worthing, West Sussex BN11 2AZ. Tel: 01903 820222

- **English Folk Dance and Song Society:** Cecil Sharp House, 2 Regent's Park Road, London NW1 7AY. Tel: 0171 485 2206

- **English Heritage:** Keysign House, 429 Oxford Street, London W1R 2HD. Tel: 0171 973 3000

USEFUL ADDRESSES

- **English Karate Governing Body:** 58 Bloomfield Drive, Bath BA2 2BG. Tel: 01225 834008

- **English Nature:** Northminster House, Northminster Road, Peterborough, Northamptonshire PE1 1UA. Tel: 01733 455000

- **English Ski Council:** Area Library Building, Queensway Mall, The Cornbow, Halesowen, West Midlands B63 4AJ. Tel: 0121 501 2314

- **English Table Tennis Association:** 3rd Floor, Queensbury House, Havelock Road, Hastings, East Sussex TN34 1HF. Tel: 01424 722525

- **Environmental Council:** 21 Elizabeth Street, London SW1W 9RP. Tel: 0171 824 8411

- **Eton Fives Association:** 74 Clarence Road, St. Albans, Hertfordshire AL1 4NG. Tel: 01727 837099

- **Expedition Advisory Centre:** Royal Geographical Society, 1 Kensington Gore, London SW7 2AR. Tel: 0171 581 2057

- **Field Studies Council:** Montford Bridge, Shrewsbury, Shropshire SY4 1HW. Tel: 01743 850674

- **Forestry Authority:** 231 Corstorpine Road, Edinburgh EH12 7AT. Tel: 0131 334 2576

- **Friends for the Young Deaf:** East Court Mansion, College Lane, East Grinstead, West Sussex RH19 3LT. Tel: 01342 323444

- **Friends of the Earth:** 26-28 Underwood Street, London N1 7TQ. Tel: 0171 490 1555

GAP Activity Projects: 44 Queen's Road, Reading, Berkshire RG1 4BB. Tel: 01734 594914

- **Girls' Brigade:** 62 Foxhall Road, Didcot, Oxfordshire OX11 7NQ. Tel: 01235 510425

- **Girls' Venture Corps:** Redhill Aerodrome, King's Mill Lane, South Nutfield, Redhill, Surrey RH1 5JY. Tel: 01737 823345

- **Golf Foundation:** Foundation House, Hanbury Manor, Ware, Hertfordshire SG12 0UH. Tel: 01920 484044

- **Grand National Archery Society:** National Agricultural Centre, Seventh Street, Stoneleigh Park, Kenilworth, Warwickshire CV8 2LG. Tel: 01203 696631

- **Groundwork Foundation:** 85-87 Cornwall Street, Birmingham B3 3BY. Tel: 0121 236 8565

- **Guide Association:** 17-19 Buckingham Palace Road, London SW1W 0PT. Tel: 0171 834 6242

- **Guide Dogs for the Blind:** Hillfields, Burghfield, Reading, Berkshire RG7 3YG. Tel: 01734 835555

- **Help the Aged:** St. James's Walk, London EC1R 0BE. Tel: 0171 253 0253

- **HM Coastguard:** Department of Transport, Spring Place, 105 Commercial Road, Southampton SO15 1EG. Tel: 01703 329100

- **Imperial Society of Teachers of Dancing:** Imperial House, 22-26 Paul Street, London EC2A 4QE. Tel: 0171 377 1577

- **Institute of Indian Art and Culture:** 4a Castletown Road, London W14 9HQ. Tel: 0171 381 3086

- **International Dance Teachers' Association:** 76 Bennett Road, Brighton, East Sussex BN2 5JL. Tel: 01273 685652

- **Jewish Lads' and Girls' Brigade:** 3 Beechcroft Road, South Woodford, London E18 1LA. Tel: 0181 989 8990

- **Jubilee Sailing Trust:** Jubilee Yard, Merlin Quay, Hazel Road, Woolston, Southampton SO19 7GB. Tel: 01703 449108

- **Keep Fit Association:** Francis House, Francis Street, London SW1P 1DE. Tel: 0171 233 8898

- **Lawn Tennis Association:** The Queen's Club, Barons Court, West Kensington, London W14 9EG. Tel: 0171 381 7000

- **Local Authority Road Safety Officers Association:** The Regional Department, Engineering Division, Road Safety Group, PO Box 47, Newton Bar, Wakefield WF1 2YN. Tel: 01924 306000

- **Medau Society:** 8b Robson House, East Street, Epsom, Surrey KT17 1HH. Tel: 01372 729056

- **MENCAP:** 123 Golden Lane, London,EC1 3PP. Tel: 0171 454 0454

- **Methodist Association of Youth Clubs:** 2 Chester House, Pages Lane, Muswell Hill, London N10 1PR. Tel: 0181 444 9845

- **Modern Pentathlon Association of Great Britain:** Pentathlon House, Baughurst Road, Baughurst, Tadley, Hampshire RG26 5JF. Tel: 01734 817181

- **Mountain Cave and Rescue Association:** 18 Tarnside Fold, Simmondley, Glossop, Derbyshire SK13 9ND. Tel: 01457 853095

- **Mountain Leader Training Board (England):** Capel Curig, Gwynedd LL24 0ET. Tel: 01690 720272

- **NABC - Clubs for Young People:** 371 Kennington Lane, London SE11 5QY. Tel:0171 793 0787

- **National Association for Maternal and Child Welfare:** 40-42 Osnaburgh Street, London NW1 3ND. Tel: 0171 383 4541

- **National Association for Outdoor Education:** 12 St. Andrew's Churchyard, Penrith, Cumbria CA11 7YE. Tel: 01768 865113

- **National Association of Teachers of Dancing Ltd:** 44-47 The Broadway, Thatcham, Berkshire RG19 3HP. Tel: 01635 868888

- **National Caving Association:** White Lion Street, Yns Uchaf Ystradgynlais, Swansea SA9 1RW. Tel: 01639 849519 (home)

- **National Federation of Anglers:** Halliday House, Egginton Junction, Derbyshire DE65 6GU. Tel: 01283 734735

- **National Federation of Gateway Clubs:** 117-123 Golden Lane, London EC1Y 0RT. Tel: 0171 454 0454

- **National Ice Skating Association of UK Ltd:** 15-27 Gee Street, London EC1V 3RE. Tel: 0171 253 3824

- **National Mountain Centre:** Plas y Brenin, Capel Curig, Gwynedd LL24 0ET. Tel: 01690 720214

- **National Rivers Authority:** Rio House, Waterside Drive, Aztec West, Almondsbury, Bristol BS12 4UD. Tel: 01454 624400

- **National Society for the Prevention of Cruelty to Children:** 42 Curtain Road, London EC2A 3NH. Tel: 0171 825 2500

- **National Trust:** 36 Queen Anne's Gate, London SW1H 9AS. Tel: 0171 222 9251

- **National Voluntary Civil Aid Services:** The Duke of Edinburgh's Award Liaison Officer, 66 Mead Fields, North Allington, Bridport, Dorset DT6 5RE. Tel: 01308 421117 Membership Secretary: 17 Edgmont Road, New Malden, Surrey KT3 4AS.

- **National Watersports Centre:** Plas Menai, Caernarfon, Gwynedd LL55 1UE. Tel: 01248 670964

- **Ocean Youth Club**, The Bus Station, South Street, Gosport, Hampshire PO12 1EP. Tel: 01705 501211

- **Order of Malta Ambulance Corps:** 83 University Street, Belfast BT7 1HP. Tel: 01232 245375

- **Ordnance Survey:** Romsey Road, Maybush, Southampton SO9 4DH. Tel: 01703 792000

- **Outward Bound Trust:** Watermillock, Nr Penrith, Cumbria CA11 0JL. Tel: 0990 134227

- **Pedigree Petfoods Education Centre:** 4 Bedford Square, London WC1D 3RA

- **PHAB:** Summit House, Wandle Road, Croydon, Surrey CR0 1DF. Tel: 0181 667 9443

- **Pony Club:** British Equestrian Centre, Stoneleigh Park, Kenilworth, Warwickshire CV8 2LR. Tel: 01203 696697

- **Raleigh International:** Raleigh House, 27 Parsons Green Lane, London SW6 4HS. Tel: 0171 371 8585

- **Ramblers' Association:** 1-5 Wandsworth Road, London SW8 2XX. Tel:0171 582 6878

- **Riding for the Disabled Association:** Avenue R, National Agricultural Centre, Kenilworth, Warwickshire CV0 2LY. Tel: 01203 696510

- **Road Time Trials Council:** 10 Derwent Place, Wombwell, Barnsley, South Yorkshire S73 0RT. Tel: 01226 753599

- **Roman Catholic Church:** Registrar, Our Lady Catechists, 6 Irving Close, The Straits, Dudley, West Midlands DY3 3BX

- **Royal Academy of Dancing:** 36 Battersea Square, London SW11 3RA. Tel: 0171 223 0091

- **Royal British Legion:** 48 Pall Mall, London SW1Y 5JY. Tel: 0171 973 7200

- **Royal Geographical Society:** 1 Kensington Gore, London SW7 2AR. Tel: 0171 591 3000

- **Royal Life Saving Society UK:** River House, High Street, Broom, Warwickshire B50 4HN. Tel: 01789 773994

- **Royal National Institute for the Blind:** 224 Great Portland Street, London W1N 6AA. Tel: 0171 388 1266

- **Royal National Institute for the Deaf:** 19-23 Featherstone Street, London EC1Y 8SC. Tel: 0171 296 8000

- **Royal National Lifeboat Institution:** West Quay Road, Poole, Dorset BH15 1HZ. Tel: 01202 663000

- **Royal Scottish Country Dance Society:** 12 Coates Crescent, Edinburgh EH3 7AE. Tel: 0131 225 3854

- **Royal Society for the Prevention of Accidents:** Edgbaston Park, 353 Bristol Road, Birmingham B5 7ST. Tel: 0121 248 2000

- **Royal Society for the Prevention of Cruelty to Animals:** The Causeway, Horsham, West Sussex RH12 1HG. Tel: 0990 555999

- **Royal Society for the Protection of Birds:** The Lodge, Sandy, Bedfordshire SG19 2DL. Tel: 01767 680551

- **Royal Yachting Association:** RYA House, Romsey Road, Eastleigh, Hampshire SO50 9YA. Tel: 01703 627400

- **Rugby Fives Association:** The Old Forge, Sutton Valence, Kent ME17 3AW. Tel: 01622 842278

- **Sail Training Association:** 2a The Hard, Portsmouth, Hampshire PO1 3PT. Tel: 01705 832055

• **Salvation Army:**
101 Queen Victoria Street,
London EC4P 4EP. Tel: 0171
332 0022

• **Samaritans:** 10 The Grove,
Slough, Berkshire SL1 1QP.
Tel: 01753 532713

• **Save the Children Fund:**
Mary Datchelor House,
17 Grove Lane, London SE5
8RD. Tel: 0171 703 5400

• **Scottish Amateur
Athletics Association:**
Caledonia House, South
Gyle, Edinburgh EH12 9DQ.
Tel: 0131 317 7320

**Scottish Conservation
Projects Trust:** Balallan
House, 24 Allan Park,
Stirling FK8 2QG.
Tel: 01786 479697

• **Scottish National Ski
Council:** Caledonia House,
South Gyle, Edinburgh
EH12 9DQ.
Tel: 0131 317 7280

• **Scottish Natural Heritage:**
12 Hope Terrace, Edinburgh
EH9 2AS.
Tel: 0131 447 4784

• **Scottish Official Board of
Highland Dancing:**
Heritage House, 32 Grange
Loan, Edinburgh EH9 2NR.
Tel: 0131 668 3965

• **Scottish Sports Council:**
Caledonia House, South
Gyle, Edinburgh EH12 9DQ.
Tel: 0131 317 7200

• **Scout Association:** Gilwell
Park, Chingford, London E4
7QW. Tel: 0181 524 5246

• **Sea Cadets:**
202 Lambeth Road, London
SE1 7JF. Tel: 0171 928 8978

• **Shelter:** 88 Old Street,
London EC1V 9HU.
Tel: 0171 253 0202

• **Ski Council of Wales:** 240
Whitchurch Road, Cardiff
CF4 3ND. Tel: 01222 619637

• **SCOPE:** 11 Churchill Park,
Colwick, Nottingham NG4
2HF. Tel: 01159 401202

• **Sports Council:** 16 Upper
Woburn Place, London
WC1H 0QP.
Tel: 0171 273 1500

• **Sports Council for
Northern Ireland:** House of
Sport, Upper Malone Road,
Belfast BT9 5LA.
Tel: 01232 381222

• **Sports Council for Wales:**
Sophia Gardens, Cardiff
CF1 9SW. Tel: 01222 300500

• **Squash Rackets
Association:** PO Box 1106,
London W3 0ZD.
Tel: 0181 746 1616

• **St. Andrew's Ambulance:**
48 Milton Street, Glasgow
G4 0HR. Tel: 0141 332 4031

• **St. John Ambulance:**
1 Grosvenor Crescent,
London SW1X 7EF.
Tel: 0171 235 5231

• **Surf Life Saving
Association GB:** Verney
House, 115 Sidwell Street,
Exeter, Devon EX4 6RY.
Tel: 01392 254364

• **Tennis (Real Tennis) and
Rackets Association:** c/o
The Queen's Club, West
Kensington, London W14
9EQ. Tel: 0171 386 3448

• **Terrence Higgins Trust:**
52-54 Grays Inn Road,
London WC1X 8JU.
Tel: 0171 831 0330

• **Tidy Britain Group:** The
Pier, Wigan WN3 4EX.
Tel: 01942 824620

• **United Kingdom
Mountain Training Board:**
Capel Curig, Gwynedd
LL24 0ET. Tel: 01690 720272

• **United Kingdom Tang
Soo Do Federation:**
PO Box 184, Watford WD1
3LS. Tel: 01582 402248

• **Welsh Folk Dancing
Society:** Fynnon Llwyd,
Trelech, Carmarthen, Dyfed
SA33 6QZ

• **Wildfowl and Wetlands
Trust:** Slimbridge,
Gloucester GL2 7BT.
Tel: 01453 890333

• **Women's Royal Voluntary
Service:** Milton Hill House,
Milton Hill, Abingdon,
Oxfordshire OX13 6AF.
Tel: 01235 442900

• **Woodland Trust:** Autumn
Park, Dysart Road,
Grantham, Lincolnshire
NG31 6LL. Tel: 01476 581111

• **World Challenge
Expeditions Ltd:** Black
Arrow House, 2 Chandos
Road, London NW10 6NF.
Tel: 0181 961 1122

• **World Wide Fund for
Nature:** Panda House,
Weyside Park, Godalming,
Surrey GU7 1XR.
Tel: 01483 426444

• **Yorkshire Dance Centre:**
3 St. Peter's Building, St.
Peter's Square, Leeds LS9
8AH. Tel: 0113 243 9867

• **Young Engineers:**
National Office, 1 Giltspur
Street, London EC1A 9DD.
Tel: 0171 294 3099

• **Young Enterprise:** Ewert
Place, Summertown, Oxford
OX2 7BZ.
Tel: 01865 311180

• **Young Explorers' Trust:**
(Correspondence) c/o The
Royal Geographical Society,
1 Kensington Gore, London
SW7 2AR. Tel: 01623 861027

• **Young People's Trust for
the Environment and
Nature Conservation:**
8 Leapale Road, Guildford,
Surrey GU1 4JX.
Tel: 01483 539600

• **Youth Clubs UK:** 2nd
Floor, Kirby House, Kirby
Street, London EC1N 8TS.
Tel: 0171 242 4045

• **Youth Hostels
Association:** Trevelyan
House, 8 St. Stephen's Hill,
St. Albans, Hertfordshire
AL1 2DY. Tel: 01727 855215

**For addresses of
organisations in Scotland,
Northern Ireland and Wales
which are not included in
this list, contact the
appropriate Territorial
Office.**

INDEX

Skills activities marked with an asterisk are available in the Skills Programmes loose-leaf folder

HEADQUARTERS ADDRESSES OF THE DUKE OF EDINBURGH'S AWARD

National Headquarters
The Duke of Edinburgh's
Award
Gulliver House
Madeira Walk
WINDSOR
Berkshire SL4 1EU
Tel: 01753 810753
Fax: 01753 810666

Fundraising Department
Award House
7-11 St. Matthew Street
London
SW1P 2JT
Tel: 0171 222 4111
Fax: 0171 222 4141

The Award Scheme Ltd
Unit 18/19 Stewartfield
(off Newhaven Road)
Edinburgh EH3 6NS
Tel: 0131 553 5280
Fax: 0131 553 5776

International Secretariat
Award House
7-11 St. Matthew Street
London
SW1P 2JT
Tel: 0171 222 4242
Fax: 0171 222 4141

The Duke of Edinburgh's Award is grateful for the support of Halifax Building Society, Head Office, Trinity Road, West Yorkshire HX1 2RG. Tel: 01422 333 333

USEFUL ADDRESSES

TERRITORIAL/REGIONAL OFFICES OF THE DUKE OF EDINBURGH'S AWARD

Scotland
The Duke of Edinburgh's Award
69 Dublin Street
Edinburgh
EH3 6NS
Tel: 0131 556 9097

Wales
Oak House
12 The Bulwark
Brecon, Powys LD3 7AD
Tel: 01874 623086

Northern Ireland
3rd Floor
177a Lisburn Road
Belfast BT9 7AJ
Tel: 01232 667757

East Midlands
*Barnsley, Doncaster, Leicestershire,
Lincolnshire, North Lincolnshire, North-East
Lincolnshire, Northamptonshire,
Nottinghamshire, Rotherham, Sheffield,
South Yorkshire, Warwickshire*
c/o Chilwell Comprehensive School
Queen's Road West
Beeston, Nottingham NG9 5AL
Tel: 0115 922 8002

West Midlands
*Birmingham, Coventry, Derby City Derbyshire,
Dudley, Herefordshire, Sandwell, Shropshire,
Solihull, Staffordshire, Stoke on Trent,
The Wrekin Walsall, Wolverhampton,
Worcestershire*
89/91 Hatchett Street
Newtown
Birmingham B19 3NY
Tel: 0121 359 5900

South East
*Berkshire, Channel Islands, East & West
Sussex, Hampshire, Isle of Wight, Kent,
Surrey*
PO Box 819, Windsor
Berkshire SL4 1AH
Tel: 01753 621622

South West
*Bath & North East Somerset, Bournemouth,
City of Bristol, Cornwall, Devon, Dorset (the
Shire), Gloucestershire, Isles of Scilly, North
Somerset, Poole, South Gloucestershire,
Somerset, Wiltshire*
Court Gatehouse
Corsham Court
Corsham
Wiltshire SN13 0BZ
Tel: 01249 701000

North East
*Bradford, Calderdale, City of York, Darlington,
Durham, East Riding of Yorkshire, Gateshead,
Hartlepool, Kingston-upon-Hull, Kirklees,
Leeds, Middlesborough, Newcastle, North
Tyneside, Northumberland, North Yorkshire,
Redcar and Cleveland, South Tyneside,
Stockton, Sunderland, Wakefield*
Border House
PO Box 2
Hadrian Road
Wallsend, Tyne & Wear NE28 6QL
Tel: 0191 262 5306

North West
*Cheshire, Cumbria, Greater Manchester,
Isle of Man, Lancashire, Merseyside*
Churchgate House
56 Oxford Street
Manchester M1 6EU
Tel: 0161 228 3688

East
*Bedfordshire Buckinghamshire,
Cambridgeshire, Essex, Hertfordshire, Luton,
Milton Keynes, Norfolk, Oxfordshire, Suffolk*
17 Lower Southend Road
Wickford
Essex SS11 8ES
Tel: 01268 571393

London
*Inner & Outer London Boroughs and
the Corporation of London*
1/1 Harbour Yard
Chelsea Harbour
London SW10 0XD
Tel: 0171 351 4455

• Regional and
Territorial Offices
of The Duke of
Edinburgh's
Award

NOTES

NOTES